Henry Hunter

Sermons Preached at Different Places and on Various Occasions

Collected and Republished in Their Respective Order - Vol. 1

Henry Hunter

Sermons Preached at Different Places and on Various Occasions
Collected and Republished in Their Respective Order - Vol. 1

ISBN/EAN: 9783337160487

Printed in Europe, USA, Canada, Australia, Japan

Cover: Foto ©Lupo / pixelio.de

More available books at **www.hansebooks.com**

SERMONS

ON

VARIOUS OCCASIONS.

IN TWO VOLUMES.

SERMONS

PREACHED AT

DIFFERENT PLACES

AND ON *Samˡ Miller.*

VARIOUS OCCASIONS;

COLLECTED AND REPUBLISHED

IN THEIR RESPECTIVE ORDER:

TO WHICH ARE SUBJOINED,

MEMOIRS, ANECDOTES, AND ILLUSTRATIONS,

Relating to the Persons, Institutions, and Events, connected with the several Subjects.

BY

HENRY HUNTER, D. D.

MINISTER OF THE SCOTS CHURCH, LONDON WALL;

Formerly of South Leith, North Britain.

VOL. I.

𝕷𝖔𝖓𝖉𝖔𝖓:

PRINTED FOR THE AUTHOR;

AND SOLD BY

C. DILLY, POULTRY; MURRAY AND HIGHLEY, FLEET STREET; AND J. JOHNSON, ST. PAUL'S CHURCH YARD.

1795.

CONTENTS.

SERMON I.

The Believer's Joy in Christ Jesus. p. 3

Acts viii. 39.—He went on his way rejoicing.

SERMON II.

The Success of the Gospel. 37

2 Corinthians, iv. 7.—But we have this treasure in earthen vessels, that the excellency of the power may be of God, and not of us.

IN CONNECTION WITH

Exodus xx. 19.—They said unto *Moses*, speak thou with us, and we will hear; but let not God speak with us lest we die.

SERMON III.

The Duty and Utility of Commemorating National Deliverances. 91

Exodus xiii. 8, 9, 10.—And thou shalt shew thy son, in that day, saying, This is done because of that which the Lord did unto me, when I came forth out of Egypt.

And

And it shall be for a sign unto the, upon thine hand, and for a memorial between thine eyes; that the LORD's law may be in thy mouth: for with a strong hand hath the LORD brought thee out of Egypt.

Thou shalt therefore keep this ordinance in his season from year to year.

SERMON IV.

The Duty of Compassion to Poor Brethren. 145

Deut. xv. 7, 11.—If there be among you a poor man of one of thy brethren, within any of thy gates, in thy land which the Lord thy God giveth thee, thou shalt not harden thy heart, nor shut thine hand from thy poor brother. But thou shalt open thine hand wide unto him, and shalt surely lend him sufficient for his need, in that which he wanteth. Beware that there be not a thought in thy wicked heart, saying, the seventh year, the year of release is at hand: and thine eye be evil against thy poor brother, and thou givest him nought, and he cry unto the Lord against thee, and it be sin unto thee: thou shalt surely give him, and thine heart shall not be grieved when thou givest unto him; because that for this thing the Lord thy God will bless thee in all thy works, and in all that thou puttest thine hand unto. For the poor shall never cease out of the land: Therefore I command thee, saying, thou shalt open thy hand wide unto thy brother, to thy poor, and to thy needy in thy land.

SERMON

CONTENTS.

SERMON V.

The Universal Extent, and Everlasting Duration of the Redeemer's Kingdom.   199

Rev. xi. 15.—And the seventh Angel sounded; and there were great voices in Heaven, saying, The Kingdoms of this world are become the Kingdoms of our Lord, and of his Christ; and he shall reign for ever and ever.

SERMON VI.

The Belief of the Gospel a source of Joy and Peace.   227

Romans xv. 13.—Now the God of hope fill you with all joy and peace in believing, that ye may abound in hope, through the power of the Holy Ghost.

SERMON VII.

The Brevity, Uncertainty, and Importance of Human Life.   321

Psalm xxxix. 4, 5.—Lord, make me to know mine end, and the measure of my days, what it is, that I may know how frail I am. Behold thou hast made my days as an hand-breadth: and mine age is as nothing before thee: verily every man at his best state is altogether vanity.

INTRODUCTION.

THE Publication of single Sermons is, in general, owing to some local, personal and transitory circumstances. They are accordingly mere *ephemera* in the republic of letters. Their sphere of circulation from the Press is not much more extensive than the circuit of the edifice in which they were pronounced; and their duration outlives *a little month*, at most, the sound of the Preacher's voice. In a country like this, however, where the press is happily open for the communication of every species of information or instruction, it is no wonder that Sermons, among other literary compositions, should advance a claim to their share of public attention, utility, and applause. What pleased and improved in a smaller circle, and on a particular occasion, it is presumed, may contribute to pleasure

pleasure and improvement on a greater scale. Every man imagines the whole world must be of his opinion on certain subjects, and it is no difficult matter to persuade an author that the voice of his friends is the voice of mankind. Public bodies, too, find their account in periodical publications of this kind. To present a man with a sermon preached for the benefit of such a charitable institution, is an indirect, and more delicate, method of soliciting his support to it, and very frequently succeeds where a blunter application would be repelled. If no great addition is thereby made to the stock of public knowledge, the cause of religion, learning and morals sustains at least no injury. Among many such productions, born to die in infancy, a few arise worthy of immortality; and modest merit is sometimes drawn forward into notice, and animated into further, and successful, exertion, by the encouragement given to an earlier and inferior performance.

All the Discourses which compose the following Volumes, one excepted, are a Republication. Having ventured to stand before

before the tribunal of the Public once already, they muſt have loſt much of both the timidity and confidence of a firſt appearance. Thoſe who have publiſhed ſingle Sermons, well know how unproductive it is as a commercial affair; and ſuch as are acquainted with the Author of theſe, will readily judge that he was as little likely, as any one, to profit himſelf by adventures of this ſort. Indeed of all of them many more were given away than ſold ; and thus ſeveral of them are actually out of print, and ſtill occaſionally called for. Many of my more immediate friends have wiſhed to procure, or to complete ſets, and it has not been in my power to gratify them. This originally ſuggeſted the idea of a COLLECTION, which is now realized. In preparing it for the preſs, I have availed myſelf of the candid remarks which have come to my ear, and of the obſervation which time and experience ſuggeſt, to retrench, correct, or amplify, as the caſe required ; and I have now endeavoured to diverſify and enliven my ſeveral ſubjects, by affixing ſhort memoirs, anecdotes, and illuſtrations,

lustrations, respecting the persons, institutions and events which gave occasion to their original discussion and publication. If the book survive me, it will inform those who may feel any interest in my memory, with what persons I lived and acted, in what services I was occasionally employed, and what train of thought I was consequently led to pursue.

The discourse which appears now for the first time, is introduced in discharge of repeated promises to repeated solicitation, that if ever I ventured to make up a volume, it should have a place.

I conclude this short address to my Friends, in the words of the younger *Pliny* to his Friend *Septitius*, who had importuned him to revise, correct and publish his familiar Epistles, " It remains for me to " express an ardent wish, that neither You " may have reason to repent of your re-" quest, nor I of my compliance."

H. H.

Bethnal-Green Road.
Sept. 5th, 1794.

SERMON I.

THE BELIEVER'S JOY IN CHRIST JESUS*.

ACTS, viii. 39.

—He went on his way rejoicing.

THIS is the conclusion of the interesting and instructive history of the conversion of the Ethiopian Eunuch. It commences at the 26th verse of this chapter, and exhibits to us a person highly distinguished by his rank in life, and much more by his piety, on his return from Jerusalem, whither he had resorted in order to join in the solemn worship of one of the great Jewish festivals, to Ethiopia, the theatre of his secular employments. To amuse the tediousness of the road, and to fix the serious impressions which the service of the temple had made upon his mind, he betakes himself to the reading of those Sacred Books, which,

---

* Preached in the Church of South Leith, April 22. 1770, after Dispensing the Lord's Supper.—First Published in Vol. IV. of the Scots Preacher.

as a profelyte to Judaifm, he received for the rule of his faith and conduct. That Providence which watches over all events, and which was haftening its gracious defigns upon him to their accomplifh- ment, at once directs to the fubject of his reading, and fends him an interpreter. The good feed of the word, being caft into a well-prepared foil, fpeedily brings forth fruit unto God; the treafur- er of *Candace*, Queen of the Ethiopians, becomes a difciple of Jefus of Nazareth: He reads, he un- derftands; he believeth, and is baptized: He is filled with peace and *joy* in believing;—" *He went* " *on his way rejoicing.*"

You have, this day, Chriftians, been recognifing your baptifmal engagements; you have profeffed your faith and hope in the *Lamb, flain from the foundation of the world:* you have been, with this illuftrious and early convert to Chriftianity, folemn- ly declaring, that with all your heart, *You believe that Jefus Chrift is the Son of God.* Would God grant the defire of my heart, concerning every one in this great affembly, you fhould with him alfo, go on *your* way rejoicing. That, by the grace of God, I may contribute fomewhat to an end fo defirable, permit me, from the circum- ftances of this fhort hiftory, or from obvious con- clufions derived from it, firft, to point out fome of

the

the sources of the believer's joy in Christ Jesus; and then to direct you to such a walk and conversation, as, by the blessing of Heaven, may conduce to your true peace and comfort through life, at a dying hour, and in the glorious world of unmixed and everlasting love and joy.

I. Then, we behold this good man *rejoicing* as he goes, that God had been graciously pleased, and by means so wonderful, to reveal to him his Son Christ Jesus, and the way of salvation through his blood. He was blessed with a teachable disposition, he had a heart turned to devotion; modest, inquiring, zealous, indefatigable, *he had come to Jerusalem for to worship*; he waited for the consolation of Israel; he was in the habit of diligently searching the Scriptures; but behold, he is, on his way homeward, still in the dark; the word that he reads is but a dead letter, *as a spring shut up, a fountain sealed*. Upon his arrival at the Jewish Metropolis, he would no doubt be informed of the late interesting events, which had so much engaged the minds, and affected the conversation of men; namely the Crucifixion of Christ, the progress of his Apostles, the martyrdom of Stephen, and the like. But whether from his ignorance of the Scriptures, and of the real character of Jesus Christ, or from the prejudices instilled into him by some Jewish teacher, who, in all probability, directed his faith and conscience, these events, however striking, had failed to make much impression. He remains still ignorant that the promised Messias was already come; and that there was *no name under heaven given among men,* whereby they could be rendered acceptable to God, and saved, but the name of Him whom the Jews had with wicked hands just crucified and slain. But, now that he is fully instructed in the meaning and application of the prophecies; now that the veil is removed from his eyes, and the great mystery of godliness stands confessed; now that he sees Christ Jesus the Lord, in what Moses instituted, David sung, and Isaias foretold; his heart overflows with gratitude and delight: and may we not suppose him, in language such as this, expressing the wonder and the joy with which his soul was filled?

" *Glory to God in the highest,* that *the Desire of*
" *all nations is come*; that the Scriptures are ful-
" filled; that the sun is risen, and the shadows
" fled away; and that it is *a light to enlighten the*
" *Gentiles,* as well as *the Glory of Israel.* But what
" am I, O Lord God, that to me this grace
" should be given? An alien! a wanderer from
" Ethiopia! ignorant, bewildered, helpless! Now
" know

"know I *of a truth* that thou art *no respecter of*
"*persons*; that he who sincerely seeks, shall cer-
"tainly find thee; that *thou wilt have mercy on*
"*whom thou wilt have mercy*. What shall I ren-
"der unto the Lord, who has made me a chosen
"vessel to convey his name, and his Son's name,
"to distant nations and regions of darkness? I
"came hither empty, but I return filled with
"good things. Once I was in uncertainty and
"obscurity, but now I am light in the Lord, for
"*the glory of the Lord is arisen upon me*. I read,
"but understood not what I read: but God has
"graciously presented me with the golden key
"which unfolds the passage to the treasures of
"Scripture, infinitely more precious than those
"which my royal mistress has intrusted to my
"care: now have I found *Him to whom all the*
"*prophets give witness*; Him whom my soul
"loveth; my Saviour and my God: And *I will*
"*go in his strength*; *I will make mention of his*
"*righteousness, even of his only*.

Have you obtained of the Lord, Christians,
like cause of rejoicing, from your attendance on
the service of his house and table this day? You
perhaps came hither, as Mary, inquiring, weeping, and complaining, "They have taken away
"my Lord, and I know not where they have
"laid

"laid him;" but are now ready to retire in the satisfaction and triumph of Simeon, "Lord, now "letteſt thou thy ſervant depart in peace, accord- "ing to thy word. For mine eyes have ſeen thy "ſalvation." *Hold the beginning of your confidence ſtedfaſt unto the end.* The eternal God *is your refuge, and underneath are the everlaſting arms; ye ſhall renew your ſtrength; ye ſhall mount up on wings as eagles; ye ſhall run and not weary, ye ſhall walk and not faint.*

II. Another evident ſource of joy to this illuſtrious perſonage, is his admiſſion into the family of Chriſt by baptiſm, and to all the privileges connected with that high dignity. Having heard and taſted of the grace of Chriſt, he cannot reſt till he is ſolemnly united to that venerable name, and he profeſſes the utmoſt readineſs to reſign every thing that might prevent, to comply with every thing that might procure, ſo great a bleſſing: "See, here is water; what doth hinder me "to be baptized?"

He had, hitherto, reckoned it a diſtinguiſhed honour to be admitted among the worſhippers of the true God, though in the outer-court of his houſe only; and, in order to obtain that honour, had cheerfully ſubmitted, at ſtated times, to the inconvenience, pain, and fatigue of a tedious journey,

journey, through inhospitable regions, and under a burning sky; and now his zeal and devotion meet with a glorious recompence, which smooths the ruggedness of the way, and tempers the ardor of the noon-tide heat. He had left the court of a great Queen, where he was respected, loved, and trusted, to do homage to the King of kings; and behold, such *love hath the Father bestowed upon us*; he is truly dignified and ennobled; he is encouraged to call God his Father, and Jesus his Friend; angels his fellow-servants; apostles, and prophets, and saints, his brethren. What joy is equal to that of considering a man's self as connected with an extensive, a wise, a virtuous, and an honourable kindred; and of contributing a share to the lustre and respect of an estimable family? And what kindred so numerous, so worthy, so respectable; what house so illustrious, as that to which the Christian belongs; into which he was received by baptism, which he strives to adorn by his virtues, where he lives in complacency and delight, and to which he is united by bonds endearing, indissolvable, eternal? And this honour and happiness have all the saints.

You have this day, my friends, been sitting at your Father's table, and eating childrens bread; tasting the heavenly manna, and drinking of the water of life; conversing with your best friends, and holding communion with God himself. However mean your condition in the world, however contracted or distressing your circumstances, the great Lord of all looks down upon you with attention; angels are ministring spirits to your necessities; and there is *a kingdom prepared for you from the foundation of the world*. And what have the children of kings to boast of, once to be compared to this?

At that table your Saviour presented you to *his Father and your Father, his God, and your God,* as his disciples, and brethren, and friends; recommending you to the care of his Providence, to the conduct and consolations of his Spirit, and to all the blessings of his love; and you can henceforth soothe all your anxieties and pains, in the belief, that the great God takes an interest in all that concerns you: your health, your subsistence, your reputation, your family: and will assuredly make *all things work together for your good*. Thus disburthened, thus supported, thus connected, must you not proceed on the journey of life, with firmness, with cheerfulness, with elevation of spirit, with joy of heart?

III. We must suppose this good Ethiopian *rejoicing* as he went on his way, in the new, the
clearer,

clearer, the more juft and fatisfying ideas he was now taught to entertain, of the Supreme Being; of his nature, his will, his worſhip. He had, indeed, already taken one great ſtep in religion, in renouncing the gods of his fathers, and in acknowledging the one living and true God: but ſo erroneouſly did he ſtill conceive of that God, ſo contracted ſtill were the views of our illuſtrious traveller, that, till now, he confined his notions of religious worſhip to one mode, and to a particular ſpot, and that ſpot far removed from his uſual reſidence. Jeruſalem, he had been inſtructed to think, is *the place where men ought to worſhip*. But the doctrine of the bleſſed Jeſus expands his mind, and inſpires nobler ideas of the Father of Spirits. As he approached the holy city in times paſt, how would his heart glow when firſt he deſcried the lofty battlements of the Temple, the place which God had choſen to put his name there: " Behold,
" O Lord, the habitation of thy holineſs and
" glory. I ſhall ſoon be where God delights to
" dwell; my feet ſhall ſtand once more in the
" courts of the Moſt High: I ſhall take ſhelter
" under the ſhadow of his wings, and mix with
" the happy, happy multitude, who are conti-
" nually before him. *Beautiful for ſituation, the*
" *joy of the whole earth, is Mount Zion*; *on the*
" *ſides*

"*sides of the north, the city of the Great King:* "*God is known in her palaces for a refuge.*" The solemnity was now over, and he is constrained, by the necessity of his affairs, to turn his back on the scene of his devout employments, and undoubtedly he did it with a heavy heart, when that God, whose presence is universal, and his power unlimited, converts the desert into a temple, kindles the sacred flame with fire brought immediately from the heavenly altar, and conveys an instructor to him on the swift wings of the wind.

How would the sacred Volume now unfold its sublime and mysterious truths to his comprehension! He would find that same prophet, who first led him to the knowledge of Jesus Christ, and him crucified, conducting him also to just and encouraging views of the majesty and condescension of God, as " the high and lofty One who inhabiteth " eternity; whose name is holy, who dwelleth in " the high and holy place: with him also, that " is of a contrite and humble spirit; to revive the " spirit of the humble, and to revive the heart of the " contrite ones." Now he is taught to consider the spacious expanse of heaven as one great temple: and how contracted, how mean does even the magnificent pile on Mount Zion appear, compared

pared to that gloriously sublime arch, that star-bespangled vault, which spreads its vast circumference over the metropolis of Ethiopia, as well as over that of Judea!

Is it any wonder that he went on his way *rejoicing*, when he proceeded in this delightful persuasion, that God attended all his footsteps, surrounding his path and his bed, and compassed him with favour, as with a shield? Is it any wonder, that the scorching heat of the sun, the dreariness of vast and frightful solitudes, and the other hardships of the way, were unfelt, or ceased to afflict? when he could read, and with full understanding of what he read, " Behold he that keepeth Israel, shall nei-
" ther slumber nor sleep. The Lord is thy keep-
" er, the Lord is thy shade upon thy right hand.
" The sun shall not smite thee by day, nor the
" moon by night." He would not now need to inquire, *of whom speaketh the prophet thus*, when employing that beautiful imagery borrowed from the state of Nature in regions with which he was so well acquainted; " *A man* shall be as an hid-
" ing place from the wind, and a covert from the
" tempest: as rivers of water in a dry place, as
" the shadow of a great rock in a weary land:"
And now that he saw accomplished, in a more exalted sense than he had hitherto apprehended,

that

that other prediction of the same great herald of the Saviour: " In the wildernefs fhall waters "break out, and ftreams in the defert; and the "parched ground fhall become a pool, and the "thirfty land fprings of water. In the habitation "of dragons, where each lay, fhall be grafs with "reeds and rufhes. And a highway fhall be "there, and a way, and it fhall be called the "way of holinefs; the unclean fhall not pafs over "it, but it fhall be for thofe: The way-faring "men, though fools, fhall not err therein. No "lion fhall be there, nor any ravenous beaft fhall "go up thereon; It fhall not be found there. "But the redeemed fhall walk there. And the "ranfomed of the Lord fhall return, and come "to Zion with fongs, and everlafting joy upon "their heads: they fhall obtain joy and gladnefs, "and forrow, and fighing, fhall flee away.

We alfo muft now retire from the temple, and purfue our journey through the wildernefs. But we travel not unaccompanied: He is faithful who hath promifed, " My prefence fhall go with you, "and I will give you reft." " I will never leave "nor forfake thee. When thou paffeft through "the waters, I will be with thee; and through "the rivers, they fhall not overflow thee: When "thou walkeft through the fire thou fhalt not be
"burnt;

"burnt; neither shall the flame kindle upon
"thee." Hence, we can rejoice in the words of
the pfalm we have been juft now finging. "Yea,
"though I walk through the valley of the fhadow
"of death, I will fear no evil : for thou art with
"me, thy rod and thy ftaff they comfort me.
"Surely goodnefs and mercy fhall follow me all
"the days of my life : and I will dwell in the
"houfe of the Lord for ever."

IV. The glorious and animating profpects which the gofpel opens to our view, exhibit another caufe of holy joy. He went on his way *rejoicing in hope of the glory of God :* in hope of a refurrection from the dead, of abfolution in the day of judgment, of reception into the kingdom of heaven, of being *ever with the Lord.* Till life and immortality were brought to light by the gofpel, futurity was covered with darknefs impenetrable : all was conjecture and uncertainty. In fome rarer inftances the foul indeed feemed to awake to the confcioufnefs, and the belief, of its divine Original, and to look beyond the grave with compofure and dignity ; yet, even fome of the greateft geniufes, who entertained this perfuafion, acknowledge, after all their reafonings and conclufions, that the doctrine of the immortality of the foul might be but a pleafing delufion ; a

truth

truth rather to be fondly wished, than clearly demonstrated. But the body was universally, and for ever, given up a prey to corruption: Not only rude barbarians, but the learned, intelligent, penetrating Athenians, treated the doctrine of the resurrection as the ravings of a madman. What a noble superiority, then, does the meanest disciple of Jesus enjoy, in the knowledge of what is most interesting to human nature! How solemnly pleasing is it, to look forward to all the events of our future existence, which Christianity discloses; to the vast revolutions which the system of nature must undergo; to the wonderful arrangements of providence which are to succeed!

What heart does not sympathize in the joy of good old Jacob, when, inconsolably mourning over the loss of his beloved son, and in a land distressed with famine, he is informed that his darling child is yet alive; alive in a land of plenty: chief governor in that land, sovereign dispenser of that plenty; and that he had sent for him, to be a witness of his greatness, to be a partaker of his honour, to be *preserved alive in famine by his bounty*, to abide with him in the choice spot of the country, to be comforted and delighted by his filial duty and affection? Rejoice, O Christian, and be exceeding glad. Your brother and friend;

friend; your tender-hearted Redeemer; He who *was* dead, *is* alive, and behold he *liveth for evermore*; liveth in *another country, that is an heavenly*; a land where spring and autumn reign in eternal union; and over which He is constituted sole administrator, *for the suffering of death,* being *crowned with glory and honour:* having *obtained a name that is above every name*; *all things* in heaven and in earth being *committed to him,* and eternal life at his disposal, to *give it to as many as he will:* And lo! he sendeth for thee, to behold his glory, to partake of the inexhausted plenty of that good land, to fix your everlasting abode in that heavenly Goshen which he is gone before to prepare for you. And O! What glorious things are spoken of this habitation of the blessed! A land watered with the *pure river of water of life, which proceedeth from the throne of God, and the Lamb;* planted and shaded with none but *the trees of life, whose leaves are for the healing of the nations,* and whose various fruits are produced at all seasons of the eternal year; a land enlightened, not with a sun, moon, and stars, but with the glory of the Most High; and peopled only with sons of light, *the nations of them that are saved:* A land where there is day without night; joy unsullied by a tear; present and perfect felicity, not subject

to

to remorse, nor checked by apprehension of change; purity unsusceptible of pollution; immortal youth and vigour liable to no age or decay; gloriously bright and smiling faces free from *spot or wrinkle or any such thing*; *perfect love* that *casts out all fear* and suspicion; and, the crown of all, eternity, that knows neither limit nor change. And is your heart, my friend, like the venerable patriarch's ready to faint at the good news? Is the vastness, and the value, of the blessing too great for belief? Let your spirits with his revive when with him you behold the vehicles which are sent to carry you, the ordinances of his grace, conducted by his spirit. What a triumphant car is this divine institution of our blessed Master! It carries the soul on rapid wheels to Christ's second coming: like Elijah's fiery chariot, it elevates to heaven, it puts us down at our Father's house, and places us with *Abraham, Isaac, and Jacob*, at a table that is never to be removed.

Go on your way *rejoicing*, for now is *your salvation nearer than when you believed*. Who would not advance with joyful speed, when such a prospect is before us! Up, up, ye travellers to Zion; *this is not your rest : Arise, let us go hence.* Take in your hand, and carefully consult, the chart of both countries, that through which your journey lies,

lies, and that to which you are travelling. Mount the carriages which your Father's care and tenderness have provided; the swift, smooth vehicles of meditation, of prayer, of praise, of the sacrament, of holy zeal, of Christian usefulness; put and kept in motion, by faith, and hope, and love, and joy; and in one or other of these, you shall, not long hence, *enter through the* everlasting *gates into the city* of the great King, to *go no more out.* What though that frightful Jordan roll between! Does not our great High Priest go before us? Do not his feet stand firm on dry ground in the midst of the channel? And while they do, its waters shall stand as a wall, on either hand, to defend, instead of a wall, in front, to oppose. Arise then, and let us take possession of the promised land; and then let Jordan roll back his tide, and for ever disjoin us from our enemies; our sins, our frailties, our dangers, our sorrows, our fears; and for ever unite us to our dearest friends; our God, our Saviour, our Comforter; our kindred angels, our fellow saints: when from this good Ethiopian's own mouth, we shall learn the wondrous story of redeeming love towards him; and with him, and all saints, for ever celebrate the grace wherein we stand.

V. Finally.

V. FINALLY, May we not suppose our Christian proselyte *rejoicing* in the prospect of being made the happy instrument of immortal happiness to thousands? How would his heart burn within him, with sacred ambition, with affectionate zeal, to think that Providence had placed him in a station so favourable to the interests of the Redeemer's kingdom, as well as of that mighty temporal empire, in the administration of whose government he had so eminent a share; that his exalted station and extensive authority might, by the blessing of God, have influence with his fellow-citizens, perhaps with his sovereign, toward the reception and acknowledgement of that faith, which he himself had embraced; and that thus generations to come might call him blessed, while they enjoyed the fruits of his labours of love; that by his means, *Ethiopia* might, according as it is written, *soon stretch out her hands unto God!* May we not suppose him, once more having recourse to the prophets, and reading, with delight, of that blessed day, when *they that be wise shall shine as the brightness of the firmament; and they that turn many unto righteousness, as the stars for ever and ever:* When he should be honoured to present himself before the eternal throne, with a numerous retinue of spiritual children, rescued from Pagan idol-

atry

atry, grofs ignorance, and barbarous manners, and received into the family of the common Father of all, bleſſed with the ſpirit of adoption, and raiſed to glory?

WE move in a ſphere much more contracted: but to every one of us there is his particular ſphere, in which he may be greatly, nobly uſeful: Let every one conſider the extent, the connections, and dependencies of his own. You have families and friends: the *poor*, and the ignorant, and the afflicted, *you have always with you.* Are there not among you, the giddy, the thoughtleſs, and the vain, to be admoniſhed with wiſdom, and reproved with tenderneſs? Are there not the impious and the profane, to be oppoſed with firmneſs, reprehended by example, reclaimed by goodneſs, interceded for with compaſſion, or ſeparated from with reſolution? Are not theſe dear, precious lambs of the flock, the hope of the preſent age, and the ſeed of thoſe which are to come, to be ſuckled, to be trained up, to be protected? Are not the poor and the afflicted of God's people, *for whom Chriſt died*, to be cheriſhed and comforted, *with the conſolation whereby we ourſelves are comforted of God?* Are theſe, and objects ſuch as theſe,

these, mean or unimportant? Are they not generally interesting? Would not success in any service, undertaken in the cause of the gospel, that is, the cause, at once, of God and of humanity, afford you the most sincere satisfaction? How silly the pride of rearing up a stately edifice, to be the seat of a family and a name, compared to the noble ambition of raising a temple for the Holy Ghost! How insipid, how transient, how unsatisfactory a gratification, is the getting before others in rank, in riches, in reputation, compared to the sublime delight of working together with God, to bring perishing sinners into the way of life and salvation? How poor an object, is that of amassing a great estate for a beloved child, compared with the divine joy of *laying up* for him *treasures in heaven*; of raising young ones up to the *lively hope of an inheritance incorruptible, undefiled and that fadeth not away!* O that the professed followers of Jesus were thus walking in the steps of their great Leader! going about doing good; never *weary of well doing*; *shining as lights in the world*; fulfilling their own joy, and promoting that of others. How pleasantly might the journey of life glide on, thus sweetened, thus variegated, thus marked, in every stage, by honour and usefulness; and thus

thus, with certainty, directed to immortal honours, and an unfading crown!

A few affectionate advices, deemed suitable to this day's service; to your professions, your engagements, and your prospects, shall conclude this discourse.

1. As I am therefore bound to wish and pray, that you may be partakers of the joy of the extraordinary person whose history we have been considering, *after* he was made to see light in the Lord so my

First direction to you shall be, to endeavour to imitate his example *previous* to the period under review; to be diligent and assiduous in the use of all the known and instituted means of grace. Read the Scriptures, with what understanding you have, though you may want much of that satisfying clearness which you wish to possess. Go at the appointed times *to the temple to worship*, though the God of the place may as yet be revealed only in part, and though you discern, *only as in a glass darkly*. Beware of *restraining prayer before God*, though the Hearer of prayer may seem to turn a deaf ear to the voice of your supplications. You have been seeking consolation in waiting upon God in *one* ordinance, and in the performance of *one* duty, and you may have missed it; be the more earnest to search after it in *every* duty and in every ordinance of Christian life. That Jesus may be found of you in the wilderness of this world, and while you are employed in the exercise of your ordinary lawful callings, who sees it meet to withdraw himself from solemn religious seasons and places. It was in the desert of Gaza, not in the temple at Jerusalem; it was when he was returning to his secular employments, not when engaged in sanctuary services, that our convert was introduced to the acquaintance of his Saviour. God acts in a manner calculated to convince us, that He is independent of every thing but his own sovereign gracious will and pleasure; but He would have us to act, as if our salvation depended entirely on the constant and diligent use of the appointed means.

2. Would you have a pleasant journey, endeavour to go on with spirit and alacrity; as if your heart were in your work. Agreeable and useful travelling is the medium between violent hurry and careless sauntering. The Christian ought not only to be in motion, he must be making cheerful dispatch. There is a sort of lazy, faint-hearted Christians, if they can deserve at all a name so honourable, whom every sultry hour, and every rough step, is ready to discourage. These would slumber it on through life, and awake in heaven as from a pleasant dream: They

They wish to be at home, but they wish to be exempted from the dangers and fatigue of the way. But Christianity, like every other work of God, connects the end with the means, and through *manifold tribulations* conducts its disciple into *the kingdom of God.* Here, those only are encouraged to look for the prize, who run in the race; and the *crown of righteousness is laid up* for those who *endure hardship as the good soldiers of Christ,* who *fight the good fight,* who *finish their course,* who *keep the faith,* who *endure unto the end.*

It is not possible that an indolent, self-indulging person, should be a prosperous and a happy Christian. What shame is it to the professed followers of Jesus, to be drowsy and sluggish in the plainest and easiest paths of duty, when he beholds the Saviour, for his sake, so ready and cheerful to tread the most rugged and forbidding path of suffering? This suggests,

3. Another direction, and it shall be delivered in the words of the apostle; " Let us lay aside every " weight, and the sin which doth so easily beset " us, and let us run with patience the race that " is set before us, *looking unto Jesus,* the author " and the finisher of our faith." Nothing tends so much to smooth and to sweeten hard weather, and a dreary road to the believer, as the sight of

his Master, just before him. *It is good for us to be here,* said Peter on the mount of Transfiguration; but it is good to be with Christ, and like him, may the Christian say, in every condition, and in every place; in the storm, in the desert, in the prison; arrayed in a *gorgeous robe,* wearing *a crown of thorns,* bearing a cross. Our Lord's first disciples, when reproach and suffering were certain consequences of the profession of Christianity, came out from the presence of their persecutors, rejoicing that " they were counted worthy to suffer shame for his name." What cause of rejoicing have we, that honour, not shame, accompanies this profession; that with us *kings* are *nursing fathers,* and *their queens nursing mothers* to the Christian church; that the road is, to us, in many places, and in many respects, strewed, not with thorns, but with flowers. Were our corrupted hearts reduced into the entire love and obedience of Christ, every obstacle would be easily surmounted, every difficulty overcome. And this is the very object of the present advice: that we *look* to Jesus for direction, for resolution, and for assistance, in putting off and laying aside those diverse sinful *lusts which war against the soul,* checking its progress, marring its comfort, wasting its strength; and that we look to him for patience under

every

every external hindrance and diftrefs; and thefe neceffarily decreafe, as inward corruption is fubdued.

4. Permit me to direct you, in order to the continuance and the increafe of your joy, to take good heed unto yourfelves that you keep in the right road, and perfevere even to the end: for in this, not only your comfort, but your very fafety is concerned. Remember you are not upon an excurfion of pleafure, but a journey of bufinefs; and that of the moft important nature. When a man's credit, or fubfiftence, or his family's welfare, depend on exactnefs and expedition, he will certainly take the readieft and the fafeft road. He will not then employ his time in digreffions after objects of amufement, fuch as gardens, palaces, and paintings. Were human life intended as paftime merely, were the world a fcene of diverfion only, and *if in this life alone we had hope*, I fhould fend you away this night, with my advice to drink as deep of pleafure as you can; to make as frequent, and as long, digreffions into the world, as inclination, conftitution, and circumftances can admit; nay, to take up your abode in it altogether. But when I confider what the world is to the Chriftian, an enemy's country, nay more, the actual feat of war, furely it is unneceffary to tell the

the good foldier of Jefus Chrift, that he has need to *walk circumfpectly*; that a holy jealoufy is abfolutely neceffary; that enemies are never fo dangerous as when they approach us with a fmiling countenance, with fair words, and with gifts in their hands. To this, let me fubjoin, that it is wife and ufeful to obferve moderation, and to practife felf-government, in the ufe of even the neceffary and lawful recreations of the way. A traveller may warrantably enjoy the pleafure of a fine profpect as he paffes along, and muft of neceffity ftop now and then for refrefhment; but he muft not dream of building an habitation in every delightful fpot, nor miftake a comfortable inn for his Father's houfe. The Chriftian is called to deny himfelf to the unbounded enjoyment of the moft innocent delights, as a feparate and independent good, now; that the poffeffion of them, as connected with, and fubfervient to the enjoyment of God, the fupreme good, may be the fweeter hereafter.

5. Finally, be daily *looking for and haftening unto the coming of the Lord Jefus*; that bleffed period which fhall put a full end to fin and all its dreadful confequences, and ufher in the eternal year of glory and immortality. Would you be truly fortified againft the hardfhips, fecured from the dangers

gers, and supported under the afflictions of this tempestuous ocean, cast the anchor of hope within the vail. *He who shall come, will come and will not tarry.* When such a prize is in view, the exertion and fatigue of a short race are unworthy of consideration; when a crown of glory is to be the reward of victory, who would shun the inconsiderable danger of a safe and easy combat? When such a mansion is prepared, what matters it that, here and there a small space of uneven ground, intersect the road that leads unto it?

You have this day, communicants, ascended an exceeding high mountain, and with the eye of faith contemplated the glories of Emanuel's land. And what have you beheld? What do you now behold? The world, and the things of the world on fire; death expiring; the old dragon chained to eternity: *hell cast into the lake of fire.* Behold, how the jasper walls of the holy city, the new Jerusalem, begin to swell upon the eye; the *gates of pearl* expand for your admission. Behold the undazzling, unterrifying splendour of the *glory of God and of the Lamb*; and *the nations of them that are saved* walking in the light thereof. *O death, where is thy sting? O Grave, where is thy victory? I know that my Redeemer liveth and that he shall stand at the latter day upon the earth. Amen, even so come, Lord Jesus.*

ADDI-

ADDITION,

THE Sacrament of the Lord's Supper is administered, and received, all over Scotland, with much seriousness, fervour, and solemnity. Not only in the Country, but likewise in the Cities and great Towns, on such occasions, every thing exhibits staid, smiling, cheerful piety. A considerable part of the preceding week is employed in exercises of public and private devotion. Young communicants assemble to converse, and pray with, to encourage and comfort, each other. The devout of the surrounding villages, according as circumstances permit, flock, " like doves to their windows," to the church where the ordinance is to be celebrated. With the zeal, simplicity and perseverance of ancient pilgrims many travel from the most distant parts, on foot, (some 50 miles, to my knowledge) to have the satisfaction of joining in christian communion with beloved pastors and friends. Hospitality, in all its native, unaffected warmth, is displayed. The spirit of primitive Christianity is revived, and the disciples of the blessed Jesus have, literally, in the purest and most exalted sense of the words, " one heart and one soul, and have all things common." The concourse is, accordingly, on many occasions so great, that the bodily, to say nothing of the mental, exertions of the minister of the

the place are wholly inadequate to the labours of the day—the fucceffion of communicants to the table of the Lord,

" From morn to dewy eve; a fummer's day,"

calling, in filent importunity, for their portion of the bread of life. This renders it neceffary for the prefiding Minifter to call in the aid of his brethren ; and a new and a delicious bond of union is formed. The patron of " my boyifh days," the friend of my youth, the pupil of my age, is invited to affift me in carrying on the divine plan of inftructing, edifying, comforting the people of God. At the folemnity which gave occafion to the preceding addrefs, not fo few as two thoufand were admitted to communion; compofed of the church of South Leith, my immediate charge : of our neighbours, with their worthy paftor, my ever to be refpected friend Dr. Johnfton of North Leith ; of a multitude from the adjoining Metropolis, and Weft-Church parifh ; of fome from the city of Glafgow and town of Paifley, befides many others from different quarters, who could not make themfelves known to me. And let me not, in making this enumeration, overlook or forget my amiable and benevolent colleague, the Rev. Thomas Scot, over whofe afhes I now fhed the tear of tender recollection, as over one of the moft placid, unaffuming, conciliatory, of mankind ; with whom I lived, amidft jarring interefts and cabals, in perfect harmony, during the fix happieft years of my life and miniftry.

It

It was at that period, and on similar occasions, I had the honour, and the felicity, of associating with my venerable departed Friends, Robert Walker, Daniel Macqueen, Alexander Webster, John Gibson, Robert Dick, James Brown, George Muir, John Hamilton, Robert Henry, and many others, whose praise will not soon expire, in the Church of Scotland; and with John Erskine, John Gillies, and a long list of my nearer contemporaries, whom I pray God long to preserve to their families and flocks, to their country, and to the Church of Christ.

This discourse was delivered in very singular circumstances. The Church of South Leith is one of the largest in Scotland, being able to contain upwards of five thousand persons. It was then completely filled. The greatness of the number who communicated, in the earlier part of the day, protracted the service to a late hour. No provision had been made for lighting up the Church for the evening-service; and the light of day failed during the prayer before Sermon. I was obliged to pronounce even the text from memory; and I feel at this moment the awful impression made on my mind, from the knowledge that I was going to address, for an hour at least, an assembly so vast, environed with darkness so profound. Silence equally profound, the preacher's voice excepted, added much to the solemnity of the scene. Could I have foreseen my situation, I should probably have shrunk from it. Involved in it, beyond the possibility of retreating, courage sprung up out of necessity: I threw
myself

myself on the help of God, and the candour of my hearers, and my trust did not betray me.

Of the great multitude which then composed my audience, how few, alas, remain to this day! Four and twenty years! what an impression they make on the human race!

How strange appeared to me the transition from communion-services such as this, to the frigid, unfrequented, unsocial celebrations of the South! How was I mortified to find, instead of the liberal, enlarged spirit of my native country, the contractedness and illiberality of sect; the Church of Christ broken into small isolated fragments; and so little cordiality among the ministers of the same religion, that the man who would invite me to his pulpit to preach the Gospel to his flock, would not, could not, durst not, admit me to the privilege of a private Christian, that of sitting down with him at the Table of the Lord! How it sounded in my ears, Such a person, such a family *belongs* to Mr. *Such-an-one*! Happy art thou, O *Scotland!* all whose ministers love as brethren; all whose Churches are *one*! " Behold, how good and how pleasant it is " for Brethren to dwell together in unity!"

THE SUCCESS OF THE GOSPEL, THROUGH THE MINISTRATION OF WEAK AND SINFUL MEN; A PROOF OF THE POWER, WISDOM, AND GOODNESS OF GOD.

SERMON II.*

2 CORINTHIANS, IV. 7.

But we have this Treasure in earthen Vessels, that the Excellency of the Power may be of GOD, and not of us.

IN CONNECTION WITH

EXODUS XX. 19.

—*They said unto Moses, speak thou with us, and we will hear; but let not GOD speak with us lest we die.*

EVER since the fatal hour, that the first Parents of Mankind furnished themselves with a humiliating reason, for flying from "the presence of the LORD GOD," and for attempting to conceal their guilt and shame amidst the trees of the garden, every personal, and immediate, approach of the Deity, has been an object of terror to them, and to their sinful posterity.

---

* Preached at the Scots Church, London-Wall, December 22, 1774, at the Ordination of the Rev. CHARLES NICOLSON, A.M. One of the Ministers of the BRITISH Reformed Church at Amsterdam.

Fear continually preſſes hard upon the footſteps of guilt; and what we fear, that we naturally ſhun. Hence we ſhould keep at a perpetual diſtance from God, did not his power compel, his juſtice drag, or his mercy allure us into his preſence. The appearance of the Moſt High, as a righteous Judge and omnipotent Avenger, were certain and ſwift deſtruction to the guilty: and, ſo fearful is the breach which ſin has made between God and Man, ſo alarming are the ſuggeſtions of an awakened conſcience, that even the gentle intimations of pity and love, if diſplayed in native, celeſtial majeſty, muſt dazzle the feeble eye, and ſtun the trembling ear, of conſcious demerit.

When, therefore, the Father of mercies was pleaſed, on ſpecial occaſions, to reveal his grace to the children of men, the voice of the Eternal did not rend the vault of Heaven, and ſhake the pillars of the earth; nor did even one of the flaming Miniſters deſcend from before the throne of God, and proclaim to an aſtoniſhed world, by the trumpet of Jehovah, the wonderful tidings of " Peace on earth, and good will to Men," but in condeſcenſion to human weakneſs, and in commiſeration of human woe, the God of conſolation, " at ſundry times, and in divers manners, ſpake unto

" unto the fathers by the prophets." He spake to sinful creatures, by men of like passions with themselves—by their fellow sinners. When angels were sent to convey the will of God to mankind, they assumed the robes of meekness, and spake in the language of sympathy and friendship.

And when, at length, in the depth of infinite wisdom, and in the riches of free grace, God thought it good to address himself to his fallen creatures " by his Son, the brightness of his " glory, and the express image of his person"— " The word was made *flesh*, and dwelt among us." When the Prince of peace vouchsafed to come for our salvation, " verily he took not on him the " nature of angels, but he took on him the seed " of *Abraham*,"—He became man, that without inspiring terror, he might converse with men, and in accents of their own, might gently persuade them of the tender mercies of God, and win them to heaven. The persons employed as ministring servants to his great design, to declare the doctrine of reconciliation, " to preach among " the *Gentiles* the unsearchable riches of *Christ*," to point out the way to eternal life, were such as needed all the blessings of that gospel which they preached to others. The precious " treasure was " committed to earthen vessels, that the excel- " lency

"lency of the power might be of God." Such has been the ſtate of Chriſtianity in every age, ſuch it is at this day, and thus it is evidently deſigned to continue to the end of the world.

The language of the text is beautifully figurative, and conveys this idea: The diſpenſation of the goſpel of peace, the moſt valuable poſſeſſion conferred by God upon mankind, is put into the hands of weak and fallible men, that its ſucceſs may appear to flow, not from the ability or ſkill of the diſpenſer; but from its own intrinſic worth and importance, and from the irreſiſtible power, the unerring wiſdom, and the ſovereign grace, of its great Author. It is like a treaſure of gold laid up in an earthen pot, or a precious jewel depoſited in a rough caſket. Theſe valuable commodities communicate a dignity and value to that which contains them, but can derive nothing from the connection. The veſſel may be broken in pieces, the caſket thrown, as a worthleſs thing, away, and yet the treaſure may retain its full weight, and the gem ſtill ſparkle in all its native luſtre.

It is my deſign, upon this occaſion, in the humble hope of divine aſſiſtance, to conſider the preſent ſtate of the Goſpel Miniſtry, and of the Chriſtian Church, in this particular point of view,

view; as an evidence of the wisdom and goodness of Providence; that we may be together led to the grateful and devout acknowledgment of it, and to an entire dependence upon that Almighty Power, which alone can render the means of grace effectual.

However it may appear upon a first, and to a superficial, observation; though it might be apprehended that perfection of moral character, and a higher order of talents ought to have been united to the ministration of a pure and perfect Religion; by attending more closely, we shall find, That the great ends which God evidently has in view, in the Gospel of his Son, are most effectually accomplished by that mode of dispensation which we see to have been established. Without insisting on the general proposition, that whatever infinite Wisdom has determined, is certainly best, the propriety of the present establishment of things in the Christian Church, conformably to the Apostle's idea in the text, will appear, whether we consider it, as respecting the Ministers of the Gospel themselves; or as respecting those to whom it is dispensed; or as it respects Him, whose message the Gospel is, and on whose blessing all its efficacy depends.

I. God

I. God has appointed the Gospel to be preached by men; to men, for the sake of its *Ministers.*

One of the most infallible methods of acquiring knowledge, of any kind, is to communicate that which we already possess, to others. While we teach, we necessarily learn; while we study the illumination of our hearers, the darkness of our own minds is thereby dispelled. Art thou called then, my brother, to the work of the ministry, to be " a guide of the blind, a light of " them which are in darkness, an instructor of " the foolish, a teacher of babes;" art thou sent of Providence to lead men to the knowledge of the truth, that they may be saved? By that call, in whatever manner conveyed, thou art invited, in the most affecting terms, to study " the " Truth as it is in *Jesus,*" upon thy own account; to understand and feel for thyself, what thou wouldst wish others to understand and feel through thy means. To all the motives, towards the pursuit of that " wisdom which is from above," and which maketh wise unto salvation, in common to thee with other men, an additional and a striking one arises out of thy particular office and profession. The great Head of the Church, the great Fountain of light has left thee no choice here, but has laid thee under a gracious and
gentle

gentle necessity, of being acquainted with the glorious Mystery of Godliness, that is, with the things which belong to thy everlasting peace. Many may, and do " perish through lack " of knowledge;" but God has mercifully secured thee on this side; and canst thou but account this as an additional instance of his goodness, and an additional claim upon thy gratitude and love?

Again, it is evident that the great Being who would have the Gospel preached to every creature, and its benefits universally diffused, must have intended, that those who were to convey such inestimable blessings to the World, should themselves liberally partake thereof. It was a Law, worthy of the bountiful and mercifully considerate Parent of the Universe, who " preserveth man " and beast," " Thou shall not muzzle the " ox when he treadeth out the corn*." " And " doth God take care for Oxen?" And are not ye of much more value than many of those? Will He, who has sent us to dispense to the poor and needy of the fulness which is treasured up in Christ, forbid us to take a supply for our own necessities? Will He, who is pleased to employ us, in directing his people to the heavenly *Canaan*, obstruct the passage against ourselves, and say,

But,

* Deut. xxv. 4.

But, "as for you, ye shall in no wise enter therein?" Shall the steward starve, while he feeds the houshold with bread? Surely not. The apostle of the *Gentiles* could, from his own sweet experience, bear testimony to the grace of God in this respect: " The God of all comfort," says he, " comforteth us in all our tribulation, that we " may be able to comfort them which are in any " trouble, by the comfort wherewith we ourselves " are comforted of God." The treasure committed to the ministers of the Gospel, is not the hoard of a miser, only to be looked at, and reckoned over; no, it is the rich, and the continually abounding, increasing store, of the bountiful Proprietor of all things, which grows by communication, and whose use is its increase.

How often has it been found, that the necessary intercourse betwixt ministers and the afflicted, the tempted, and the desponding children of God, hath, through the divine blessing, proved the means of alleviating the distresses, of subduing the temptations, of removing the doubts, and of healing the painful wounds of the former as well as of the latter; of conveying peace and joy to the minister, as well as to them among whom he ministered? Besides, by conversing with men in all the varieties of situation in human

man life, and in religion, the teachers of Christianity may be, and often are, led to the discovery, and the improvement, of many important particulars in their own character and conduct, to which they had not attended before; and which, but for their office, they might not have found out, till the season of profiting had been lost.

Farther, It is meet that the Gospel "treasure should be in earthen vessels," not only for the purposes of extending the knowledge, and of promoting the edification and comfort of ministers; but also in order to form their tempers, to impress their characters, and to regulate their behaviour, into the similitude of their divine master, the meek and lowly JESUS. The grand and comprehensive aim of Christianity is to teach men humility. For this end, "CHRIST humbled "himself, and became of no reputation;" for this end, He would have his Gospel preached by such as, in this respect, bore some resemblance to Himself; and for this end, He furnished his ministring servants with every argument to exemplify, and to inculcate, humility. Their name, their office, their personal characters, their relation to the blessed JESUS, and, above all, his example, call upon them, with an united voice, to be lowly in heart, that they may teach the world to be humble

ble. The diſtinctions which prevail among men upon earth are calculated to feed the pride and vanity of the diſtinguiſhed; and the badges of ſuperiority are carefully contrived to conceal or to efface, as much as poſſible, every thing mean and mortifying in the condition of him who wears them; but this order is quite reverſed in CHRIST's kingdom; one of the great and fundamental laws of its conſtitution runs thus, " Whoſoever, will " be great among you, let him be your miniſter; " and whoſoever will be chief among you, let him " be your ſervant: Even as the Son of Man came " not to be miniſtered unto, but to miniſter."

To riſe in any kingdom is to approach towards the Sovereign, and to reſemble him: From the nature of CHRIST's kingdom, then, and from the character of Him who ſits upon the throne of it, to be advanced there, is to deſcend; to acquire dignity, is to grow in humility; to be qualified for a ſtation near the Prince, is to poſſeſs a meek and quiet ſpirit; to be honourable in the ſight of God and angels; to be fitted for the ſociety of juſt men made perfect; to enjoy inward compoſure—is to be. " poor in ſpirit," for that is to inherit the kingdom of heaven. When this is conſidered, it is matter of joy that the goſpel treaſure is committed to *earthen veſſels*—to men, whoſe

* Matt. xx. 26, 27, 28.

whose employments, and whose hopes, are an habitual exhortation to the study and practice of humility; and besides, whose own minds will suggest many private and personal reasons to the same effect. It is happy for the world, for the church, and for the parties themselves, that if ministers will be proud, peevish, or self-sufficient, it shall not be through want of arguments to the contrary, arguments, in which conscious frailty, without much expence of thought, will instruct them.

Another useful and important ingredient, in the character of a Gospel-Minister, is furnished from the same store, namely, a humane, compassionate, and patient disposition. The best teachers, in any art or science, are those who arrive at excellency, through much pain and labour. A quick and penetrating genius can hardly form any notion of a slow capacity, and with difficulty accommodates himself to the progress of such; whereas, one who recollects that his own dulness often tried the patience and temper of his teacher, must be both in the habit, and under the inclination, of shewing lenity and tenderness toward those who learn of him.

A physician who has never known pain and sickness himself, wants at least one important auxiliary to skill, and one irresistible recommendation

tion to his patient; one useful quality, which experience only can bestow upon him. It is an amiable view of the great Physician of souls, in this respect, with which the Apostle presents us: " In all things it behoved him, to be made like " unto his brethren; that he might be a merciful " and faithful High-priest, in things pertaining to " God, to make reconciliation for the sins of the " people; for in that, He himself hath suffered, " being tempted, he is able to succour them that " are tempted*." And, again, " For we have " not an High-priest who cannot be touched with " the feelings of our infirmities; but was in all " points tempted like as we are, yet without sin||." Providence has, for the same reason, wisely and graciously so ordered it, that priests and ministers, taken from among men, should have heart-felt motives to pity the ignorant, the weak, the miserable. They are " ordained for men, in things " pertaining to God, to have compassion on the " ignorant, and on them that are out of the way, " for that they themselves also are compassed " with infirmity†."

I have reckoned this among the *advantages* of a Minister's situation; for though a feeling heart

---

* Heb. ii. 17, 18. || — iv. 15.   † — 1, 2.

heart be often a fource of the acuteft anguifh, and of the moft overwhelming diftrefs, which a felfifh mind is always ftudious to avoid, yet there is a decency, there is a dignity in it, which conftitute the nobleft characteriftic of humanity. While it confers upon its poffeffor the moft laudable and the moft advantageous afcendant toward the fuccefsful difcharge of his duty, it beftows the jufteft title to confidence, it brings all a minifter's other talents into the way of their fulleft and moft promifing exertion, it leads by the fhorteft, and the fafeft road, to extenfive utility. The tender-hearted will bear me out, if I add, that, in the very paroxyfms of fympathetic woe, there is a joy which the felfifh are not honoured to tafte, with which the ftranger muft not afpire to intermeddle. And this painful fenfibility, at worft, is more than compenfated, to the man who lives not for himfelf merely, by the delightful employment of it, in removing what gave it exiftence—the mifery of others. I now proceed,

II. To confider, for what reafons, in the wifdom of God, the Gofpel is difpenfed by the hands of frail and imperfect men, as thofe reafons affect the perfons *to* whom the word of this falvation is fent; or rather, as they affect their joint interefts and mutual relations, for thefe are fo blended, as to render a feparation of them impoffible.

THE

The address of the children of *Israel* to *Moses*, which we have read, affords one very obvious and striking reason. A dispensation coming *immediately* from GOD, was clothed in too many awful circumstances, to admit of recollection and composure. Though the chosen tribes had every encouragement to believe that the glorious JEHOVAH was peculiarly propitious to them, and had promulgated his Law, not in anger, but in kindness; yet they could not support the enunciation of it from his own lips. And had you, Christians, stood with them, trembling under the awful terrors of *Mount Sinai*; had you heard the thunderings, and seen the lightnings; heard the noise of the trumpet resounding from rock to rock; seen the mountain smoking and quaking, and heard the voice of GOD himself bursting through the thick cloud that veiled his Glory; you would, doubtless, have been disposed, with them, to remove and stand far off, and to join in their request, " Let not GOD speak with " us, lest we die"—for " so terrible was the sight, " that *Moses* himself said, I exceedingly fear and " quake." The appearance of the ALMIGHTY unto *Elijah*, in *Horeb*, recorded 1 *Kings* xix. 11, 12. is another instructive and striking illustration to this purpose, while, at the same time, it beautifully

tifully points out the difference between the legal dispensation and the evangelical; the terrifying solemnity of the one, the mildness and gentleness of the other——"And behold the Lord passed "by, and a great and strong wind rent the "mountains, and brake in pieces the rocks be- "fore the Lord: But the Lord was not in the wind."—Else, how could a frail, sinful mortal have supported his presence? "And after the "wind an earthquake; but the Lord was not in "the earthquake: and after the earthquake a fire; "but the Lord was not in the fire:" The glory of GOD, thus manifested, had been too much for even an *Elijah* to bear: What then? "And after "the fire, a still small voice:" This at length encouraged the Prophet to attend, and to approach towards the entrance of the cave, though not without wrapping his face in his mantle, that he might hear what GOD the Lord would say, in a voice to which he could listen without astonishment. And it is thus that our merciful heavenly Father deals with us in the Gospel of his Son; He speaks to us in a still small voice—the words, the accents are those of a man to his friend; fearful, trembling sinners are invited to the throne of grace, in language which they understand, and which dissipates, not confirms and strengthens their apprehensions.

The ministration even of angels, superior, though created intelligences, would be unsuitable to the present weak, depressed state of humanity; for, not to mention the terror inspired by the appearances of those exalted beings, under a dispensation calculated to display, chiefly, the majesty of the divine power, holiness and justice; we find that, under the gentler reign of grace and mercy, the presence of an angel was an object of fear, to the best of men, as well as to the bold and guilty. "For fear of him," who attended upon the resurrection of the Lord Jesus, "the keepers did "shake, and became as dead men." This is not much to be wondered at; but *Zacharias* himself, though employed in the most solemn religious service, in obedience to the express appointment of God; though accustomed to make solitary approaches to the most solemn and secret recesses of the temple; and though free from the horrors which an ill conscience excites in the guilty soul, yet "when he saw the Angel of the Lord stand- "ing on the right side of the altar of incense, he "was troubled, and fear fell upon him. At the sight of him who announced the nativity of our Lord, the shepherds of *Bethlehem* were "sore "afraid."

No passion unhinges the mind more than fear. It distracts the attention, misrepresents the object, overwhelms

overwhelms the understanding, and renders the performance of a reasonable service utterly impossible; it is, therefore, inconsistent with a worship to be rendered "in spirit and in truth," such as the Father of spirits requires. We are not, then, invited to it, and assisted in it, by creatures whose nature is superior to our own—by sinless and perfect beings; because their devotion, however elevated and intense; their zeal, however fervent; their love, however pure; their capacity, however enlarged; their labours however executive and assiduous, could be no examples of, no incentives to, ours. The advantages which they possess, in these very respects, would prove the means of damping, of discouraging, of intimidating us. It is the evident design of the gracious Author of the christian dispensation to draw men to himself with "cords of a man, with bands of love;" and therefore *men* are employed in this benevolent, this hope-inspiring service.

As it is the gracious intention of GOD, that his people should not be *terrified*, in receiving the proclamations of his love, by the dignity and the distance of the persons sent on this errand; so, by choosing his messengers from amongst the frail, the sinful and the miserable, he has wisely cut off all occasion of *their* exacting an undue respect

respect, and has forbidden the world, more than by an express interdiction, to yield them reverence on their own account. Nothing about them challenges veneration, nothing is peculiarly estimable, except it be the office which they bear, and the message which they bring.

There is a well-known propensity in human nature, to transfer the attention which is due to an useful and important piece of intelligence, by an easy, and seemingly excusable, transition, to the person of him who delivers it; at least, it is natural to share the respect between them. And it is as natural for those who are intrusted with any weighty and honourable commission, to take state upon it, and to expect submission and regard on their separate score; and these propensities, acting upon, and aiding each other, have filled even the Christian world with idols and idolaters. But it is also observable, that when an attempt was made to deify a christian minister, a claim of infallibility was advanced in his behalf; the earthen pitcher was by a kind of magick transmuted into a vase of gold; for so long as it sensibly retained the base and contemptible qualities of the former, it was impossible, with all the natural bias of the human heart towards idolatry, to erect an altar unto it. It is no less observable, however,

however, in opposition to this, that the nearer we approach to the pure times of Christianity, and the higher that we mount on the scale of apostolic and angelical perfection, with the greater firmness and abhorrence do we find all improper respect disclaimed and rejected. " See thou do it not," said the Angel to *John*, when he would have fallen down to worship before his feet, upon being shewn the glories of the *New Jerusalem*; " for I
" am thy fellow-servant, and of thy brethren the
" prophets, and of them which keep the sayings
" of this book; worship GOD." When *Paul* and *Barnabus* discovered, in the inhabitants of *Lystra*, an intention to render them the homage due to deity, in the belief that they were superior to mortals, " they rent their clothes, and ran in
" among the people, crying out and saying, Sirs,
" why do you these things? we also are men of
" like passions with you, and preach unto you,
" that ye should turn from these vanities, unto
" the living GOD"—and so restrained the people. When *Cornelius* met *Peter*, and fell down at his feet and worshipped him, *Peter* took him up, saying, " Stand up, I myself also am a man."

But what occasion is there, it may be asked, for making these remarks, in the present state of things? These, surely, are not the times, nor is
this

this the land of idolizing the priesthood; of consecrating altars to the ministers of the despised *Galilean*; these are not the days of implicit faith and blind attachment. And can you indeed believe, Sirs, that it was never said, except by the *Corinthians*, and eighteen hundred years ago, " I " am of *Paul*, and I of *Apollos*, and I of *Cephas*, " and I of *Christ*." Does the Bishop of *Rome* alone lay claim to supremacy and infallibility? Or, Is prelacy peculiar to the church of *England*? Did there never exist in the church but one " *Diotrephes*," never but one, " who loved to " have the pre-eminence"? Do *Presbyterian* parity, and the levelling hand of *Independency*, alway repress the lofty pretensions of arrogant individuals, and prevent the people from " having mens per- "* sons in admiration?" Alas, my friends! it is not a *system* that can check the usurpations of pride and ambition: It is not a form of church-government that can settle the dispute between the just demands of a righteous GOD, and the passions and worldly interests of men, or between the opposite and discordant claims of men upon each other. There have been, there are, and there will be, till human nature be thoroughly purged of its dross, men of all persuasions, ready to ask, and to yield, what belongs to no man what-

whatever. When the people are intelligent, a requisition of personal regard, in whatever manner advanced, is always sure to defeat itself, and to meet with deserved contempt; and when it is otherwise, when men will fall down to gods of their own raising, it is wisely and well ordered, that the idolatry should expose its own folly 'and absurdity. In this process, men *act* as they often *reason*—in a circle. Designing, covetous, and ambitious priests worship and exalt the people; that the people, in their turn, may elevate and support them; and both are equally repugnant to " the wisdom that is from above," which has committed this treasure to earthen vessels, that " none may think of himself more highly than " he ought to think; but to think soberly, ac- " cording as God hath dealt to every man the " measure of faith."

The extreme opposite to superstitious homage and veneration, is likewise guarded against, by this wise establishment in the christian church. Though the ministers of it derive no title to exercise authority, or to demand respect, as men, from their sacred office, yet, on the other hand, that very office ought to be a full security against insult and disrespect. The bearer of even an unwelcome message ought not, in reason, to be maltreated;

treated; for the offence, if there be any, comes not from him, but from his employer. The brittle phial which contains a precious elixir muſt not be handled rudely, left, in cruſhing it, the medicine ſhould periſh. This has an evident reſpect both to miniſters and people; the former, in the perſuaſion that they are appointed of Providence to convey the beſt of tidings to mankind, cheerfully commit the care of their perſons, and of all their temporal concerns, to that Providence; and, under it, to the tenderneſs and affection of thoſe who partake of the ſpiritual bleſſings which they diſpenſe. The people again, in the perſons of their miniſters, have continually before their eyes an object whereon to exerciſe ſome of the worthieſt principles of their nature—gentleneſs, ſympathy, benevolence, kindneſs. For what picture, I beſeech you, does a miniſter of the goſpel preſent to the world? He preſents to us a man loaded with all the infirmities, and liable to all the diſtreſſes incident to humanity, with the additional weight, peculiar to himſelf, of a momentous charge, intruſted to him by God, in the certain proſpect of rendering a ſtrict account of it; a man conſtrained to ſtand daily at the bar of any one who may be pleaſed to ſit in judgment upon him, and uncertain when he may be called

to

to appear before the more tremendous tribunal of the great Judge of all: a man who has voluntarily refigned the great, and the gainful walks of life, and the means of whofe very fubfiftence, in many inftances, depend on the good-will of others: a man whofe profeffion has obftructed to him moft of the ufual avenues leading to fame and to fortune, and whofe fpirit fhould abhor every indirect road to either: a man who has undertaken, not an eafy and commodious employment, but a truft full of care, of anxiety, of danger. In fuch circumftances, are not the injunctions of Scripture, concerning the treatment of the chriftian miniftry, at the fame time alfo, the conclufions of reafon, the dictates of confcience, the obligations of gratitude, and the gentle calls of fenfibility? Even " to know them which " labour among you; and are over you in the " Lord, and admonifh you; and to efteem them " very highly in love for their works fake." If there be then any virtue, if any praife, in employing and exerting the nobleft and beft principles of which the human mind is fufceptible, you have reafon to blefs God, that he has furnifhed the occafion, and fpread the field for fuch exertion, by the manner in which, and from the character and fituation of the perfons by whom,

the

the gospel is dispensed. It remains, that we consider,

III. That great and weighty reason which is urged by the apostle in the text, why the all-wise GOD has thought fit to send his Gospel to the children of men, by the hands of their frail and sinful brethren, it is " that the excellency of the " power may be of GOD, and not of us."— " The *excellency* of the power;" that is, its superiority to every thing human or created. The effect designed to be produced by instruments so weak, must be so great and astonishing, as to constrain the beholder to transfer the praise from the visible to the invisible agent ; from the feeble creature to the omnipotent Creator, who has given such power unto men.

The apostle, in the preceding part of this chapter, had been considering " the knowledge " of GOD" under the idea of light shining out of darkness : This light was displayed at first in meridian brightness, in the person of his Son, " in the " face of *Jesus Christ*."—After, and under, Him, it was transmitted through a more obscure medium, the ministry of his apostles. But even then, its rays were so quick and penetrating, as fully to evince its divine original, and to satisfy

every

every impartial observer, that it was indeed an emanation from the pure source of eternal and uncreated light. In *Jesus*, the world " beheld " the glory of the only begotten of the Father, " full of grace and truth," native, underived splendor; but *we* have this treasure in earthen vessels; the glory is one, the fountain of it one, its effect constant and uniform; the end still one and the same: the medium of transmission alone differs. In *Christ, all fulness was pleased to dwell*; to him the Spirit was given without measure; and from that inexhaustible fulness, which is treasured up in him, do all his ministring servants, whether angels or men, receive continual supplies of *grace for grace*, according as they need, and as He is pleased to communicate.

The grand, combined system of nature, of providence, and of grace, is evidently hastening to one great consummation, a general and full manifestation of the glory of the great Lord of all. Into this vast ocean, the various and innumerable instruments, employed by his sovereign hand, are pressing forward, to empty their several little urns: " The Kings of the earth," to use the lofty language of *Revelation*, " do bring their glo- " ry and honour into it, and the nations of them " that are saved shall walk in the light of it*;"

that

Rev. xxi. 24.

that God may be all in all; that every thing glorious and excellent in the creature, may be finally resolved into that, by which, and for which, the universe was brought into existence—the glory of the Creator. Every attempt to subvert this order, or to frustrate this end, must be highly displeasing to that God, who is jealous of his honour, who will neither resign it, nor suffer it to be taken away from him; and who has, accordingly, so settled the government, both of the natural and moral world, as most effectually to prevent the ascribing to any other, what is due to him alone. And, particularly, the administration of God's kingdom of grace is so contrived, as to render an alienation, or a partition, of praise, impracticable and absurd, " For after that, in the wisdom of God, the
" world by wisdom knew not God, it pleased
" God, by the foolishness of preaching, to save
" them that believe. Because the foolishness of
" God is wiser than men, and the weakness of
" God is stronger than men;" to demonstrate which, " God hath chosen the foolish things of
" the world to confound the wise; and God hath
" chosen the weak things of the world to con-
" found the mighty; and base things of the
" world, and things which are despised, hath
" God chosen; yea and things which are not, to
" bring

" bring to nought things that are, that no flesh
" should glory in his presence, but that he who
" glorieth, should glory in the Lord."

When we behold any wonderful and striking effect, it is natural to investigate the cause of it, and to compare them together; having discovered the apparent and proximate, and, as we think, an adequate cause, we are too apt to stop short, to rest there, and to forget God. He is pleased, therefore, in many instances, to disturb us in such processes and conclusions, and to confound and expose our shallow or presumptuous reasonings, by exhibiting effects, betwixt which and the apparent causes, there is no manner of proportion, that He alone, " for whom are all things, and by whom " are all things," may be acknowledged and adored.

When we read of one king, attended with an hundred thousand men, going out to meet another king, who is advancing against him with an equal number; when, after a long and fierce conflict, we behold victory at length dropping into either scale, we presently endeavour to account for the event, by considering, and comparing, the skill or misconduct of the generals; the bravery or cowardice of the soldiers; the advantages or disadvantages of the ground, and such like circumstances,

cumſtances, which might have contributed toward the victory or defeat: But when we read of the hoſt of the *Midianities* and *Amalekites**, like "graſhoppers for multitude," diſcomfited by the "three hundred which lapped," and theſe armed only with trumpets, lamps, and empty pitchers; and a whole camp overturned, as by "a "cake of barley bread, rolling down upon it," it is impoſſible to ſtate a compariſon betwixt the cauſe and the effect, we are conſtrained to riſe at once to the great firſt Cauſe of all things, and to cry out, "This cometh forth from the Lord of "Hoſts, who is wonderful in counſel, and excellent "in working." When I ſee the walls of a great and ſtrong city, though ſhaken by no convulſion of the earth, ſunk by no mine, ſhattered by no battering ram, or other warlike engine, yet falling down flat to the ground; I cannot ſtop to think of † "ſeven unwarlike prieſts, with their ſeven "trumpets made of rams horns;"—but muſt immediately revere the arm of JEHOVAH, and aſcribe the ſucceſs to the appointment and interpoſition of Heaven.

But the hiſtory of the Goſpel exhibits wonders ſtill greater than theſe, and places the divine perfections in a ſtill more aſtoniſhing point of view.

Had

* Judges vii. 12. † Joſhua vi. 22.

Had the Saviour of the world chosen his apostles from amongst the celebrated philosophers and orators of *Greece* and *Rome*; or commissioned the great, the mighty, and the affluent of the earth, to instruct their fellow creatures in the way of salvation; the sagacity, the eloquence, and the authority of the preachers, would certainly have become objects of attention; it might justly have been enquired, How far men may be led to embrace a religious system through the submission which is usually yielded to superior rank, or the charms of oratory, or the respect implicitly paid to apprehended wisdom, independent of knowledge and conviction? Whatever effects might have been produced, through the intervention of human power and genius, would, in part at least, have been ascribed to their exertion; and the doctrine itself, conveyed through such channels, must have received, at most, a divided praise.

When we look back to the infant state of Christianity, nothing seems more improbable, according to the ordinary rules of judging, than its continuance in the world beyond the short and uncertain lives of its first professors. Full well was the prediction of the Psalmist accomplished*, in the early, obstinate and rancorous opposition which was made to the

---

* Psal. ii. 2.

the religion of the blessed *Jesus,* "The kings "of the earth set themselves, and the rulers take "counsel together against the Lord, and against "his anointed." The improbability of success was greatly increased by the internal character and spirit of the Gospel, and by the condition and character of its first ministers; the former contradicted and exposed the most favourite maxims, disallowed and condemned the generally prevailing practices of the world: The latter seemed calculated rather to hurt a popular cause, than to recommend one that was odious and disgusting. To a mind engrossed by the wisdom, the pleasures, the riches, the honours, which the human heart naturally affects and pursues; what could be more ungainly and forbidding, than the aspect of a doctrine which pointed out, which enjoined, which imposed the cross; which professed to level every high mountain of pride, to dry up the very fountain of carnal Joy, to lay the axe to the root of ambition, and which proposed, to the covetous, treasures in Heaven?

And by what instruments were purposes of such hazardous and difficult enterprize to be effected? By men destitute of authority, of influence, of ingenuity, of address. By men, whom their natural abilities, their country and parentage, their persons and occupations

pations, expofed to contempt rather than to hatred. An infidel of thofe days might have found plentiful food for his fpleen and ridicule, in the contemplation of a fect which was in time to overfpread the whole world; at the head of which ftood a little handful of fimple, unlettered fifhermen. But what is the fact? The hated doctrine, and the defpifed minifters of a crucified *Jefus*, furmounted all oppofition, triumphed over the hoftile powers of earth, and the malice of hell, and, without the affiftance of force, or guile, or gold, nay against the united ftrength of all thefe, vigoroufly and zealoufly engaged on the other fide, conftrained men to embrace the crofs, once the object of their averfion and difdain. When, therefore, we behold the great " Author and finifher of our faith," employing, at firft, a feeble and fcanty band of fimple men, furnifhed with a few fimple and unoftentatious, though notorious facts, for the purpofe of converting a prejudiced and fin-enflaved world, to a mafter; a doctrine, a converfation which the world naturally defpifes and abhors; and by means of fuch meffengers, armed with fuch weapons, actually fubverting Satan's kingdom, fupported by all the learning, paffion, power and temporal intereft of man; and when, to this day, we fee the fame difficulties overcome, the fame work

F profpering

prospering, the same ends attained; and still through the instrumentality of men of moderate parts, of feeble eloquence, of little authority, and for the most part of very slender fortune; men of many personal and of some professional infirmities; when we observe all this, do we not hear, at the same time, a voice from the most excellent glory, saying, " The work is mine, the " praise be mine, and I will not give my glory " to another?" And can we but reply, in the words of the heavenly host, " Blessing, and ho- " nour, and glory and power be unto him who " sitteth upon the throne, and unto the Lamb " for ever and ever?"

From this subject,

I. CHRISTIAN *Ministers* are instructed in the nature of that rank and station which they occupy in the church of CHRIST; and the obligations which arise out of these. It is surely of importance, men, brethren, and fathers, that the vessel which contains Gospel blessings, for the benefit of others, should itself be seasoned with grace. It is an awful thing for a man to be the publisher to another, of an act of indemnity, which contains in it a positive and express exception against himself; to preach the doctrine of reconciliation to others, and be himself a cast-away. The distinct knowledge of
this

this treasure, and the application of it to our own necessities, ought certainly to précede the communication of it to our fellow-sinners, both for their sakes and our own. Mankind, at large, will assume and exercise a liberty of studying or neglecting Christianity, according to their pleasure, and they must abide by the consequences; but the very name of minister supposes the choice to be already made, and that necessity is laid upon him who bears it, to study, know, love, and practise the truth, as it is in JESUS.

He whose office it is to go between opposite and contending, but reconcileable parties, ought to be acquainted with the mind, the condition, and the dispositions of both. A message not fully understood, never can be faithfully delivered. A minister must deliver what he has received of the Lord, not what his own inclination, or the taste of his hearers, may relish or approve. A trust reposed must, in order to prove a man faithful, be surrendered without increase or diminution. To conceal any part of the counsel of GOD, is to be unjust to the people, who have a heaven-derived claim to the whole; to pretend to add any thing, is to be highly presumptuous against GOD, who is the only competent judge of what is enough. But this by no means precludes the exercise of prudence,

prudence, of delicacy, of boldness, according as various circumstances may require. Now that calls to the ministry are not miraculous, but providential; our talents, as men, are to be carefully cultivated, and strenuously exercised. If we would be faithful to God, and useful to men, we must add, to an entire reliance upon Almighty Grace, the full exertion of all those powers, natural and acquired, which the great Dispenser of every good and perfect gift has bestowed upon us.

The idea of the text suggests to ministers, their intrinsic weakness and worthlessness, but, at the same time, their utility and importance, as instruments in the hand of God for carrying on his work. This distinction, properly understood and felt, is the only preservative from pride and self-conceit, on the one hand, and a listless indolent affectation of humility on the other. The idea of the text suggests to ministers their fragility, their mortality. " Our fathers, where are they? the pro-
" phets, do they live forever?" Ah, no! yet a little while, and " the silver cord shall be loosed,
" and the golden bowl broken, and the pitcher
" broken at the fountain, and the wheel at the
" cistern." A consideration how affecting, a motive how urgent, to do the work of the day, while the day lasts! Did we consider our sermons

as

as the addresses of dying men, to dying men, surely they would often, in many important respects, differ from their present tenor. May God give us a deeper sense of the worth of precious souls, and make us to feel, in all their weight and importance, the powers of a world to come.

II. The *Hearers* of the Gospel are, by this subject, instructed in sundry interesting and important particulars of their duty and situation in the Church of Christ. They are taught gratitude to the grace and condescension of God, who, in making known to them the counsels of his will, has been pleased to lay aside the thunder of his power, has suppressed the awful voice which makes earth shake to her centre, and hell to tremble in the agonies of despair; and has sunk the Sovereign and the Judge, in the Father and the Friend. And ought that message to be less welcome, which encourages hope, which invites to peace, which soothes the soul to rest—not confounds the understanding, not drinks up the spirit; which extinguishes the hell within the breast, and brings the means of escape from the hell beyond the grave? Because God is gentle and condescending, shall men be trifling and negligent? Of all punishments, that of despised mercy, of slighted grace, is surely the justest, and will be the most severe.

If you feel this, Christians, you are already informed how to conduct yourselves towards your ministers; you are already guarded against putting them in the place of God, on one hand, or setting " them with the dogs of your flock," on the other. You have already learned to revere their office, to listen to their message, to love their persons, for their work's sake, to consider their outward circumstances, to imitate their virtues, to commiserate their infirmities, and to be merciful to their faults. In behalf of their vices, I have nothing to urge; would to God they had none that needed indulgence; but in behalf of their many failings and infirmities, I would venture to plead, were this the proper time and place. Ministers are indeed, in all respects, their ministry alone excepted, so very like yourselves, that you have only your own hearts and consciences to consult, in order to make a proper estimate of them, to determine your opinion of their conduct, and to regulate your behaviour towards them.

III. To conclude: Both *Ministers* and *People* are hereby taught to acknowledge God chiefly, God only, in all things; to refer all the good which they do, or receive, to the great Parent of good; to cease from man, from each other, from themselves; to rejoice in the establishment of the
divine

divine glory, upon the ruins of human pride. This view, my friends, abforbs the fpirit of party, annihilates contention, brings heaven down to earth, and places men among angels. By entering ferioufly and heartily into it, we fhall feel pride languifh and die, zeal burn with a more pure and placid flame, Love to GOD and Men wax ftronger and ftronger, the world and its lying vanities difappear, the *New Jerufalem* in all its glory unveil itfelf. Let thy Will be done, O heavenly Father, by men on earth, as by the angels in heaven. "Fulfil in us the whole good pleafure of thy "goodnefs, and the work of faith with power, "that the Name of our Lord JESUS CHRIST "may be glorified in us, and we in him." *Amen.*

ADDITION TO SERMON II.

Memoir of the late Rev. CHARLES NICOLSON

MR. CHARLES NICOLSON, A.M. was the son of a clergyman of the Church of Scotland, in the neighbourhood of Aberdeen. It is very customary in North-Britain, for ministers who have families, (and most of them possess that blessing) to bring up one of the sons to the father's profession. The general practice, influenced by the particular circumstances of the case, pointed this out, early in life, as *Charles's* destination.

A placidity of temper, which adorned the youth, and afterwards endeared the man; an ingenuousness and innocence of disposition, which never forsook him, united to an aptitude for literature far above the common, were, it must be allowed, a happy basis whereon to rear the character of a minister of the gospel. Young *Nicolson's* school and academical career was accordingly accomplished much earlier than usual, greatly to the satisfaction of those who superintended his education, and greatly to the credit of his own capacity and diligence. Classical learning was, from the beginning

ginning his darling purfuit; and he devoted himfelf to it with an avidity, and an intenfenefs of application which would have overwhelmed a conftitution lefs vigorous, and exhaufted a fpirit lefs ardent than his. Frequent and conftant were his vifits to the Pierian fpring; long and delicious were his draughts at that harmlefs fountain, and ftill his thirft increafed as he drank. It is unneceffary to fay that, with fuch capacity, induftry, and perfeverance, he made the Greek and Roman claffics all his own. Providence, no doubt, kindly directed this tafte, with a view to the future condition and exigencies of the man. It was to be his lot to fpend a confiderable proportion of his days in exile, feparated from the land and the friends he loved, amidft the marfhes of Holland, and in the no lefs inclement air of the Thracian Bofporos. His beloved claffics were the conftant companions of his peregrination and folitude. In them he fought and found delight, whether by the fide of a putrid Batavian canal, or on the pleafanter banks of the Propontis.

Befides his high attainments in Greek and Roman claffical lore, what is not often the cafe, he had, before he reached his twentieth year, become a refpectable proficient in oriental learning. Nor were his Theological ftudies meanwhile neglected. On the contrary, he had become a mafter in fcripture criticifm, for which his fkill in both the languages of the facred Books eminently qualified him: and had read and digefted the feveral fyftems of Divinity commonly aught in our colleges; preferring, on deliberate enquiry

quiry and reflection, what is commonly denominated the orthodox, or calvinistic, system of doctrine. I said, *on deliberate enquiry and reflection*; for Nicolson was at no period of life a man disposed implicitly to adopt any one's opinions; and his conduct afterwards demonstrated, in very trying circumstances, that no allurement, on the one hand, and no menace, on the other, could induce him to deviate from what he thought the path of truth and rectitude. In the character and colour of his Theology, the goodness of Providence to honest Charles was again conspicuous: for he was to be sent to people with whom system, orthodoxy, a confession and a catechism, are every thing; and the heart and life a mere nothing. He had all their coldness and rectitude in opinion, and they left him to the undisturbed enjoyment of all the benevolent feelings of his good and honest heart.

That the university of Aberdeen should, at the proper season, decorate such a man with the academical feather, A. M. is not to be wondered at; that they never swelled it into a complete plume, has often been to me matter of surprize. In respect of learning, of real dignity, of unaffected goodness, few seminaries in Europe could boast his equal, as an alumnus, no one, his superior. The university which conferred its highest possible title of respect on Charles Nicolson, minister of the British Church at Amsterdam, or chaplain to the British Turkey Company at Constantinople, and to his Majesty's Ambassador at the Sublime Port, would have done itself the highest honour.

Earlier

Earlier than it is generally attained, as early indeed, almoſt, as the rules of the Church of Scotland permit, Mr. Nicolſon was admitted, by his native Preſbytery, to the rank of preacher of the Goſpel, or, as it is termed in Scotland, probationer for the holy miniſtry. I take the opportunity, which this era of my lamented friend's public life preſents, briefly to detail the practice preſcribed, and obſerved, in my native diviſion of the Iſland, reſpecting the admiſſion of candidates for the Goſpel miniſtry.

The private ſchool education being finiſhed, the young man muſt be entered at one of our four univerſities, as a ſtudent in Humanity and Philoſophy. In the minuter ſtudy of the learned languages, and of logic, mathematics, phyſics, ethics, and the *belles lettres*, four years are generally employed; and in the cloſe of the fourth year, if ſuch be his deſtination, he is entered as a ſtudent in divinity, on proper evidence being produced, to the profeſſor, that he has reputably performed his claſſical and philoſophical courſe. Here a new courſe of particular, theological ſtudy commences. Attendance muſt be be given on the public lectures of the Divinity-Hall, for a ſeries of years. The letter of the law ſays ſix, and the ſpirit only in rarer inſtances falls ſhort of it. The ſtudent muſt be not only a hearer of lectures from the profeſſorial chair, but is required to perform publickly, from ſubjects preſcribed, a certain number of exerciſes of a particular deſcription, ſubject to the criticiſm not of the profeſſor only, but of the other ſtudents. This being accompliſhed

accomplished, and the regulation, both as to length of time and nature of study, being complied with, the candidate is entitled to offer himself to a Presbytery to be taken on trials, in order to be licensed as a preacher. On his making such application, a committee of Presbytery is appointed to converse with, examine, and encourage him. Circular letters are then ordered to be written to all the Presbyteries in the Synod, or Province, informing them of the application made, and desiring their concurrence. That being obtained, the young man is admitted to trial; and the several pieces prescribed, are contrived in such a manner, as to obtain a fair and impartial view of his dispositions and talents; of his progress in learning; of his knowledge, in particular, of Divinity; and of his qualifications as a public speaker. The whole course of trial, and it is deliberate, serious and impressive, concludes with what we call the *questionary* trials; the meaning of which is, every member of Presbytery has a right, which is generally exercised, to put to the candidate whatever question or questions he thinks proper, on subjects relative to the profession, to languages, criticism, science, ecclesiastical history; and to require an answer. If all are satisfied, the moderator from the chair declares the judgment of the Court, and with a suitable exhortation to the probationer, pronounces the Presbytery's licence to him to preach the Gospel.

In the event of his being invited to undertake the pastoral charge of a particular vacant Parish, he must, previous to ordination and induction, submit to a second sond course of trial similar to the former, before the presbytery within whose bounds such parish is situated. If he is still approved, a day for the ordination is appointed, of which notice is given all over the district; and particular proclamation is made at the door of the Church to be supplied, after morning service on the Lord's day, ten days at least previous to the ordination, that if any one has any thing to object to the doctrine or life of the person to be ordained, he would appear and substantiate his charge. If nothing is alleged or proved, the presbytery proceeds, at the time fixed, by solemn prayer and imposition of hands to set apart the candidate to the work of the ministry, and appoint him to his particular charge.

From this it will appear that no one grossly ignorant, or notoriously immoral, can possibly find admission into the Church of Scotland. And to her scrupulous attention to the literature, and morals, of all her members, it is owing that one of the most meanly endowed of the reformed Churches, ranks with the highest, in the purity, piety, learning, eloquence, and general respectability of her Clergy. I return to Mr. Nicolson.

Having attained the rank of preacher, and exercised his talents with acceptance in the city of Aberdeen and its vicinity, the height of his ambition was to obtain the charge of a quiet country parish, where he could find leisure for prosecuting his favourite studies, and where he could have a decent competency on which to subsist. No prospect, however, of this kind

kind opening, he was induced, in 1770, partly from curiosity and a desire of seeing the world, (the passion of young and cultivated minds,) and partly in hope of finding creditable, useful and productive employment, to visit the North-British metropolis; and it was then and there I had the happiness to form an acquaintance with him, which was quickly mellowed into mutual friendship, not to be dissolved even by death.

The year after, I received and accepted a call to undertake the pastoral charge of the Scots Church London-Wall, become vacant by the death of that excellent man and Minister, Mr. Robert Lawson. As my friend Charles found his prospects at Edinburgh not greatly brightened, it was no difficult matter to persuade a man, who had so often, and with such exquisite delight, traced the wanderings of an Ulysses, while

Πολλῶν δ' Ἀνθρωπῶν ἴδεν ἄστεα, καὶ νόον ἔγνω,

to proceed in his progress to visit another city, and to converse with men, in situations unknown, untried before. Soon after I settled in London, then, I was followed, to my great satisfaction, by Mr. Nicolson. He was furnished with very little above the bare necessaries of life, but ever appeared with a face of serenity and satisfaction, which it is not in the power of wealth always to bestow. London is happily adapted to a man of such a disposition, in such circumstances. There, you may either display affluence, or conceal poverty,

at

at pleasure. Nicolson lodged in a garret, in Bartholomew-Close Smithfield, with a journey-man mechanic; lived on bread and beer; never wore his only suit of apparel a single moment when at home; and thus maintained his independence, in the midst of extreme indigence. When called to go abroad, no dignitary of the Church ever made a more respectable appearance. He was always one of the best dressed, most cheerful looking men, in every company he frequented; and when a little extraordinary expence became necessary or decent, his half crown was ready among the first. He was now, indeed, in his element; at the fountain of Science; enjoying complete leisure, and unlimited access to men, and books, and objects of every other kind, that could either amuse or instruct.

In the spring of 1772, Charles and I, together with Louis Balfour of Pilrig, planned and executed a peripatetic expedition to Oxford, and the circle of which the road from the metropolis to the university is the radius. On this perambulation it was, that the stores of a good and honest heart, of a manly, liberal, independent spirit, and of an enlarged and cultivated mind, displayed themselves to an advantage I had not hitherto apprehended. Every object was new and interesting, it was the jocund season of the year, when

——————— Nature
Wantons as in her prime, and plays at will
Her virgin fancies;
With every assistance, therefore, which health, good humour, cordiality, and novelty could minister, we
performed

performed the magic round of beautiful nature, scientific research, and royal magnificence.

O noctes cœnæque Deum!

After strolling the livelong day through the academic groves planted on the banks of the Isis, or panting over Blenheim's ample domain, or climbing to contemplate "Windsor's towery pride." Never did Chancellor of University, or puissant prince of Woodstock, or proud potentate of Windsor, enjoy these lordly, envied possessions, with half the relish and glee that the three dusty pedestrians felt in visiting them.

It would be ingratitude not to acknowledge, in this place, the benefit derived, on our excursion to Oxford, from the benevolence and extensive information of Mr. James Williamson, who then taught mathematics privately in the university, with much reputation and success, and who has since acquired greater celebrity by his edition of Euclid's Elements, with original Dissertations. Through the friendship of that gentleman we were admitted to every repository that could gratify curiosity, and were enabled to examine every object with superior advantage.

All this while, however, poor Charles was unprovided for. He had unfortunately no patron in his native country; and his pulpit-talents, though solid, wanted that brilliancy which attracts popular favour. "In patience," notwithstanding, he "possessed his soul." Retirement in London was still preferable to retirement any where else. Change of books, select society, and

the

the perpetual novelty and variety of that great city were always in his power: and the chriſtian maxim was with him a practical one, " Sufficient unto the day " is the evil thereof."

At the end of about eighteen months, a dawn of hope appeared. The ſecond charge in the Britiſh Church at Amſterdam had become vacant, and application was made to Miniſters, both at London and Edinburgh, to look out for a proper perſon to ſupply it. Mr. Nicolſon, ſeemed to be completely formed for ſuch a ſituation. His friends, accordingly, beſtirred themſelves on the occaſion; proper credentials were procured, and, without waiting for a formal invitation, he embarked for Holland, on very ſhort notice, and arrived long before any other candidate was thought of. This precipitancy had almoſt proved fatal to the deſign, but, eventually, favoured it. Dutchmen have no idea of proceeding but in the old beaten track; and certainly Charles appeared at Amſterdam unſent for; and was on the point of being ſent back, by the way that he came. Fortunately he had been warmly recommended to a reſpectable family in the Church, nearly allied to the venerable Mr. Longueville, the ſenior miniſter. This procured for him an invitation from the good man, to ſupply his place on the Lord's-day following. His preaching gave ſuch general ſatisfaction, that the Conſiſtory condeſcended to relax a little, and ſo far to diſpenſe with rigid form, as to requeſt him to preach, both parts of the day, the Sunday after. He was all the while gaining

ground

ground, wherever he went, by the gentleness of his manners, and the charms of his conversation; with some, by the gravity of his deportment. His suavity, his learning, his unaffected modesty, particularly endeared him to Mr. Longueville, who at that time, was respected as an oracle all over the Provinces. He continued to please as a preacher, on repeated trials, and returned to London in full confidence of being appointed to the vacant charge. Nor did his confidence betray him. In a few weeks the choice of the Consistory, confirmed by the approbation of the Burgomasters, was formally notified to him; and this was accompanied with a request to the Scots Presbytery in London, to proceed to his ordination in due form, in order to his exercising the pastoral office. This was joyfully undertaken, and accomplished; and to that solemnity the preceding sermon owes its existence. The other ministers who assisted in it, were David Muir, John Patrick, George Turnbull, George Stephen, James Fordyce, D.D. and William Smith A.M. of whom the last two alone and I " remain unto this day," the rest, with him whom they that day set apart to the work of the ministry, " are fallen asleep!"

Mr. Nicolson was thus raised to an honourable, useful, and, to him, affluent situation; his revenue being 1700 gilders, or £155 per annum; punctually paid by the States of Holland. Being fixed in his new charge, in addition to his other literary attainments, he thought it his duty to acquire the language of the country in which Providence

vidence had settled him: and to this he applied with such industry and perseverance that he could, in less than a twelvemonth, not only read Dutch correctly, and converse in it with ease, but preach with equal fluency in Dutch or English.

He enjoyed his amiable and excellent colleague little more than eighteen months. The only strife they ever knew, was the strife of paternal and filial tenderness. It was Charles's study and delight to soothe, to relieve, to cheer the old man's decline of life; it was Mr. Longueville's pride and joy to encourage, to introduce, to recommend, to exalt his youthful colleague and successor; and as a mark of affection he bequeathed him books from his library, to the value of twenty pounds, of Mr. Nicolson's own selection.

On the death of Mr. Longueville, Mr. Nicolson succeeded, of course, to the first charge of the British Church, with an additional stipend of five hundred gilders. And thus, in the course of not many months, was my friend translated from obscurity, penury, and a garret in Smithfield, to respectability, wealth and usefulness in Amsterdam; and he who had borne adversity undepressed, and submitted to poverty without losing dignity, rose into distinction and consequence without pride or self-sufficiency.

In this enviable state, about seven years of undisturbed tranquility rolled quietly away; and, excepting the society of a few friends, whom he dearly loved, and who with equal cordiality repaid his affection, honest

Charles enjoyed every thing this world could bestow. And thus, without strife, happy, and making happy, he pursued "the noiseless tenor of his way" till the year 1781, when the rupture took place between Great-Britain and Holland; a rupture which involved, among its other consequences, the comfort and independence of the unfortunate subject of these memoirs.

From the period that England and Holland became rival and hostile maritime powers, the Dutch have employed against their enemies not only the thunder of naval artillery, but the more tremendous ordnance of devotional execration. Accustomed in their creeds coolly to consign about nineteen twentieth parts of the human race to the bottomless pit, it is not to be wondered at, if, in the moment of rage, they should devote a bitter foe to hell and destruction. A dreadful anathema against England had been composed, in order to be used in churches, on every return of hostility between the two nations, and was devoutly addressed to the God of mercy, every returning Lord's day, by men in black cloaks and starched bands, in aid of men in long trousers with lighted matches in their hands. It had now so quietly and harmlessly slumbered and slept for upwards of a century, that it was considered as dead and buried; when lo, the sudden departure of Sir Joseph Yorke from the Hague, and the capture of St. Eustatius, re-animated its ashes: and the Burgo-magisterial mandate enjoined every pulpit through the united Provinces to resound with curses upon curses

against

against poor old England! The terrible injunction was laid on Mr. Nicolson, among the rest. Charles was full of " the milk of human kindness." He would at any time have gone a mile round rather than crush a worm that might crawl in his path. He had no idea of cursing any person or thing whatever. What then was it, to think of cursing that dear land where his heart was deposited, and all those dear friends who were the constant subjects of his daily orisons? He would have forfeited the triple mitre, rather than do such a violence to all that was human in him. He well knew the consequence; but firmly rejected the injunction. Dutch phlegm knows not what it is to relent; and Batavian resolves, though tardy, are decisive. A pair of shoes and staff, the Belgic summons to depart, were presently at Mr. Nicolson's door; and he had the pleasure of quickly following his Majesty's Ambassador to England.

And thus, by a jerk of the political wheel, was the Minister of the British Church at Amsterdam, in the very prime of life, hurled from the zenith of ease and affluence, cast afresh on the wide world, and reduced to that poverty out of which he had so providentially emerged. But his conscience was clear, his constitution sound, his friends numerous; and he bore his disaster like a man, a philosopher, a christian. Having never married, and being, from his youth up, trained in habits of frugality, he had been able to save a considerable proportion of his revenue. He could live on little, and be content with it; and in London he again found all he either wanted or wished.

Among other acquisitions of value, made in Holland, the friendship of a gentleman already mentioned, Sir Joseph Yorke, afterwards Lord Dover, was not the least. Mr. Nicolson's qualifications could not escape the discernment of so excellent a judge of merit, and could not be discerned without conciliating favour. Sir Joseph honoured him for the sacrifice which he had made, sympathized with him under his depression, and was animated with a sincere desire to do him service. But what interest he had was limited to the sphere of the Church of England, and Nicolson was not of that description. Tired, at length, of languishing out his best days, idle, unemployed; having no patronage, and therefore no prospect of a settlement, in Scotland, he began seriously to reflect on Sir Joseph's reiterated advice to conform, and take orders in the Church of England. Reflection produced resolution, and soon after his episcopal re-ordination, he was appointed Chaplain to the Turkey Company, and to his Majesty's Ambassador at Constantinople.

This was, indeed, going into exile, but an honourable exile. It was *otium*, but *cum dignitate*. His appointments were liberal, the duties of his station easy and pleasant. He was a member of Sir Robert Ainslie's family; he breathed in classic air, and trod on classic ground; and Nicolson found himself in his element. Not being confined to a rigid residence, he

made

made frequent and short rambles, in every direction round Byzantium. Again he applied successfully to the study of the language of the country. Habits of œconomy, had they been yet to learn, would now have been forced upon him, for he had no opportunity of spending money, and every year he lived was making provision for some future year, should some other reverse, peradventure, toss him once more on the boundless ocean; or

———————to be his foster nurse,
When service should in his old limbs lie lame,
And unregarded age in corners thrown.

SHAKESPEAR.

But these were mortifications which Providence graciously spared him. It had long been an object of desire with him to stroll over the plain of Troy, with Homer in his hand; and few men were more qualified to have made such an excursion, with equal pleasure and advantage. I see him, with my " mind's eye," tracing the current of the Simois and Scamander; weighing every particle of venerable dust; measuring the distances of ill-fated Ilium from Ida, from Tenedos.

Hic Dolopum manus : hic sævus tendebat Achilles :
Classibus hic locus : hic acies certare solebant.

VIRGIL.

As a preparation for this classical banquet, he had whetted his appetite in the air of the far-famed isles of the Egean sea. In order to travel with more comfort, he had assumed a dress better adapted to an Asiatic climate. But his habit of body, now inclining to corpulency, and never having been accuftomed to take exceffive care of his perfon, he expofed it, once too often, to an inclement fky; the noon-tide fun fmote him; the fever quickly pervaded the mafs of blood, in a region where difeafe makes fhort work with the patient; and, in twenty-four hours from his being attacked, the fpirit of Charles fled to join " the fpirits of juft men made perfect."

The compofition of this fhort memoir of a man I dearly loved, has fomewhat tended to alleviate the affliction of his lofs. It will perhaps be no unacceptable prefent to his numerous friends in Scotland, in London, in Holland, in the Eaft; and it will convey to thofe who knew him not, a faint fketch of one of the moft innocent, ingenious, unaffuming, amiable of mankind.

SERMON

SERMON III.*

THE

DUTY AND UTILITY OF COMMEMORATING

NATIONAL DELIVERANCES.

* Preached before the Society which supports the Lord's-Day Morning Lecture at little St. Helen's Bishopsgate-Street, at their Anniversary Meeting, August 12th, 1777: and Published at their Request.

TO

THE GENTLEMEN

WHO SUPPORT THE

LORD's-DAY MORNING LECTURE,

AT

LITTLE St. HELEN's, BISHOPSGATE-STREET,
LONDON;

THIS SERMON,

PREACHED BY THEIR APPOINTMENT, AND PUBLISHED

AT THEIR REQUEST,

AS A SLENDER BUT SINCERE TESTIMONY OF UNFEIGNED

GRATITUDE,

IS MOST RESPECTFULLY INSCRIBED

BY THEIR OBEDIENT

HUMBLE SERVANT,

HENRY HUNTER.

*Hackney, August
14th, 1777.*

THE
DUTY AND UTILITY OF COMMEMORATING NATIONAL DELIVERANCES.

EXODUS xiii. 8, 9, 10.

And thou shalt shew thy son, in that day, saying, This is done because of that which the LORD did unto me, when I came forth out of Egypt.

And it shall be for a sign unto thee upon thine hand, and for a memorial between thine eyes; that the LORD's law may be in thy mouth: for with a strong hand hath the LORD brought thee out of Egypt.

Thou shalt therefore keep this ordinance in his season from year to year.

THE application of this passage of Scripture to the design of our present meeting is obvious. It refers to a very memorable interposition of Providence in behalf of the Children of Israel: and *We* are assembled to commemorate an event of similar importance to Great-Britain. *Israel*, in possession of the land of promise, must remember

remember their diftrefs in Egypt, and their deliverance: And *Britons*, in the full enjoyment of religion and liberty, reflect on the danger which once threatened both, with the pleafure and the gratitude which flow from the recollection of danger efcaped, fear difappointed, and expectation exceeded.

To neglect that inftitution which annually brought to remembrance the downfal of Egyptian tyranny, and Ifrael's releafe, was, in a fon of Abraham, not only difgraceful, but criminal. Jofeph was now dead: And there had arifen a new king over Egypt, who knew not Jofeph. A total change of meafures enfued. Ifraelites were no longer confidered, and treated, as favourite guefts, but as odious and defpifed flaves. They were made to ferve with rigour. The full quantity of labour was exacted, while the neceffary materials were withheld: Infult was added to cruelty. The royal mandate doomed every male-child to deftruction; the fweeteft fruit of conjugal endearment was turned into gall. Life was fo embittered that it became a burden. If fuch woe could be heightened, it was heightened, by the feverity of hope deferred; and by repeated efforts to fhake off the yoke, which had proved ineffectual. They were in poffeffion of a divine prediction

prediction in their favour, which feemed far from accomplifhment; and of a promife of peace, of liberty, of a country, which was not likely to be realized: Their portion was mifery, their profpect defpair.

But the time to favour GOD's afflicted church and people at length arrived. The LORD himfelf gives the word; the LORD himfelf appears; all Nature flocks to his ftandard; every element engages in his caufe. Stroke after ftroke is inflicted: by an army of frogs and of flies, the ftrength of Egypt is broken, and the pride of Pharaoh dafhed to the ground. At laft, in one dreadful night, by one awful blow of JEHOVAH's out-ftretched arm, the blood of ten thoufand innocents is avenged: the firft-born over all Egypt fall; compliance is enforced; the enemy is confounded; Ifrael is faved.

To preferve the memory of this great deliverance, GOD was pleafed to inftitute the ordinance of the paffover: and the ceremonies attending the celebration of it, were intended ftrongly to affect and imprefs the minds of that generation; and to engage attention, and roufe a fpirit of enquiry in all future ages. They were defigned to furnifh parents, to the lateft pofterity, with the nobleft

and

and moſt intereſting ſubject of diſcourſe to their children; the pureſt ſource of uſeful knowledge; the moſt powerful argument to gratitude, to love, to obedience. The paſchal lamb muſt be eaten every year, on the ſelf-ſame day on which ſalvation was wrought, that the aged might not become forgetful, nor the young remain uninformed; and the obſervance of this law was injoined under a ſanction no leſs formidable, than that of being cut off from the congregation of Iſrael.

Let us ſhift the proſpect.—Let Britain be the ſcene, not Egypt. From the dangers, the diſtreſſes, the deliverances, and the duties of Iſraelites, let us turn to the conſideration of our own.

Not to be acquainted with the great events which gild this illuſtrious day of the revolving year, is, in a citizen of Great-Britain, an argument of the moſt ſhameful ignorance, or the moſt contemptible indifference. To know them with a heart unkindled by the hallowed flame of patriotic love, is to be dead to the fineſt, nobleſt, and moſt honourable feelings of our nature. To know them, and to glow at the recollection of them, without aſcribing the glory and the praiſe of all, to that God, who alone hath done for us great wonders, is to be chargeable with the groſſeſt impiety, and the blackeſt ingratitude. Whatever can touch us

as

as men; whatever can animate us as Britons; whatever can infpire and elevate us as Chriftians; our perfonal rights, our public liberty, our religious privileges—all, all prefs upon our thoughts, on the return of the twelfth of Auguft, and loudly call us to thankfgiving and joy.

We are affembled, Men, Brethren and Fathers, to celebrate the aufpicious, the happy acceffion of the illuftrious houfe of Hanover, to the Throne of thefe united Kingdoms: an æra which has proved a plentiful fpring of bleffings innumerable, not to them only, but to Europe, but to mankind, during a period of more than threefcore* years. We are affembled to celebrate the great, the important, the eventful day, when the chief corner ftone was placed of that fair, that well-proportioned, that majeftic, that venerable ftructure, the materials of which had been collecting and preparing through many ages; whofe dimenfions were marked out, and whofe foundations were laid, at the Revolution; whofe walls and columns rofe in beauty, in ftrength, and in comely proportion, under the government of William III. whofe fplendor dazzled the world, during one half of the fucceeding reign; and whofe high towers tottered

from

* Now fourfcore.

from the bottom to the pinnacle, during the other. We are assembled to celebrate the day, which gave birth to the eldeſt hope of this great realm: And propitious be it to the generation following; while we join in the moſt affectionate wiſhes and fervent prayers for length of days, and increaſing proſperity to HIM, under whoſe mild and gracious government we have the happineſs to live.

We will " keep this ordinance, in his ſeaſon, " from year to year." Britons! are all our old men mindful, is all our youth informed, of what God has at ſundry times, and in divers manners performed in behalf of theſe nations? Or are there no national bleſſings to be acknowledged; no wonderful and unexpected interpoſitions of Providence to be remarked; no miraculous deliverances to be commemorated? O ſhame! Indignation! attempts were made, attempts almoſt ſuccefsful,—are they forgotten? to make Britons ſerve with rigor; to twiſt inglorious chains about their free-born necks; to reſtrain their manly ſpirit; to fetter conſcience; to bend their ſturdy knees to a popiſh idol. And this, not in a foreign land, an houſe of bondage: in ſuch a caſe, dire neceſſity, the hard, the heavy hand of power, might have broken the mind to
the

the sufferance of it: but at home, in the inheritance of their fathers, an inheritance purchased, defended, transmitted at the expence of blood,— the blood of valour, of liberty, of wisdom, of virtue: And this, not by a foreign tyrant, by unknown despots; but by those whom office place and station, whom duty and int rest, called upon to be " nursing fathers, and nursing mothers" to their native land. And this, not in the rage of victory, not in the pride of triumph, not in the insolence of acquired superiority; but in the malignant gloom of superstition, but in the sullenness of revenge.

I call upon you, friends, countrymen, to reflect upon these things. I call upon you, fathers, to instruct your children in these things. With the rising Israelites, they will perhaps be saying to you, " What is this ?" Why do you observe the twelfth of August ? I shall endeavour, in the spirit of the text, to assist you in giving, somewhat more at large, an answer to these questions. And, in so doing, it shall be my study, to speak of things as they are, neither extenuating any thing, nor setting down aught in malice.

" You wish to know, my son, why I devote this day to joy and praise: Listen attentively to what I shall relate, and then judge what reason God has given me, and these lands, to address his throne with songs of thanksgiving. That you may the better comprehend, and the more devoutly feel the interesting event of which this is the anniversary, it may be necessary to lead your attention to the situation of this country during a period of about thirty years preceding it, and to the transactions which gave rise to, and are more immediately connected with, it."

" Know then, that a century ago, your native country had the infelicity to be governed by a prince of a licentious and dissipated character, Charles II.—who came to the throne in circumstances peculiarly favourable to his personal and domestic prosperity, as well as that of the kingdom; but who during the whole course of a reign of twenty-five years, through misapprehension, perverseness, or neglect, pursuing the private and separate interest of the sovereign, disregarded that of the state, and thereby sacrificed both the one and the other. He is said to have possessed much good-nature, and yet by his authority he patronized and encouraged the cruelty of others. He was cold to all religion ; and, perhaps, except in his own practice, not an enemy to the religion

of

of his country, yet permitted its harmless professors to be discouraged, obstructed, persecuted. Engrossed in the pursuit of pleasure, he attended little to the duties of his station. Unjustifiable attachment, ill-judged partialities, inveterate prejudices, indolence of temper, and ignorance of the proper arts of government, led him to form foreign connections, inconsistent with his own honour and dignity, and destructive to his people. Hence the nation was repeatedly reduced to great distress, involved in disgrace, and threatened with ruin. But, through the goodness of Providence, while the corrupted manners and the pernicious politics of the court were wickedly employed to weaken and dissolve the national strength, public virtue preserved it."

" The next heir to the crown was, avowedly, a determined and inflexible adherent to the Church of Rome; whose spirit breathes nothing but hostility to the most valuable rights and privileges of mankind. Britain had every thing to fear from the succession of such a prince. The horrors of a former Popish reign occurred to the minds of men. Freemen and Protestants, appalled at the thoughts of prisons rebuilt, of fines renewed, of persecution revived, of fires rekindled, for the punishment of those whom Popery might deem heretics, had united in vigorous efforts for the exclusion of the Duke of York. But through the partiality of the reigning monarch to his brother, not improbably to his brother's principles, these just and generous efforts succeeded not. Accordingly on the death of Charles in 1685, James mounted the throne. What ensued? Vehement protestations of a determined resolution to maintain the established government, both in church and state, were made: Measures subversive of the constitution, were adopted and pursued. Revenues were levied by royal authority, without deigning to ask, or wait for, the concurrence of parliament. Royalty with all its ensigns, and in the face of the sun, went in solemn procession to join in the illegal, and abhorred service of the mass. A messenger was dispatched to Rome to prostrate the majesty of England at the feet of the Pope; and measures were concerted for the solemn readmission of this Protestant kingdom into the bosom of the Roman-Catholic Church. A power of dispensing with the laws of the land, was claimed and exercised. Military tyranny was encouraged and supported: The British seat of justice was converted into a Spanish tribunal of inquisition: An inhuman Jefferies finished the

the horrid scene of blood which a savage Kirke had begun. Neither age, nor sex, nor innocence, could save those, whom a cruel, vindictive, unrelenting court had resolved to destroy."

" Three unhappy kingdoms lay bleeding, almost three years, at the feet of a sanguinary prince, whose tender mercies were cruelties. Protestants of every denomination, without regard to any other distinction, endured all that malice could dictate, or revenge inflict."

" It would shock humanity, and excite resentment, at the distance of ninety years elapsed*, to enter into a particular detail of the enormities which disfigure this period of British history. It is the painful and disgusting province of the historian, to describe them at large; and you have heard enough, my young friend, to rouse up all that is virtuous and manly in you. Happily, the court was too violent, and the nation too spirited, to admit of a long continuance of such scenes. The insulted genius of an injured people at length awoke to just vengeance, and speedily exhibited an example, formidable to violence and tyranny, highly honourable to the actors in that great scene, and to their country

* Now one hundred and six years.

country, encouraging to virtue, and inſtructive to mankind."

" Men of all parties and denominations ; the parliament, the church, the army ; conformiſts, diſſenters; the city, the country, filled with indignation, reſolved to reject the gloomy and bigotted tyrant, who had dared to trample upon the deareſt rights, the hereditary privileges of Britons. Wearied out with the perſevering violence and oppreſſion of a court, which no ſubmiſſion could mollify, no intreaties could bend, no terrors but thoſe of ſuperſtition could intimidate, and no teacher but experience could inſtruct, the Nation, as one man, looked for ſuccour, to a neighbouring prince, whoſe conſort was the apparent heireſs of the crown, and the darling object of Britain's fondeſt hopes and wiſhes, and who himſelf poſſeſſed wiſdom and virtue, and was attended with a ſucceſs, which have long, and deſervedly, been the favourite theme of Britiſh tongues and pens. He engaged in the generous deſign of aſſiſting an injured and inſulted people. Providence ſmiled on the attempt, and he proſpered.—James, who had made himſelf obnoxious to all, was now deſerted of all; his timidity, in flying from danger, equalled his former ſtupidity in deſpiſing it. Having

ing no resource in the affections of his subjects, in the approbation of his own mind, nor in the support of Heaven, he precipitately abandoned a throne, which he could not fill with wisdom and honour; and the heroic William received from the hands of a gallant and grateful people, that crown which the violent and imprudent James had shaken from his own head."

" From this memorable period, distinguished, in the annals of British history, by the name of THE REVOLUTION, the nation possessed of wisdom and virtue, to form and to establish a system of government favourable to liberty and happiness, began to enjoy the sweets of it. To render this enjoyment complete, it became necessary to provide a security against future evils, of the same nature with that which had been applied as a remedy to the past. The security proposed and effected, was a law which entirely, and for ever, excluded from all hope of succession to the crown, the popish posterity of the exiled sovereign; and which settled it, in favour of the Protestant family of Hanover, whose right of blood was indisputable; whose religion, being that of the nation, warranted the continuance of this invaluable blessing; and whose character for valour, wisdom, and moderation, promised that
public

public felicity, which long experience has happily realized.

" Toward the conclusion of Queen Anne's reign, the tempest gathered again, and threatened the public tranquility. The happy settlement of the succession, which King William had so anxiously laboured to establish, was brought into imminent danger. Those Ministers who had steadily and uniformly exhibited a regard to Revolution principles, that is, to the civil and religious rights of mankind; and who had served the Queen faithfully and succefsfully for several glorious years, were now dismissed; and their places were filled by men of a very different spirit, who, against the declared sense of the nation, conceived the fatal design of setting aside the succession, and of calling back to the throne, upon the Queen's demise, the rejected issue of the Popish tyrant. What were then, Britons, Christians, Protestants, What were then your feelings? What were then your fears? Some are yet alive to tell, and to shudder at the horrid recollection. It pleased GOD in his great mercy again to interpose, and to disperse the thick cloud. He brought about the Revolution, by employing men as his instruments; but, here, He took the great work, immediately into his own hands. The LORD, who

removeth

removeth kings, and setteth up kings, who causeth *the wrath of man to praise him, and restraineth the remainder* thereof, He sends forth his awful messenger, death; the breath departs; the throne is vacated; the half-finished design evaporates into empty air; the much to be remembered first of August dawns upon the British Isles; the shades of night flee away; GEORGE reigns; and sorrow is turned into joy."

" Protestant dissenters had peculiar reason to rejoice in this event. They had distinguished themselves by their zeal and activity, in the settlement of the succession in favour of the present Royal Family; they were, to a man, determined to maintain it; they had thereby rendered themselves peculiarly obnoxious to a Jacobitish ministry, who were endeavouring to alter it. Resentment had already marked them out for punishment; nay, the attack was actually begun. A Bill breathing cruelty and revenge against Dissenters was framed, and, after a vehement struggle, about a month before the Queen's death, passed into a law. The alarm was general, the approaching distress great; no deliverer appeared. Mark again, and adore the wonder-working hand of heaven! On the 1st of August, this vindictive act was to have taken place: and that very

day,

day, so it pleased the great Ruler of all events, terminated Queen Anne's life, confounded the enemy and the avenger, plucked the sting from the oppressive statute, and defeated its malicious intention. If, then, Protestant dissenters suffered so severely, and had so much greater distress to fear, under a female and a Protestant administration of high prerogative principles, what had they not to apprehend and to suffer, if God, in his displeasure, should have permitted a male tyrant, trained up in the despotism of France, and the bigotry of Rome, inheriting his father's prejudices, and actuated by family resentments, to mount the throne of these kingdoms? Who must have fallen the first victims to the fury of stern James's posterity? Those surely, who were most active in bringing about the Revolution, and in preserving the Protestant succession. Had the horrid design proved succesful, they, they would have been marked out for signal vengeance. Had the wicked scheme of Anne's last Ministry been matured, or their counsels remained united, or the Queen's life prolonged—gracious Heaven! instead of assembling, as at this day, under the countenance and protection of civil Government, to worship GOD according to our consciences, and to express our mutual congratulations and satisfaction, we might have been skulking in corners, venting our complaints in silent

lent tears, shocking the eye of humanity with our torments, tainting the air with our mangled limbs, or, still more shocking, committing such barbarities as nature recoils at, upon our fellow creatures. Therefore, we observe the twelfth of August, because that on it GOD was graciously pleased to scatter the thunder-impregnated cloud, which was ready to burst on this Nation, by sending us a wise and a moderate Prince to reign over us, the rule of whose conduct was law, not passion; and because He has given, and promises to continue, a succession of Princes, of the same spirit, as of the same Blood. Is not a tranquility of sixty-three Years*, worthy the commemoration of a few hours? While that tranquility is lengthened out, is not the annual acknowledgment of it, our honour and privilege, as well as our duty? Let us measure our gratitude by our danger and our deliverance, and it will be the employment, not of one day, but of all the days in the Year."

" In the case of Israel in Egypt, you know, my Son, GOD interposed, by his command, to secure a perpetual remembrance, as he had before interposed, by his power, to rescue from bondage. As your mercies are not inferior, let your gratitude be at least equal. To use the beautifully expressive language of Moses on that occasion, let this day's
solemnity

* Now fourscore.

solemnity " be for a sign unto thee upon thine hand," like a ring, worn in memory of some departed friend, or in respect to one at a distance, or out of affection to one greatly beloved; " and for a memorial between thine eyes," as a legible and distinct inscription on a monumental pillar, commanding the attention as often as you frequent the place of public resort; " That the LORD's law may be in thy mouth," as the watch-word in the camp, the sign of union, and the bond of safety. " Thou shalt therefore keep this ordinance in his season from year to year."

Having endeavoured, with as much brevity as the case would permit, to suggest an answer to the question, which the young, the uninformed, or the stranger might put, on seeing us assemble together at this season; I shall employ the remainder of the discourse, in attempting to justify, and to recommend, our practice, by shewing the utility and importance of it, in a *political*, *moral*, and *religious* view.

I. The occasional and anniversary recollection of great events, is highly useful and important in *a political light*. In order to excel in any art or profession; in order to make a man exert himself with vigour in any enterprize, and to give him delight in the enjoyment of any blessing, a tincture of enthusiasm is absolutely necessary: And nothing has a more direct tendency to kindle, and keep alive that spirit, than the social intercourse of persons embarked in the same cause, united by a common interest, suffering the same calamities, or enjoying the same benefits. Communication is the fuel of zeal. As united fires burn more vehemently, and "as iron sharpeneth iron," so is the holy ardor of patriotism lighted up to a purer flame, and the spirit of friendship whetted to greater keenness and brightness, by the blessed interchange of animated looks, acceptable words, and social employments. Who has not observed, who has not felt the celestial fire, quick as the stroke of electricity, or the lightning's flash, dart from soul to soul, while men were engaged in the same acts of devotion, or even in partaking of the innocent, convivial delights of a social, temperate meal, which brought to their remembrance some amiable friend, some common benefactor, or some public deliverance? And is not the union and the ardor of her sons, the glory and the strength of a Nation?

The very extravagances of patriotic enthusiasm, if not praise-worthy, are at least pardonable. I could wish all my countrymen to believe, that their Island is, by far, the finest in the world;

their

their form of government the beft; their rivers and cities, their fhips and fortreffes, their admirals and generals, their feamen and foldiers, far fuperior to all of the fame kind, in any other country. For the belief of thefe things, actually makes them fuch. I could even wifh it to be believed, that Providence is more propitious to us than to our adverfaries, nay, than to our neighbours; for fuch perfuafion makes Providence to be more acknowledged, reforted unto, and confided in, and deliverances already wrought, while they produce gratitude upon the recollection, lay, at the fame time, a foundation of pleafing hope for the time to come.

The world has lately been prefented with a refinement on Chriftianity*, which attempts to fmother the flame, which we wifh to kindle; and which, in my apprehenfion, is not warranted by the conftitution of human nature, nor the conclufions of right reafon, nor the genius of the Gofpel. This modern refinement would reprefent the fpirit of patriotifm, the love of one particular country, as too narrow and illiberal to confift with the comprehenfive, the generous, the benevolent religion of Jefus Chrift. The world is held up, by it, as our country, and all mankind, as our fellow citizens

* Soame Jennings's Tract.

citizens. The heart rejects this idea; for He who made it, taught it to glow with affection, not for the globe, but for Athens, for Rome, for Jerusalem, for Britain; and to rejoice, at meeting, not with a man, but with a friend, a countryman, a fellow citizen. Reason acknowledges it not, for reason discovers, at one glance, that the world, and the whole human race, are objects too vast for the mind to take in'; and that every attempt to stretch it beyond what its texture will bear, diminishes its strength, and renders it incapable of exertion otherwise within its compass. The wise and the good of every age and nation have ranked the love of our country, among the first of virtues; and most of the splendid actions which adorn the historic page, and delight mankind, are derived from this source. To ascribe such a notion to the Gospel, is doing it a manifest injustice, is a palpable misapprehesion, or misrepresentation of its Author, its nature and design. Jesus Christ loved his country, and his countrymen, notwithstanding their cruelty, unnaturalness, and ingratitude to him: Witness his particular and anxious concern about *the lost sheep of the house of Israel:* Witness his affecting tears, and pathetic lamentation over the devoted metropolis of his country: Witness his charge

I   to

to his disciples, to begin their progress of preaching and teaching at *Jerusalem*. The Gospel surely was never intended to eradicate the honest and the virtuous feelings of our nature, but to improve them. The Gospel considers man in his present confined, imperfect state; proposes to him objects within his reach; inspires sentiments suited to his condition, and prescribes rules of conduct, which have respect to his ignorance, his frailty, his depression, as a limited creature. An angel of light, or a saint in glory, may be capable of entertaining those enlarged and comprehensive views: but in a being so contracted and so imperfect as man upon earth, all just and useful sentiment, all proper and praise-worthy conduct, must necessarily move within certain bounds. He must commence with the individual, he may in progress, comprehend a great multitude; but the law of his nature forbids him to arise to universality. The intenseness of our affections, and the efficacy of them, must be in proportion to the number of their objects, and the extent of their sphere. The world, and mankind, are ideas altogether indistinct, and never can excite distinct, that is, vigorous, efficacious, useful emotions. The man who hath no country but the globe, and no fellow-citizens but mankind has really no country

at

at all, and will hardly be a tolerable citizen in any place. This refined notion of patriotifm expands the mind over a furface much too large for it to cover, and ftretches it out to a confiftency, which its natural frame and ftrength will not bear; like a piece of folid gold, beaten out into leaf, or drawn into wire; what it gains in extent, it lofes in value and folidity: its ufe is totally changed, it is no longer a valuable and effectual inftrument of commerce among men; it is only fit for gilding baubles, and glittering in the eye.

Our object this day, my dear countrymen, is to praife GOD, for his goodnefs to Great-Britain: And your hearts, your underftanding, and your religion, concur in calling you to this divine employment. You cannot but wifh that this highly-favoured land, fhould ftill flourifh and profper; that your pofterity fhould have the bleffings which you poffefs, tranfmitted to them; and, as an expreffion of this wifh and defire, you have affembled, to ftir up your own minds, by way of remembrance, and to put the rifing generation upon enquiry, that they may learn betimes to love, and reverence their country, to perform the duties which they owe to it, and to blefs GOD who has diftinguifhed it among the Nations.

And verily, my friends, you shall not lose your reward; your honest endeavours shall succeed: And if the breast of so much as one generous youth, be kindled into the sacred flame, you have done an essential service to your country; for individuals are that to the state, which Samson's celebrated locks were to him; his glory and his strength at once; each particular hair contributing its proportion of virtue, and consequently possessing its proportion of value and consideration.

II. Your practice, in the observance of the Twelfth of August, is defensible, nay highly commendable, in a *moral* as well as in a *political* light. By what means did God save these Nations, at the periods to which we have been referring? By the public and private virtues; by the good sense, the piety, the prayers, and the spirited and strenuous efforts of your venerable ancestors. The same means which were employed to save in the time of danger, must be employed to preserve, in the calmness of safety and peace. A state of tranquility ought not to be a state of indolence and security. The arguments to vigilant, active virtue, are as obvious, striking and conclusive, as if there were apparent danger of an invasion of our religion and liberties. By commemorating the mercies

of

of GOD, and the diftinguifhed virtues of good men, you, in effect, exhibit the moft powerful motive to the ftudy of wifdom and goodnefs. By teaching men to love their country, you directly inculcate upon them the practice of every private and public virtue. Indeed I know but of one way, in which the generality have it in their power to render effential public fervice, and to difcover a real fpirit of patriotifm. It is to look well to one particular citizen; to reform the vices, to improve and increafe the virtues of a certain individual, to whom every one has continual accefs; with whom he may, whenever he pleafes, become throughly acquainted; over whom he poffeffes no flender degree of influence; who has a great deal in his power; and whofe power he may at any time call forth into exercife. You will eafily perceive I am not going to mention a prince, nor a minifter of ftate. In truth, my friend, this great, this confequential perfon, is no other than yourfelf. On you, and you, and you, the fate of your country depends; on you, it depends, whether Great-Britain is to recover any of her glory which may have departed, and preferve what ftill remains, and acquire new fplendor: Or whether fhe is to fink in accumulated fhame and diftrefs, involving in her ruin, her guilty, inconfiderate, degene-

rated

rated children, who refused to know the things which belonged to their peace, till they were forever hid from their eyes. Would you save your country, be a good man. If you succeed, you will have the consolation to think that you have contributed your slender aid; if general corruption brings the wrath of heaven upon a sinful land, you will at least have the satisfaction to reflect, that you have borne an honest, though humble testimony to GOD and truth; and that though you suffer in the public calamity, your inward peace cannot be broken, nor the virtues of a holy life be taken away from you.

It was reserved for modern sagacity and refinement; for we have, in this sentimental age, refinement in all sciences; it was reserved for modern sagacity to discover, that profligacy and patriotism were entirely consistent; that the public man might be an object of respect and veneration, while the private character was an object of just aversion, disgust and contempt. Such pernicious doctrine may go down with the profligate themselves, and be perhaps connived at by some of the better sort, in the fierceness of contention, and the intoxication of party-rage; but happily for the world, it cannot impose on mankind in the calm hours of reflection. As the tide

of

of faction subsides, the sophistry appears, and no sooner appears, than it is rejected with proper indignation, for the insult it presumes to offer to the human understanding. For corrupted as the world is, to the praise of its remaining good sense and discernment, private vice sooner or later proves a milstone about the neck of public profession, and overwhelms it in merited disgrace. I conclude with remarking,

III. That observances of this sort, are useful and important in a *religious* view. They lead us to God our maker and preserver. They teach us our constant and entire dependance upon Him. They mortify pride; they kindle, and keep alive the flame of gratitude and love. It was evidently for these ends, that God was pleased to institute that ordinance to which my text refers. He would have the operations of his hand carefully observed, devoutly acknowledged, and faithfully recorded; that while his people remembered they were Israelites, and heirs of an earthly Canaan, they might not forget their higher character, as citizens of another country, that is an heavenly.

The study of the divine Providence, is, of all others, the most pleasing, and the most useful. While it improves the understanding, it makes the

heart

heart better. From the partial and imperfect views given of it, in paſt events and tranſactions, we are led forward in trembling hope, to the grand conſummation of the mighty plan, when the myſterious intricate chain, which we now behold only in ſeparate links, in detached fragments, ſhall be ſeen extended at full length; its intricacies unravelled, and the connection and dependance of the ſeveral parts clearly diſcerned.

Religion alone can reſolve the difficulties, and decypher the perplexities of hiſtory. If we advert only to ſecond cauſes, if we conſider the Revolulutions which have taken place in human affairs as the effect merely of human counſels, the ſtudy is altogether unprofitable and unſatisfactory; the proſpect is melancholy and diſpleaſing. The whole is a vaſt chaos, a huge aſſemblage of indigeſted diſcordant materials, deſtitute of beauty and utility. Empires formed, flouriſhing, falling to pieces, as it were by accident, aſtoniſhing the world, now by their ſplendor, now by their ruins, till theſe very ruins are ſwallowed up, and they are remembered no more. But if we permit religion to be our inſtructor in the ſtudy of hiſtory; if we are impreſſed with the belief, that *the Lord reigneth,* that He who is *wiſe in heart, and mighty in ſtrength*

continually

continually fuperintends and directs the affairs of men, then light breaks out as in the beginning, at God's command, and pervades the obfcure mafs. By degrees, the ill-proportioned members are reduced to their proper fize, by being brought to their proper place. Under the all-fubduing hand of Omnipotence, a void, formlefs, jarring chaos, becomes a beautiful, majeftic, harmonious world. Then our own place in this glorious fabric is confidered with more attention, and improved to greater advantage: then the hiftory of our own country is ftudied with greater pleafure, and is productive of fuperior benefit.

Has GOD diftinguifhed us amidft the Nations? Has nature bleffed us in our infular fituation, and in our nearnefs to the moft important continent on the Globe? Has Providence watched over the formation and maturing of the conftitution of our civil Government? Are our religion and liberty fecured to us, by every fanction of law, by the watchful genius of the people, and by the guardian power of Heaven? And fhall this queftion, after all, opprefs us, " Wherein are ye better than " others!" Can we ftand the expoftulation, which God employs in fimilar circumftances? in that beautiful allegory, Ifaiah v. 1, 2, 3, 4, *My well-beloved hath a vineyard in a very fruitful hill.*

And

And he fenced it, and gathered out the stones thereof, and planted it with the choicest vine, and built a Tower in the midst of it, and also made a wine-press therein; and he looked that it should bring forth grapes, and it brought forth wild grapes. And now, O inhabitants of Jerusalem, and men of Judah, judge, I pray you, betwixt me and my vineyard. What could have been done more to my vineyard, that I have not done in it? Wherefore when I looked that it should bring forth grapes, brought it forth wild grapes? Shall I repeat the sequel? Hoping it may, by the blessing of God, prove an useful warning, I will; *And now go to; I will tell you what I will do to my vineyard; I will take away the hedge thereof, and it shall be eaten up: and break down the wall thereof, and it shall be trodden down. And I will lay it waste; it shall not be pruned nor digged, but there shall come up briers and thorns: I will also command the clouds that they rain no rain upon it.*

To prevent consequences so fearful, let us return together to the Lord from whom we have revolted; let us break off our sins by righteousness; in this *our* day, let us consider the things which belong to our peace, before they are hid from our eyes. Does not an argument arise out of every passage of our history, out of every privilege we enjoy, out of the service of this day, out of our present com-

comfortable circumstances, to love God more, and serve him better than we have done.

I sum up all in the words of an elegant author*: " Whilst we glory in the title of Englishmen and Britons, let us not forget that we are to support the still higher titles of Men and of Christians. Let us remember, that however reasonable and praise-worthy it may be *at present*, to cultivate the more private affections, the love of a family, a particular society, a country; yet the time will come, when all these partial affections, these narrow attachments shall be obliterated; when the godlike plan of Christianity shall have its full effect, when our heart shall be enlarged, and every bosom filled with universal benevolence. The time will come when all distinctions shall be forgotten, but those eternal distinctions of the virtuous and the wicked; and when the worthy and the good of all Nations shall be united together, in eternal bonds of love."

" Looking forward therefore to that time, and with all the affection that becomes us for our own country, joining all the benevolence that is due to others, let us with the good Patriarch confess that

---

* Mr. Rotheram's Sermon on the Anniversary of his Majesty's Inauguration.

that we are ftrangers and pilgrims on the earth; and whilft we enjoy, and are thankful for our prefent happinefs, let us, like him, wait for thofe better promifes, of which we have a profpect far off; and being with him perfuaded of them, and embracing them in our minds, let us direct our defires towards that better, that common, that heavenly country, where we truft that the good felected from all mankind fhall meet in endlefs blifs."

ADDITION

ADDITION TO SERMON III.

THE republication of this discourse brings powerfully to my recollection the man to whom its first appearance is principally to be ascribed, and to whose memory I take this opportunity of paying a merited tribute of affection and respect.

Mr. THOMAS WELLINGS, late Chymist in the Poultry, and, for many years, Chairman of the associated Livery of London, was, at the date of this Sermon, Treasurer to the Morning Lecture, and indeed its life and soul. The ministers engaged in it, twelve in number, were of various denominations, and differed widely from each other in respect of religious sentiment. Mr. *Wellings*, while he maintained his own particular opinions with unassuming firmness, always treated those of others, who differed from him, with candor and deference. His attendance at the Lecture was punctual, whoever was the Lecturer: his attention was in unison with his punctuality, and the smile of benevolence irradiated his countenance, whether the doctrine delivered coincided with, or contradicted his own ideas.

I never

I never knew the love of order so perfectly exemplified as in the conduct of this worthy man. In his person, his domestic œconomy, his business, his political engagements, his conviviality, all was method and arrangement; and all this, without the appearance of fetter and constraint. Impressed with the value of time, he never indulged himself, nor encouraged others, in a solemn or a careless trifling with any portion of it. If he said, *Two o'clock*, he meant it, and kept it, to a moment. Indeed, it is hardly possible to conceive a greater indecency, or a grosser insult than for one man gravely to tell another, that in an appointment, of his own making, for two o'clock, he meant three. The accurate person, who prizes time, who subdivides it in subserviency to the necessity of his affairs, who is faithful to a clearly expressed stipulation, by the absurdly prevailing practice, is robbed of an hour, injured in his feelings, disturbed in his arrangements, and if he ventures to complain, has insult added to injury : " My dear Sir, did not you know that " Twelve o'clock always means One precisely ?" Mr. *Wellings* used severely to reprobate this worse than ridiculous absurdity, and he acted decidedly in contradiction to it. If you went to dine with him, to transact business with him, half an hour later than the notice specified, your opportunity was, for that season, lost. When he entered into the place of worship, it was exactly time for the minister to begin the service. He never waited for any one, be his rank whatever it might; and no one ever had occasion to wait for him. This habit of regularity largely contributed

tributed, no doubt, to an uninterrupted hilarity of temper, to the preservation of a vigorous state of health to a good old age, and to the honourable acquisition of an easy, independent fortune.

If the present publication is so happy as to impress but on *one* mind this recent and respectable example of *doing all things decently, and in order*, the Author will not have altogether missed his object. He has the satisfaction, in any event, of having contributed his little handful of spicery toward embalming the remains of a much respected friend.

NOTES.

" He patronized and encouraged the cruelty of others." page 102.

The whole Administration of the affairs of Scotland, was a shocking proof of this.—The Duke of York, in person, frequently presided in the councils of that kingdom, during the latter years of Charles's reign, and the cruel and oppressive measures of Government seem to have extinguished there the passion of liberty, and in many instances to have driven men to madness.—The Earl of Argyle, for no other crime but that of urging, in council, a conscientious scruple respecting an absurd and contradictory test, recently enacted by the Scots Parliament, and offering an explanation

planation in his own behalf, was, a few days after, committed to prison, indicted for high treason and perjury, and after a trial, in which not even the semblance of Justice appeared, was adjudged to have forfeited honours, life, and fortune; sentence past against him accordingly, and was executed.

A gentleman, of the name of Weir, was tried and condemned for having kept company with one who had been a rebel, though that person had never been pointed out by process or proclamation. At this time, a prosecution by the Government, and a condemnation, were, in Scotland, one and the same thing. Above two thousand persons were outlawed, on pretence of their having conversed with rebels, and they were continually hunted in their retreats by soldiers, spies, informers, and oppressive magistrates. People living peaceably in their own houses, were by these wretches assailed with ensnaring questions; and upon their refusing to answer, or answering disagreeably to the court-creed, were, without regard to age or sex, dragged to capital punishment.
Wodrow, vol. ii. *Hume's History of Britain*, chap. lxix.

" Permitted its harmless professors to be " discouraged, obstructed, persecuted." p. 103.

The horrid custom then prevailed, in Scotland, of extorting confession by the torture; and the Duke of York was accustomed personally to assist at these barbarous ceremonies, and to contemplate the agonies of
the

the unhappy sufferers, with that closeness of attention which one would bestow on some curious experiment. Three women were apprehended on a charge of attending prohibited religious assemblies; and upon refusing to abjure a declaration, which the violence and cruelty of Government had driven them and their persecuted associates to make, respecting publick measures, were condemned to die by drowning. One of them was of an advanced age: the other two were very young; one eighteen years old, the other only thirteen. Even these inhuman persecutors were ashamed to execute the sentence upon the youngest: But the other two were carried out, and tied to stakes, within the sea-mark, at low water, that the bitterness of death might be increased by its gradual and lingering approach. The elderly woman was placed farthest in, and, by the influx of the tide, was first suffocated. The younger, shocked with the sight of her companion's death, and overcome by the supplications of her friends, consented to put up a short prayer for the King, which was the test of submission: upon which the spectators called out, that she had saved her life, and she was accordingly loosened from the stake: but the officer who guarded the execution, having again required her to sign an abjuration of her former principles, and she again refusing, he ordered her instantly to be plunged into the water, where she was choaked.

Wodrow, vol. II. p. 505.

Can Charles, with any colour of propriety, be termed a good-natured man, who could, in cold blood, authorize

authorize the perpetration of these, and numberless such barbarities?—Can there be a greater object of detestation than the calm, unrelenting tyrant, who could abuse his brother's authority to such horrid purposes; and who could bring himself to be a calm spectator of scenes, the bare description of which must shock the feelings of every one who is not dead to the impressions of Humanity? His administration in Scotland, where he was but Charles's representative, afforded England a most alarming prospect of what she had to fear, if ever he should ascend the throne of that kingdom; and the event dreadfully evinced, that these apprehensions were but too well founded.

" But through the partiality of the reigning "Monarch to his Brother," page 104.

I cannot resist my inclination to copy the portraits of the two brothers, as they are sketched by the masterly pencil of one who had studied them well, who cannot be suspected of prejudice against them, and who lived severely to repent an attachment to the family which involved him in merited disgrace and ruin.

" The two Brothers, Charles and James, became infected with Popery to such degrees, as their different characters admitted of. Charles had parts; and his good understanding served as an antidote to repel the poison. James, the simplest man of his time, drank off the whole chalice. The poison met in his composition, with all the fear, all the credulity, and all the

obstinacy

obstinacy of temper, proper to increase its virulence, and to strengthen its effect. The first had always a wrong bias upon him: He connived at the establishment, and indirectly contributed to the growth of that power, which afterwards disturbed the peace, and threatened the liberty of Europe so often; but he went no farther out of the way: The opposition of his Parliaments and his own reflections stopped him here. The Prince and the People were indeed mutually jealous of one another, from whence much present disorder flowed, and the foundation of future evils was laid. But his good and bad principles combating still together, he maintained, during a reign of more than twenty years, in some tolerable degree, the authority of the crown, and the flourishing estate of the nation. The last, drunk with superstitious, and even enthusiastic zeal, ran headlong into his own ruin, whilst he endeavoured to precipitate ours. His parliament and his people, did all they could to save themselves by winning him. But all was vain: He had no principle on which they could take hold. Even his good qualities worked against them, and his love of his country went halves with his bigotry. How he succeeded, we have heard from our fathers. The Revolution of 1688, saved the nation, and ruined the king."

Lord Bolingbroke's Letter to Sir William Wyndham.

Whoever is desirous of having full satisfaction respecting the expediency, and indeed the necessity, of the Revolution, and of the Hanover succession, let him carefully peruse the whole of this very elegant performance. It is the testimony of an adversary, and therefore may be trusted. Lord Bolingbroke is well known to have been but a cold friend to the Revolution, and to have done all he could to defeat the Succession; and yet this Letter, whose primary object is a vindication of his own conduct to his Jacobite friends, is, perhaps, the best defence of both that ever was made.

" Military tyranny is encouraged and supported." page 104.

Upon the suppression of the Duke of Monmouth's ill-concerted insurrection, a loose was given to every species of cruelty. Colonel Kirke, who was trusted with a very extensive command, had served long at Tangiers, and had largely imbibed the savage spirit of that country. Immediately upon his entrance into Bridgewater, he hanged up nineteen persons, without making any inquiry into the merits of the cause. In the very wantonness of barbarity, he would order a certain number to be executed, while he and his company drank the health of the King, or the Queen, or Judge Jefferies. Observing the convulsive motions of their limbs in the agonies of death, he said he would give them music to dance by, and commanded the drums to beat, and the trumpets to sound. He would, by way of experiment, hang a man up three or four times, and ply him at every interval with insulting questions. A beautiful young damsel threw herself at his feet, to beg her brother's life: The charms of youth, beauty, and innocence, heightened by distress,

inflamed

inflamed the monster's appetite, without softening his heart: he promised to pardon the brother, if she would consent to gratify his lust. Sisterly affection prevailed over the abhorrence of prostitution, and she did consent to the shocking condition. He ordered the windows of the chamber where they passed the night to be opened by break of day; and the violated maid on her first looking abroad, was presented with the dreadful spectacle of her beloved brother hanging on a gibbet, secretly erected on the spot, by Kirke's particular direction. Indignation and remorse took possession of her mind, and the total loss of reason was soon the consequence. The inhabitants of Somersetshire and Devonshire, innocent as well as guilty, were exposed to the ravages of this infernal barbarian. The soldiery were let loose upon the country, and his own regiment animated by the exhortation, and instructed by the example of their commander, distinguished themselves by every kind of brutality. With a pleasantry suited to such a character, he called them *his lambs*, an appellation which was long remembered with horror in the West of England.

Hume's History of Britain, Chap. lxx.

" An inhuman Jefferies finishes the horrid
" scene of blood which a savage Kirke had begun."
page 104.

The Western counties soon experienced, in the progress of Jefferies, that the severity of law, could equal, at least, the outrages of unrestrained military tyranny.

He set out upon his circuit with a savage joy, anticipating that plentiful harvest of blood and death, which his soul longed after: And he glutted himself to the full. At Dorchester two hundred and ninety-two received sentence of death, of whom eighty were executed. Exeter was the next stage of his cruelty; two hundred and forty-three were there tried, and a very considerable number of them condemned and executed; many were ordered for execution immediately on receiving sentence. Taunton and Wells, in succession, exhibited like scenes of horror. The whole country was strewed with the heads and limbs of traitors. Every village, almost, beheld the mangled carcase of a wretched inhabitant. Stern Justice, untempered by the smallest infusion of Mercy, equally confounded and intimidated prisoners, juries, and spectators. Every footstep of Jefferies was marked with characters of blood. The innocent and the virtuous were the particular objects of his fury. Let the two following instances serve as a specimen:

Mrs. Gaunt was an Anabaptist, noted for a beneficence, which extended to persons of all professions and denominations. One who had been in arms under Monmouth, knowing her humane disposition, had recourse to her in his distress, and was by her concealed in the hour of danger. A proclamation being issued, which offered indemnity, and promised rewards to such as should discover criminals, this ungrateful wretch took the opportunity of it, to betray his benefactress, and upon his evidence she was condemned.

He was pardoned for his treachery: fhe was burned alive for her charity.—Lady Lifle was profecuted for harbouring two rebels, the day after the battle of Sedgemoor; and Jefferies pufhed on the trial with the moſt unrelenting violence. The venerable Woman pleaded in her defence, that the perſons on whoſe account fhe was charged, had never been put into any proclamation or had been tried and convicted before any court: that no evidence was adduced of her having any knowledge of their guilt; that it was notorious in the whole neighbourhood, fhe had ever been of loyal principles, had carefully inſtilled them into her ſon, and that fhe had actually ſent him out, at that very time, to fight for his king, againſt thoſe very rebels, whom fhe was accuſed of protecting. Theſe arguments made a deep impreſſion upon the Jury: Twice they brought in a favourable verdict: Twice they were ſent back with threatenings and reproaches from the bench, with whom it was determined to make a ſacrifice of the aged priſoner: At length they were terrified into compliance, and brought her in guilty. Every application for her pardon was fruitleſs; the cruel and unjuſt ſentence was executed. The inflexible, compoſed tyrant coolly refiſted all importunity in her behalf, by ſaying, he had given Jefferies a promiſe not to pardon her.

"Three unhappy Kingdoms lay bleeding, al"moſt three years," page 105.

In Ireland the maſk was wholly taken off.—There the king thought himſelf at liberty to go every length

that

that zeal and violence prompted. The proteſtants were diſarmed, and left naked to the fury of their catholic enemies. The officers of the army, to the number of three hundred, were broke, becauſe they were proteſtants, though many of them had purchaſed their commiſſions. About four or five thouſand private ſoldiers were diſmiſſed for the ſame reaſon, ſtripped of their regimentals, and turned out to ſtarve in the ſtreets. A barbarous banditti, more fierce than even diſciplined ruffians, were let looſe on that wretched country, and the horrors of the former maſſacre were renewed. *Hume's Hiſtory of Britain, Chap. LXX.*

" Proteſtants of every denomination." p. 105.

James indeed attempted a ſtroke of policy, from which he expected great things, as it carried the appearance of lenity. He affected to be a great patron of toleration; he expreſſed a diſlike of all perſecuting laws; he ſuſpended them by his authority, and publiſhed a declaration of general indulgence. This was a bait thrown out to catch the Diſſenters, with a view to detach them from the intereſts of their country; and at the ſame time to ſcreen Papiſts from the pains of law. But the artifice was diſcovered. Proteſtant non-conformiſts knew the King, and underſtood their principles too well, to become the dupes of ſuch an inſidious kindneſs. Had they been ever ſo much diſpoſed to ſhut their eyes on the preſent occaſion, and to accept the proffered indulgence, the King's treatment of the Preſbyterians in Scotland muſt have undeceived them.

He

He had juft applied to the Parliament of that Kingdom for an indulgence in favour of the catholics alone, without comprehending the prefbyterians, which that Affembly had the fpirit to reject.

" He engaged in the generous defign of affift-
" ing an injured and infulted people." p. 106.

A train of remarkable circumftances attending this important expedition, has engaged the attention of ferious minds in reflecting upon it. The Prince of Orange's Fleet, on its firft fetting out, was put back by a violent ftorm; but the delay of a few days was all the lofs fuftained. That of the King, had almoft got out of the river to oppofe him, but by a fudden change of the wind, it was faft locked in; and the Prince, of courfe, being as much favoured by it, again put to fea, paffed the ftreights of Dover without moleftation, and arrived fafely in Torbay on the fourth day from its fetting fail, being the 5th of November, and the anniverfary of the Gunpowder-Treafon. Part of his fleet, by a miftake of the pilot, had failed beyond Torbay and Dartmouth harbour, the places of rendezvous, and was under great apprehenfion of being forced into Plymouth. Such a feparation might have proved very unfavourable to the caufe, efpecially as the affections of the governor of Plymouth were doubtful, if not unfriendly. But the wind unexpectedly fell, and permitted them in a few hours to work back into the bay to join their companions. The coaft was found wonderfully commodious for difembarking

the

'the troops, and a calm which immediately enſued, forwarded that ſervice without any interruption. The mildneſs of the weather had brought out the King's Fleet, and they advanced, in the purſuit, as far as the Iſle of Wight. Providence again interpoſed; a violent gale of wind ſprung up from the weſt, which, after toſſing them about for ſeveral days, forced them at length, in a very ſhattered condition, into Portſmouth, where they remained unſerviceable all the reſt of that ſeaſon.—*Burnet's Hiſtory of his own times.*

" the rejected iſſue of the popiſh tyrant." 108.

It was, at leaſt, greatly doubted, and not without an appearance of reaſon, by a great part of the nation, whether the child, produced as Prince of Wales, really was the iſſue of James II. Nothing has carried men greater lengths than religious bigotry: and James was capable of doing any thing that the ſpirit of Popery could ſuggeſt. It is certain, that the exhibition of this Child, by the indignation it raiſed among the people, and the apprehenſion with which it filled the Prince and Princeſs of Orange, from the danger that threatened her title, accelerated the Revolution, and, if it was an impoſture, ſpeedily puniſhed itſelf. To us, it is a matter of no conſequence whether a fraud was committed in this caſe or not. Whoever was the Father, the Son and his Poſterity are *legally* cut off from inheriting the Crown of Great-Britain: an excluſion

clusion more formidable and more satisfying, than even a direct proof of imposture. Providence has at length extinguished the claim of the house of Stuart by reducing it to an aged Roman Catholic Priest, precluded at once by nature and profession from the possibility of having issue.

" The much to be remembered first of August."
page 109.

It is not superstition, it is patriotism, it is gratitude to GOD for his great goodness, which considers the first, now, by the alteration of the style, the 12th of August, as a day which wears an aspect of peculiar benignity to this country. On that day, in the year 1714, Queen Anne died, and George I. succeeded to the throne. On the 12th of August, 1759, the important and decisive victory on the plains of Minden was obtained over the French, by the blessing of God upon the arms of Britain. On the 12th of August, 1762, the Moro Castle was taken by storm, and the Havannah with the Spanish Fleet, and of course the whole Island of Cuba, fell into the hands of his Majesty's Army and Navy. On the 12th of August, 1762, GEORGE, the present Prince of Wales, was born, almost at the very moment of the day, that his Great-great Grandfather acceded to the Throne, forty-eight years before. And on the 12th of August, 1763, the immense treasure, taken on board the Spanish Galleon *Hermione*, arrived at the Tower of London. If it be a
weakness

weakness to make this enumeration, the enthusiasm, which is naturally excited by anniversary commemorations, will, with the good-natured and the candid, plead its excuse.

"A Bill, breathing cruelty and revenge." page 106.

It is well known by the name of the *Schism* Bill, and was directly levelled against Protestant Dissenters. Among other things, it meant to enact, "That no person in Great-Britain or Wales, should keep any public or private school, or seminary; or teach and instruct youth, as tutor or schoolmaster, who had not first subscribed the Declaration to conform to the Church of England, and had obtained license from the respective Diocesan or Ordinary of the place: or, upon failure of so doing, should be committed to prison, without bail or mainprize. And that no such license should be granted, until the party produced a certificate, of his having received the Sacrament, according to the communion of the Church of England, in some parish-church, within a year before obtaining such license. That if any person should teach any other Catechism, than what is set forth in the *Common Prayer*, his license should be thenceforth void, and he be liable to the penalties of the intended act."

What a rod of iron might this act have proved in the hands of the arbitrary wretches who contrived it, and who certainly meant to execute it with rigor! What an argument to gratitude, that thefe things were known to our fathers only by apprehenfion, and to us only by report!

" Private vice fooner or later proves a milftone
" about the neck of public profeffion, and over-
" whelms it in merited difgrace." page 120.

In the life of 'Colley Cibber, we have an anecdote which well deferves the attention of every one who appears in a public character. A celebrated contemporary female performer, was notorioufly of fuch an abandoned private life, that the town would not permit her to perfonate certain virtuous dramatic characters, though it was univerfally allowed that her talents, for the exhibition of thofe characters, were fuperiorly exquifite.

SERMON IV*.

THE DUTY OF

COMPASSION TO POOR BRETHREN.

NON IGNARA MALI MISERIS SUCCURRERE DISCO,
VIRG. ÆN. l. v. 634.

---

* Preached at the Scots-Church, London-Wall, before the Scottish Corporation in London, at their Anniverſary Meeting, St. Andrew's Day, 1778, and publiſhed at their requeſt.

TO HIS GRACE

HENRY DUKE OF BUCCLEUGH,

PRESIDENT OF THE SCOTTISH CORPORATION
IN LONDON

My Lord,

NEVER did the magnanimity of the Roman people shine more conspicuously, than when it voted thanks to the unfortunate General, who lost the battle of Cannæ, *because he had not despaired of the Common-wealth.* Such a spirit must ever ensure victory in the end. Happily for Great-Britain, this spirit is roused in every rank of her people, and affords a most encouraging prognostic of approaching triumph over all her enemies.

Your Grace has stepped forth at a critical period, to exhibit, to kindle, and to direct the manly ardor of patriotic enthusi-
L asm,

asm, in the national defence. Permit me to solicit your attention to an object, of indeed very inferior importance, but yet of importance. The Scottish Corporation is greatly on the decline: and a spirit of languor and despondency is unhappily gone forth, which threatens it's dissolution. It is easily in your GRACE's power to prevent this: you have but to avow yourself it's patron: A multitude will soon appear to support that cause which the Duke of Buccleugh is known to favour. It is the cause of good-will among fellow citizens, for promoting one of the best of purposes, the relief of the aged, the poor and the miserable.

Your countenance, my LORD, will put success beyond a doubt; and you will have your reward, in the satisfaction which a good mind feels, in contemplating the happiness, which it has communicated to others.

I am, with profound respect,
your GRACE's most obedient,
and most humble servant,
HENRY HUNTER.

OF COMPASSION TO POOR BRETHREN.

DEUT. xv. 7.—11.

If there be among you a poor man of one of thy brethren, within any of thy gates, in thy land which the Lord thy God giveth thee, thou shalt not harden thy heart, nor shut thine hand from thy poor brother. But thou shalt open thine hand wide unto him, and shalt surely lend him sufficient for his need, in that which he wanteth. Beware that there be not a thought in thy wicked heart, saying, the seventh year, the year of release is at hand: and thine eye be evil against thy poor brother, and thou givest him nought, and he cry unto the Lord against thee, and it be sin unto thee: thou shalt surely give him, and thine heart shalt not be grieved when thou givest unto him; because that for this thing the Lord thy God will bless thee in all thy works, and in all that thou puttest thine hand unto. For the poor shall never cease out of the land: Therefore I command thee, saying, thou shalt open thine hand wide unto thy brother, to thy poor, and to thy needy in thy land.

MUCH of the beauty of this great universe consists in the wonderful and pleasing variety, arrangement, and connection of the several parts of which it is compofed. Some of thefe, examined feparately, may difguft or terrify; but viewed in their relation to the whole, and to each other, they never fail to aftonifh and delight. Hence, vaft caverns and frightful precipices, volcanos and comets, afford a pleafure equal, if not fuperior, to that which flows from the profpect of the moft beautiful, and highly cultivated, rural fcenes, or from the contemplation of all the fettled and majeftic harmony of the hoft of heaven.

In the government of the world we obferve the fame delightful contrafts, variety, fucceffion and change, which its ftructure exhibits. The great Creator and Ruler of all feems to take delight, in continually miniftring to our joy. With pleafure we obferve in perpetual rotation the gentle fragrance of Spring, the dazzling glories of Summer, the luxuriant fulnefs of Autumn, and the magnificent horrors of Winter. Charmed and inftructed we behold, alternately, the river gliding modeftly within its banks; and proudly fwelling over the adjacent fields: the ocean, now prefenting a furface tranfparent and fmooth as the polifhed mirror; and anon agitated into rage, and raifing its billows to the fky: and the celeftial vault, this hour ferenely refplendent, *fretted with golden fire*; the next, deformed with clouds, *a peftilential congregation of vapors*;

vapors; and inſtead of the murmuring breath of the zephyr, the ſeven thunders of God uttering their voices.

From the *natural* let us make the eaſy and obvious tranſition to the *moral* world; and, with a moderate degree of attention, we ſhall diſcover equal cauſe of aſtoniſhment, gratitude and joy, in that diverſity of talents, of rank, and of ſucceſs; and in that important connection of circumſtances which the ſtate of civil ſociety preſents to our view; in the wife diſtribution, and regulation, of which, divine Providence unites, ſupports, and bleſſes the children of men.

To this intereſting and uſeful ſubject of reflection, my dear Friends and Countrymen, the return of this day, the deſign of our meeting in this place, and the paſſage of Scripture, now read, at once invite us.

At the time when the inſtructions in the text were delivered, God was conducting the children of Iſrael to that good land, which he had long before promiſed to Abraham their forefather. They were there to enjoy a ſtate of proſperity and affluence, altogether ſingular and unprecedented. But the peculiar felicity of the climate and ſoil to be beſtowed upon them, was never deſigned to abolish,

bolish, or to prevent, the wise, useful and necessary distinctions, which Providence had from the beginning established among men; and, even, " a land flowing with milk and honey", was not intended to pour out it's precious store to all, in equal measure. Of the descendants from the same common stock, some were, in the ordinary course of events, to arrive at riches and honor; while others should *wax poor and fall into decay*. The provision of the rich was to flow immediately from the bounty and blessing of heaven; of the poor, from the goodness of God, through the tenderness and liberality of their happier brethren. And to this purpose tend the merciful and compassionate injunctions, which have been recited: injunctions worthy of the great Parent of mankind, who has " of one blood, made all nations of men, to dwell on all the face of the earth;" who beholds all, with an equal eye; who in wisdom permits temporary distinctions to take place; and who will, at last, reduce all to one common level, in the grave.

In discoursing farther on this subject, I shall endeavour, in hope of your patient and indulgent attention, to recommend to your observation,

I. The

I. The wifdom and propriety of the divine procedure in this particular allotment of things, *the poor fhall never ceafe out of the land* :

II. The original and permanent relation of man to man, amidft all the variety of rank and condition, that of *brother*.

III. The obligation, arifing from fuch relation, upon the great, the affluent, and the profperous; to protect, affift, and relieve the weak, the indigent, and the miferable : And,

IV. The utility and importance of the voluntary affociations, which are inftituted in the view of promoting brotherly affection, and of alleviating the diftreffes of the poor, the aged, and the infirm. I propofe,

I. In fome inftances to evince, the wifdom of Providence in this allotment of things, *the poor fhall never ceafe out of the land*. The abfolute and univerfal equality of mankind is a favourite topic with fome moral and political writers. This fuppofed equality has been confidered as a circumftance entirely favourable to intercourfe and union among men. But nearer infpection and experience prove, that natural equality is the very thing which disjoins and fcatters the human race.

The history of our species, in its rude and early state, exhibits indeed faculties both of mind and body, very similar, if not exactly the same, in all; and the external condition corresponds to the general character. We see men indeed on a level; their powers, their pursuits, their attainments, their rank, the same: but it is a sameness which fills us with mortification and disgust. We are presented, not with men, but with solitary, straggling individuals, pursuing, apart, their only employment, hunting after prey, for food; shunning one another, or destroying one another, as fear or hunger impel: resembling each other in their minds, because in all, the nobler powers of mind lie dormant, through want of exertion, and want of an object; resembling each other in their bodies, because irresistible necessity constrains all to follow the same exercises: resembling each other in condition, because their state admits of no variety. This is not theory, but fact. Savage nations have always been found divided into small wandering tribes, ignorant of, and unsociably disposed towards, their nearest neighbours. But men, in an advanced state of civilized society, compose populous empires and commonwealths; build, and inhabit, towns and cities. Patriotism and public spirit spring up; genius discovers itself; the soul awakes; society assumes

assumes a form; the several members occupy their proper places, and adapt themselves to their several stations and employments. Mutual dependence and obligation attract and unite men to each other: but the idea of dependence and obligation destroys that of equality. If, therefore, it be a blessing to live in civilized society, in preference to a state of nature, the inequality, which is so often, and so ignorantly, complained of, will be found, not only a necessary, but a wise and merciful institution.

Again, the business of the world, in every department, must of necessity be carried on by the assiduity and the strength of the *many*; and every man needs a motive to engage him to exert his strength and industry; and no motive is so powerful and persuasive as necessity; and there is no necessity so cogent, as that of having daily bread. This, therefore, likewise discovers a reason, why *the poor shall never cease out of the land*. Poverty, that is, the necessity of having food, is the mighty spring, which puts and keeps the great machine in motion. It is poverty which sets invention to work, which whets the genius, which braces the nerves, which supports the spirits. It is poverty that plunges into the mine, and penetrates into the polar regions; that yokes the patient steed, and

and puts the plaſtic loom in motion: that ſpreads the ſail, rears the column, and embattles the hoſt. It is poverty which, of courſe, gives ſtrength and ſecurity to ſtates, and majeſty to kings; which creates wealth, and diffuſes happineſs. It is the labour and the induſtry of the multitude, excited by poverty, which permits the philoſopher to purſue, at leiſure, his ſpeculations, and the ſtateſman to form and proſecute his plans; which provides inſtruments to learning, embelliſhments to beauty, and comfort to human life.

In this view, the *poor of the land* are the virtuous, the wiſe, the important, the reſpectable part of ſociety; and the ceaſing of ſuch out of the land, neceſſarily implies the diſſolution of the ſtate.

But others are *poor* in the peculiar ſenſe of that word, and them the text holds up to our particular notice, challenging, in their behalf, the utmoſt attention and reſpect. Behold that man riſing early, with a cheerful countenance; and hands ſtrong to labour; purſuing his toil to the going down of the ſun, and alleviating its preſſure by the lively ſtrain; retiring at the cloſe of the day to his humble cottage, to recruit exhauſted nature, with the homely bread which he has juſt earned with the ſweat of his brow, and prepared

pared for him by the hand of conjugal tenderness: and, at length composing his weary limbs to rest, on his pallet of straw, and closing his eyes with a clear conscience, and a thankful heart, to enjoy " the gift of sleep." I pity him not; he is not poor; he is rich; he is happy: princes may look up to him with envy. But ah! my friends, there is in the world, poverty pining under sickness, poverty racked with pain, poverty distracted with anxiety and fear, poverty groaning under oppression, poverty sinking in despair! This poor man labours to the wasting of the flesh, and the drying of the bones, yet he filleth not his hand. His children cry for bread, and there is none to give them. Disease has taken possession of his wretched mansion. Industry, frugality, and an honest disposition, have not been able to prevent the worst of human ills—he is fallen into debt. With confusion he avoids the presence of a gentle creditor; and shudders at the thought of meeting a surly one. The companion and friend of his better days passes carelessly by, and he who formerly did eat of his bread, now pays him with reproach. The chords of sensibility, once attuned to the voice, and the looks, of love, now, stretched beyond their pitch, utter only the shrill and discordant notes of woe. And is it necessary,
men

men and brethren, that such misery should exist? Is it thy will, O most merciful and compassionate Father, that these should *never cease out of the land?*—It is—it is thy will, that the great and the affluent, the giddy and the gay, the prosperous and the proud, should be reminded, warned, admonished; reminded of their mercies, warned of their danger, admonished of their duty. It is thy will, O my God, that the generous and beneficent should be furnished with opportunities of doing good; that the compassionate heart should be fitted with suitable objects of regard; that distinguished worth should have a sphere wherein to shine, benevolence a field wherein to expatiate; and that examples should be displayed to demonstrate, that man may still resemble his Maker, by scattering blessings, and by relieving distress.

Finally, Providence permits this mixture in human affairs, for the sake of the poor and afflicted themselves. Our heavenly Father is more concerned about our virtue than our temporal success. Our dispositions are of infinitely more importance in his eyes, than our circumstances: that is good, with Him, which tends to make us wise and good. If by the distribution of natural good and evil, moral good be promoted and extended, the ends of God's government are attained.

ed. If the wealthy and prosperous learn mercy, and pity, and charity and kindness: and if the poor and disappointed acquire patience and meekness, contentment and resignation, then piety has levelled the inequalities which Providence had permitted, and the divine perfection is more gloriously illustrated, than if these inequalities had never taken place. A world composed entirely of great, rich, and successful men, were a world of proud, thoughtless, ungrateful monsters; a world of poor, afflicted, desponding creatures, were an assemblage of wretches, whose private distress, depressed by the weight of universal woe, would convert creation into one vast dungeon of despair. Blended as they are, they present us with a picture painted by the hand of the sovereign Master, where light and shade in regular and just gradation, and disposed in exact proportion, at once delight and instruct. I proceed,

II. To lead your attention to the original and permanent relation of man to man, amidst all the variety of condition, that of *Brother*. It surely deserves notice, that some of those things which remove men farthest from each other, and go the greatest length in destroying the idea of Brother, are things entirely out of our power, independent of our will, and consequently undeserving either

of

of praise or of blame. They ought, therefore, neither to excite pride, nor occasion shame. Such, in particular, is the circumstance of birth, and it's corresponding advantages or inconveniencies. High birth is then a real benefit, when it serves as an incentive to noble actions; and obscure extraction is honourable distinction, when the man compensates the meanness of his origin, by the lustre of his virtues.

It were tedious and impertinent, to present this Audience with a long detail of the particular respects in which man may be considered as *brother* to man, notwithstanding that almost infinite variety of circumstances, which shew men different one from another. I shall not, at present, speak of their common Father in Heaven, nor of their descent from one and the same earthly parent—of the similar structure of their bodies, and contexture of their minds—of their common degeneracy and corruption, and consequent subjection to pain, and sorrow, and remorse—of the sameness in their manner of subsisting in the world; and the necessity to which all are subjected, by the same irrevocable sentence, of leaving the world, and of descending into the grave, that " house appointed for all living." But I will at this time, and on this occasion, and in addressing this Society,

seek

seek the proof of *brotherhood* in the breasts of the respected friends and brothers, before whom I stand. Let me appeal to the affectionate emotions of your hearts, the glistening of pleasure in your eyes, the shining of your countenances, on a day sacred to patriotism and friendship. Let me appeal to this affectionate effort to preserve union, to improve the spirit of love, to promote the endearments of charity, to support the godlike design of doing good to your younger, poorer brethren, as a proof, at once pleasing and satisfactory, that men are still the friends of mankind; that prosperity has not made you forget there is misery in the world; that elevation has a hand to raise up the dejected; that the gifts of Providence have not hardened, but humanized the soul; and that the past experience of calamity hath taught, to many, sympathy with the miserable. If with any I fail in my proof here, I must take other ground, and inform the hard-hearted and the proud, that however far beneath them, in some respects, the children of poverty and distress may be, in others, and those far more important, they may be, and often are outdone, by those whom they would disdain to "set with the dogs of their flock." He who is but thy younger brother, my friend, as to the gifts of fortune, may

probably

probably be far superior in the gifts of Nature, and in the still more valuable attainments of wisdom and goodness. For, notwithstanding external appearances, the gracious Dispenser of " every good and perfect gift," distributes his blessings in more just and equal proportion, than is commonly apprehended. The loftiest have ever something mingled in their cup, to mortify and depress them; and the meanest can always fix upon some circumstance in their condition, to cheer, console and support. Son of pride, that poor man whom thou passest by in silent neglect, or beholdest with scorn, looks down on thee, perhaps, and with juster reason, in commiseration of thy vanity and selfishness; and comforts himself, in secret, with the thought, that the God who has placed him in a low condition, has given him discernment to see, and a spirit to despise, thy cruelty and insolence. Favourite of fortune, unless thou art a man of probity, of humanity, of mercy, the virtuous beggar has cause to be ashamed to acknowledge thee as his *brother*.

Permit me to suggest one consideration more, to induce the rich and the great of this world, to acknowledge the relation of *brother* to the needy and the wretched—it is the possibility, not to say the probability, of a turn in Providence, revolution

volution of affairs, an exchange of condition. The gilded fly, now perched on the summit of the wheel, may, by one light motion, be crushed in the dust; and the crawling insect, now depressed to the bottom, may, by the same motion, be elevated to the top. "Surely," says the Psalmist, concerning the impiously prosperous, "Surely, thou didst "set them in slippery places, thou castedst them "down into destruction:" And O how fearful that destruction, how mortifying that reverse, which overtakes a man swelling with self-importance, despising his brother! and defying his Creator! Think, my happy friend, O think, if thou art a child of God, and if thy poor neighbour also enjoys that honourable distinction, then by the strongest and noblest tye, ye are *brethren*. If you are to meet in your father's house at length, is it fit, is it decent, that you should be strangers to each other by the way? If his poverty, and your riches, be improved, to the pursuit and the attainment of eternal riches and honour, the great end of both is happily attained. Your inequality of condition is now of little, and will soon be of no, importance. Be not then ashamed of thy bone and thy flesh; have the greatness of mind to acknowledge thy connection with the haunts of poverty, and the vale of obscurity. Be not ashamed to own thyself a man:

M "Take

"——Take physic, pomp;
" Expose thyself to feel, what wretches feel,
" That thou may'st shake the superflux to them,
" And shew the Heavens more just."

SHAKESPEARE'S LEAR.

I am now to attempt,

III. To shew the obligation, arising from this permanent and indelible relation, upon the great, the affluent, and the prosperous, to protect, assist, and relieve, the weak, the indigent, and the miserable. It is an obligation to which duty and interest lend their combined force.

The very ideas which are affixed to the various connections in life, and particularly that of *brother*; the absolute dependence of all upon the universal Parent; the sanctions by which divine Revelation has enforced the law of charity; and the example of the affectionate Brother, and compassionate Friend of mankind: all, all proclaim, That man was not made for himself alone, and that he who lives merely for his little self, counteracts the design of Providence, offends the Governor of the world, sins against his own soul, dishonours the Christian name, and pours contempt on the blessed Jesus.

I appeal to the constitution of human nature, whether compassion to the miserable be not your duty.

I

I appeal to that pure flame which glows in the bosom of the humane, when the tear is wiped away from the eye of woe; and to the dying throbs of tenderness in the heart of the selfish man, as he hardens into stone—to the violence he must do to himself, while he turns away his face, suppresses his sigh, and closes his hand. I appeal to that honourable testimony, that tribute of praise, which all good men have agreed to bestow upon generosity and compassion. I appeal to every page of these Sacred Records, where God has written to the eye, what he had before engraved upon the heart: and, with peculiar satisfaction, I appeal, to what outweighs all precept, to that amiable, that attractive, that perfect pattern of all excellence, which the Saviour of the world exhibited. From what height does the argument for charity fall, when the Son of God is displayed as the living model of it? What a pleasing aspect does duty assume, when we behold the practice, in the great Author and Finisher of our faith? Consider, I beseech you, my christian friends, consider, *the grace of our Lord Jesus Christ: though he was rich, yet for your sakes he became poor, that ye through his poverty might be rich.* He condescended to be ranked as the *brother* and friend of men; of the meanest and most wretched of men.

In these relations, fulfilling all righteousness, He acknowledged in himself, as well as enforced on his disciples, the obligation of charity; and by the gentlest affability, the most winning attention, and the kindest offices of humanity, illustrated, in his own person and example, the amiable nature, and the divine charms of that benevolence, which is the spirit of his religion.

It is truly mortifying, to observe the practice of a duty so clearly enjoined, and so forcibly recommended, yielding to the most paltry considerations, and the most childish reasonings. Let us hear a few of them, and estimate their weight:——" We have met with ungrateful returns from " those whom we have endeavoured to serve, and " are thereby discouraged from shewing kindness " to others." But the failure of others in the performance of their duty, can never release us from perseverance in doing our own. " I have " given much away, and with an intention to do " good: but instead of reaping praise, have in-" curred censure." It was your object then, it seems, to purchase fame, rather than to shew mercy. " My designs have been frustrated, my charity misapplied, my bounty perverted." That was the fault of another, not yours. " It is impossible to relieve every

every object." Can you seriously urge this as a reason for relieving none? Will you contribute to the support of this charitable institution? "No." Why? "It is declining, and therefore I do not "chuse to join in it." It must infallibly die, if all men think and act in the same manner. "I "am engaged in the support of so many other "charities." My friend, do you always answer the solicitations of pleasure, and of appetite so? Strange! that men should have so many arguments at hand, to plead for the omission of their duty; while at the same time, all the reasons which God and conscience can urge, are insufficient to restrain them from the indulgence of one sinful passion.

But, deaf to the calls of duty, perhaps the voice of interest may make itself heard by you; and I am now to shew, that it is clearly the interest of men to be charitable and compassionate to their poor brethren.

In the text, God expressly annexes a promise of success and prosperity, to a humane disposition, and a bountiful hand: *Because that for this thing, the LORD thy God shall bless thee in all thy works, and in all that thou puttest thine hand unto.* In many passages of Scripture, the cause of the poor is represented as the cause of God; when we relieve them

them, our Maker condefcends to become our debtor in their room, and promifes ample recompence, *He that hath pity on the poor lendeth unto the* Lord: *and that which he hath given will he pay him again**. If the poor be neglected, the Saviour of the world is infulted in them; *In as much, as ye did it not to one of the leaft of thefe my brethren, ye did it not to me*†. If then the promife of Him who is *faithful,* of Him who is *true,* be a fecurity; if the approbation of Him who fhall judge all men, be defirable; if men be difpofed to ftudy either their temporal welfare, or their eternal happinefs; and if the dictates of Scripture, as in this cafe, correfpond to the emotions of the heart, it is evidently our intereft to be merciful and beneficent.

But intereft may be placed in another view, and thereby gain the attention of fome who utterly difregard it, as now ftated. The pooreft, meaneft of mankind, are, or may be, of importance to the mightieft. You are a lofty man indeed, if you be entirely out of the reach of all your little fellow-creatures. What! are you indeed abfolutely independent? Who dare affirm it? A time may come, when the moft obfcure, unconnected, remote, defpicable wretch that you can imagine, may have it in his power to hurt, or to help you. And had you not better fecure a friend,

* Prov. xix. 17. † Matt. xxv. 45.

friend, though an humble one, by a little condescension and generosity, than create an enemy, by insolence or unkindness? The bountiful man is the friend of mankind, and is therefore befriended of all: the unfeeling and the proud, have declared war upon their own species, and they will quickly be made to feel, that mankind is a party much too strong for them.

Experience enforces the argument, in the same point of view; for she can marshal a whole host of witnesses to prove, that what men lay out upon works of charity, in the days of wealth and prosperity, is literally a stock put out at more than common interest, against the day of adversity. Charity is alternately the parent and the child. First, the tender mother which suckles the perishing infant; and then, the dutiful and affectionate " Grecian daughter," supporting her perishing aged parent, with the milk of her own breast. Were it either necessary or proper to enumerate examples, many might be adduced, of the pupils of benevolent institutions, living to be, in advanced life, the principal supporters of that which instructed and cherished their childhood; and of the decline of life cheered, and the pressure of want alleviated, by the munificence of youthful days, and affluent circumstances.

I intended

I intended to speak a few words,

IV. Of the utility and importance of those voluntary associations, which are instituted for maintaining brotherly love, in the view of relieving the distresses of the poor, the aged, and the infirm. But this surely were altogether unnecessary, in a city where one can hardly move a step, without beholding an edifice, or an inscription, sacred to the genius of friendship, or of mercy. And the importance of this is so great, in the eyes of an excellent and ingenious moral writer*, that he justly considers a nation, where justice is administered with so much impartiality, and charity dispensed with so much munificence, as at present they are in Great-Britain, as very far from a state of total corruption, whatever vices may prevail, whatever symptoms of danger may appear.

Indeed the utility of such designs, both in a private and public view, forces itself upon our observation, and commands our assent and applause. I shall only, therefore, in pursuance of the design of this day's meeting, recommend, in a few words, to your attention and support, that

---

* See Brown's Estimate of the Times.

that pious inftitution, which is immediately before our eyes.

The Scottish Corporation is now venerable for it's antiquity; having been formed, foon after the reftoration of *Charles* II. for the mutual affiftance and relief of North Britons refiding in London. It was happy in receiving, in early infancy, the patronage of fome of the moft diftinguifhed characters of that age, in refpect of rank, fortune, and virtue, of our own country; and fome of the Englifh nobility too honoured it with their countenance, and promoted it by their bounty. It was then dignified by the fanction of a Royal Charter. As the intercourfe between England and Scotland increafed, in confequence of the Revolution, and afterwards of the Union, the object of the Corporation increafed in proportion. It flourifhed by the favour of the great and affluent; it was in a condition to do much good; and it did not fail to improve the opportunity and the means. Now, alas! the love of many has waxed cold; and the caufe of the poor and needy droops and languifhes. We wifh to revive the fpirit of days that are paft; to rekindle the love of your country, and fellow citizens; to engage you in the protection and fupport of your *poor brethren fallen into decay,*

God

God forbid I should be so wicked as to attempt to rouse a narrow, illiberal, selfish, national spirit; which had better be for ever extinguished; a spirit founded in ignorance, prejudice, pride, and folly. When I intreat your favourable regards to one generous design, it cannot be my intention to decry any, or every, other. When I invite Scotsmen to give their aid to an institution of which North Britons are the object, I do not wish to tie up their hands, or shut their hearts against any pious action, whatever, to which occasion may call, inclination lead, and fortune be propitious. But it were surely an unnatural and absurd refinement, on the other hand, for you, my dear Countrymen, to neglect an useful charity, merely because it is Scottish.

Such is the amiable spirit of the times, that our attachment to each other, for the generous purposes of the present institution, will meet with general approbation. And if a few vulgar, ignorant, illiberal persons shall reproach us with an intention which we disavow, and a spirit which we detest, we will repay such treatment with pity, and kindness; and if we be upbraided with our love and services to one another; to abuse on this score, we shall reply in the spirit and words of David to Michal, " We will be be yet more vile:" what you charge us with as infirmity and dishonour, we glory in, as just praise.

But the great misfortune is, they who have it in their power, to give us the most effectual aid, will not give us an opportunity of soliciting it. Involved in the maze of business, ingrossed in the pursuit of pleasure, or dissipated by the endless formalities and avocations of high-life, the feeble and modest voice of woe can find no vacant, no favourable moment of access to their ears. Strangers to want themselves, and seeing only scenes of grandeur and gaiety, they never reflect there is such a thing as want in the world; they turn away their very thoughts with abhorrence, from the haunts of hunger and nakedness. Ah! would the great and the happy but consider what blessings they might diffuse, by a slight degree of attention; would they but consider that a few hours, once in the year, stolen from the demands of business, or of pleasure, might be the means of cheering aged poverty, of feeding a numerous starving family, of making the widow's heart to sing for joy; they could not surely reckon the sacrifice too great. Their bounty might do much; their countenance would do still more; for

many

many are difpofed to encourage and promote that caufe which one eminent man is known to have efpoufed.

But the coldnefs, of thofe who move in the fuperior walks of life, to works of charity and mercy, can with no colour of reafon, be employed, by perfons in the middle and lower fpheres, as an argument to indifference and hardnefs of heart. Diftrefs is more frequently before their eyes: they themfelves are accuftomed to bear it: their own feelings inftruct them in their duty.

To you therefore, men and brethren, I now apply: with you I leave the caufe of the infirm, the declining, and the unfortunate. As you value the honour of that land where you firft drew breath; as you prize the character of humanity; as you regard your own intereft; as you wifh to promote your real happinefs; as you refpect the will of your Creator, and venerate the character of the Redeemer of mankind, let your heart devife liberal things; " open your hand wide unto your poor brother." And may God return a thoufand-fold into your bofom. Amen.

A BRIEF

A BRIEF HISTORY
OF THE
SCOTTISH CORPORATION
IN
LONDON;

FROM ITS INSTITUTION IN 1665,
TO THE PRESENT YEAR, 1794.

WORKS of charity and mercy conſtitute, perhaps, the brighteſt glory of the Britiſh Empire. Great in arms and arts; great in literature and commerce; rich in genius and taſte, BRITAIN is ſupereminently great and rich in benevolence and compaſſion. Beſides the legal proviſion made for the indigent, in every region of her cities and towns, in every village, almoſt in every hamlet, the delighted eye meets an inſcription, an edifice, an inſtitution ſacred to ſuffering humanity; eſtabliſhed and ſupported by cheerful, voluntary beneficence. No ſooner does a new ſpecies of diſtreſs appear, than an effectual exertion is made to relieve it. Be the circle of miſery ever ſo wide, mercy ſweeps a wider circle, and embraces it.

When a particular charitable purpoſe is to be recommended to public attention, the orator finds his ground already pre-occupied; every imaginable topic of addreſs is anticipated, exhauſted: but repetition
neither

neither cloys nor offends. The good people of this truly great Country ſtand in need neither of argument to convince the underſtanding, nor of eloquence to intereſt the affections, on the ſide of the poor and the afflicted. The well-known and juſtly admired ſentiment of the Poet,

Homo ſum: Humani nihil a me alienum puto*.

Terentii Heautontim.

is not merely on an Engliſhman's tongue; no, it gliſtens in his eye, it glows in his heart, it diſtils from his hands.

Amidſt the innumerable Inſtitutions for the relief of the miſerable, which dignify and decorate this metropolis, the SCOTTISH CORPORATION is neither the leaſt reſpectable, nor the leaſt efficient. Its nature and objects are by no means ſo extenſively known as its utility and importance juſtly merit. The very exiſtence of the Inſtitution is unknown to multitudes in every part of the Iſland, who need nothing but information to be induced to patronize and promote it. Ignorance and prejudice have, in ſome few inſtances, endeavoured to miſrepreſent it.

A conciſe hiſtory of the CORPORATION, therefore, may be acceptable to thoſe who are already Members of it: may poſſibly communicate information to well-diſpoſed ſtrangers, which will conciliate their good-will

and

---

* I am a man; and can deem nothing incident to humanity a matter of indifference to me.

and procure their support: and, by unfolding its real nature and design, may obviate misrepresentation and silence ignorance.

During a long and dismal period, the inhabitants of England and Scotland, whom nature destined, from the beginning, to be brothers and friends, were animated with fierce and implacable national hatred. Frequent, bloody, and desolating wars were the consequence. From the first dawning of British history down to the REFORMATION, in the sixteenth century, this fell spirit raged with unrelenting, almost unremitting, fury. At that era, A. D. 1560. union in religious sentiment, and common danger, from Popery the common enemy, cemented a political friendship between the sagacious Elizabeth and the Scottish Reformers*. This, however, produced so little personal intercourse between the two nations, that in 1567, the ninth year of Elizabeth's reign, while commerce had attracted no less than 3838 Flemings to London, religion and politics had allured no more than 58 Scots to that metropolis‡.—But the accession of James to the throne of England in 1603, produced a mighty change; for the multitude which accompanied or followed the monarch to his new dominion, and particularly to the seat of government, was such, as to excite jealousy and give offence, in the southern kingdom§.

---

* Hume ch. xxxix. ‡ D'Ewes, p. 497. Hume ch. xliv.
§ Wilson in Kennet p. 662. Hume ch. xlv.

The turbulent and unhappy reign of Charles I. could not possibly be favourable to social intercourse between the two nations; and still less the period of the Commonwealth, which was established on the ruins of Monarchy; for no intercourse then took place, but what was of a hostile nature. The Restoration in 1660, again, and finally, opened the communication between England and Scotland: and the first charter of Incorporation is itself the most undoubted historical evidence of the extensive migration, which, in the course of a few years, had taken place, from the northern kingdom to the southern metropolis. The Scots are naturally restless, bold and enterprising. The higher state of cultivation, and the more extended commerce of England, invited hither multitudes of adventurous and industrious mechanics, of all descriptions, seamen, labourers; who at once benefited themselves, and contributed to the population and wealth of the Country which received them: for the Scottish Commonalty are amongst the best educated in the world; they are trained up from infancy in habits of order, temperance, and industry; the moral and religious principle is strong in them. These principles and habits; their skill, sobriety, and industry; their early and prolific marriages, were undoubtedly therefore, a very valuable acquisition to the cities of London and Westminster. While health and vigor remained, they were able, not only themselves to subsist comfortably, but, many of them, to rear families, and to educate

and

and provide for them. Few however, in comparison, had the power of acquiring independence, or even of forming what is called a settlement. No degree of economy or industry was sufficient to make provision against "the thousand natural ills that flesh is heir to"—disease, accident, old-age. Overtaken by all, or any one of these, absolute misery followed. They were still aliens in the land which they were helping to people and to enrich. Journeymen, labourers, lodgers, from the beginning, they continued so to the end. No claim to parochial assistance had been established, and of course, no provision made for the dark season of life. To beg, or to perish, was the dreadful alternative.

Time was continually increasing the evil, by multiplying the number of objects, and aggravating their distress. It became a bitter reflection, after an absence of many years, that they were far from their native land, and destitute of the means of returning thither; that they had become personally unknown to their nearest relations, or had survived most, if not all, of the friends and companions of their better days: in a word, that they had no where a kinsman, a friend, a home, a parish, a country.

Even so early as 1665, five years after the Revolution, the distress of the lower order of Scotsmen in these Cities, though not yet arrived to its height, was sensibly felt and deplored; to such a degree, that the more affluent of the Scottish Nation, resident in London

don, found themselves prompted by compassion to take the case of the poor into serious consideration, and to devise a remedy. A voluntary association of respectable Merchants, Tradesmen and others, was formed, and it was agreed to petition the Crown for a Charter of Incorporation, in order to procure co-operation, and to give effect, to their plans of relief to their distressed countrymen. This was without hesitation granted, and Letters patent, under the great Seal of England, for the purpose desired, were issued accordingly, bearing date the 30th of June, 1665. By these, the persons described in the Charter were empowered to erect an Hospital in the City and Liberty of Westminster, for the maintenance of old or decayed artificers of the Scottish Nation, and for training up their children to handicraft employments.

With so much ardor and unanimity was the cause adopted, and patronized, by persons of all ranks, English as well as Scots, that in 1673 the Corporation was enabled to erect a Hall, with six adjoining tenements, for fulfilling the purposes of the Charity, in Black-Friars, one of the Suburbs of the City of London.

But experience speedily evinced, that the powers granted by the Charter were inadequate to the design. The very situation of the Hall had been determined by local and temporary considerations, without regard to the express terms of the Charter. The Corporation was likewise put on a scale far too small for an undertaking

taking of such magnitude; the number of Governors being restricted to eight, with powers almost as limited as their numbers. It became necessary, therefore, to make a second application to the Crown, for an enlargement of the Corporation's numbers, powers, and privileges. This too was readily obtained, and new Letters Patent under the great Seal issued accordingly, bearing date the 16th of November 1676; by which thirty-three assistants were added to the eight Governors; liberty was granted to establish their Hospital either in London or Westminster, as might be most convenient: and they were empowered to purchase and to hold lands, to the yearly value of five hundred pounds, by the name and style of *The Master, Governors and Assistants of the Scottish Hospital, of the Foundation of King Charles the Second.*

But how limited, alas, is human foresight! From the tenor of both these charters it appears, that the original intention, and this intention followed up for eleven years together, was to erect a house of reception for all the objects of the Charity, whatever their cases might be; old, young; men, women; persons suffering under casualty, lunacy, debility, disease, all assembled within the same precinct. The impropriety, the absolute impracticability, of this, was quickly demonstrated. What funds could have supported the expence of an establishment so enormous; and that establishment incessantly on the increase? The inconveniency and discomfort attending the separation of married persons from their families and friends, at a season when sympathy and assistance are most necessary, and most acceptable, pleaded powerfully against the idea of a public, general receptacle. The uncouth mixture, and improper communications, of such a motley assemblage of patients must have produced indecencies and immoralities not to be mentioned. The design of an Hospital, therefore, was abandoned, almost as soon as adopted: and in its place was substituted the wiser mode of assisting and relieving the poor objects at their own habitations. Thus the slender funds of the Corporation were rendered more extensively efficient, for there was no expensive fabric to be raised and supported; the distressed objects were succoured in a manner more congenial to their feelings: and the jobbing, but too generally connected with all great establishments, was completely prevented.

It was an idea entertained under the original plan, to make the labouring part of the community, which might be eventually cast on the charity of the Corporation, to contribute a small pittance of their earnings, in the season of youth and prosperity to the general fund, as the foundation of a claim to relief, when they were overtaken with sickness or age. Subscribing members were accordingly admitted at the easy rate, first, of one shilling, and afterwards, of four shillings a quarter. Even the largest of these sums was considered as a mere trifle, to a man in full health

and

and full employ; especially as it conferred on him a title to expect and to demand affiftance, in the hour of need.

The Scottifh commonalty are, in general, actuated by a laudable pride. It is with extreme reluctance they fubmit to the degradation of being deemed a burden to the public. Neceffity alone can humble them to this. There is no poor's rate in any part of the proverbially poor kingdom of Scotland. Frugality, induftry, and the art of living on a little, prevent the multiplication of *paupers* there. The fhillings and fixpences of the rich, the pence of the farmer and tradefman, and the farthings of the poor, caft into the plate, as they enter or leave the Church, on the Lords-Day, is all the provifion that is made, and all that is found neceffary for the relief of the abfolutely indigent. The land-holder is indeed obliged by law to make up the deficiency, fhould any exift; but no occafion, except in very rare inftances, has occurred, of reforting to that expedient. The idea of a parochial Charity-Work-Houfe is unknown all over the country. Inftead of looking to fuch an afylum with hope and defire, a Scottifh ruftic or artificer would regard it as filling up the meafure of his wretchednefs.

The admiffion of the lower order of tradefmen, as fubfcribing members of the Scottifh Corporation, at the rates formerly mentioned, was undoubtedly favourable to this honeft pride. The man paid with cheerfulnefs as long as he was able, for he knew he was thereby laying a foundation for time to come, and purchasing a title to consideration, and corresponding support, when his powers should be impaired or exhausted. Another benefit flowed from this arrangement: the regular, quarterly call for the quarterly subscription, was a frequent and gentle admonition to the contributor, to be frugal, to be sober, to be diligent; and though the sum of such contributions could not greatly swell the public treasury, it was a gracious offering, and did good so far as it went.

The more affluent were, mean while, endeavouring, with various success, to keep alive and promote the cause, by stated, by occasional, by honorary donations; by convivial meetings and testamentary bequests. But the increase of fund by no means kept pace with the increasing demands made upon it. Few of the Nobility, and not many of the Gentry, had been induced to give it warm support, either by their attendance, or their munificence. During the short and unhallowed reign of James II. the public mind was in a state of fermentation too violent to admit of attention to sober plans of mercy and compassion.

The union of spirit, and of operation, in the two kingdoms, which effected the glorious REVOLUTION in 1668, happily paved the way for the incorporating act of UNION in 1707, by which the two were consolidated into one great Kingdom, and the distinction of England and Scotland began to disappear, and to melt away, into the auspicious, common name of GREAT-BRITAIN. There being, from that eventful epocha, but one legislature for the whole Island; one seat of Government; one Court of appeal in the last resort; one civil, commercial, and political interest, the intercourse of the two countries became, of course, unbounded. The English Court of Exchequer travelled northward, and carried with it to Edinburgh, English-Law, English Judges, English practice, and English manners. The doors of both Houses of Parliament, on the other hand, opened for the admission of the Scottish Delegates; and this interchange was highly beneficial to both.

From the very nature of the case, however, and from the well-known character of the Scottish Nation, the influx from North to South must have been out of all proportion greater than the reflux from South to North. London had now become the alone seat of Civil Government, as it had long been the great centre of commerce, of science, of arts, of industry, of amusement, of opulence. All those, therefore, who were fired with ambition, or stimulated by avarice; prompted by curiosity, or pressed by want; all who had suits at law to determine, or literary pursuits in hand; all who possessed talents, or imagined that they possessed them—all flocked to London, as to the field of fame, of fortune, of enjoyment.

The number of successful candidates was undoubtedly very great: but the disappointed, the unsuccessful, the unfortunate increased in full proportion. Time, which brings every thing to the test, at length demonstrated, that even the second Charter, that of 1676, had put the Corporation on a scale still too small to be of very extensive utility and effect. It was found that the slight exertions of a great multitude must be inconceivably more efficient, than the most violent efforts of a few, however well these might be disposed; and that, of consequence, this very important charitable Institution must either sink, or an attempt be made to support it by numbers.

Under this impression, and after very mature deliberation, it was resolved to make application to his present Majesty, for a new Charter of Incorporation, conveying a farther extension, as to number of Governors, and as to powers and privileges, such as were adapted to the exigencies of the case. This application too was successful, and a third charter was accordingly obtained, bearing date the 28th of November 1775; by which the Corporation is re-established, under the ancient name and style of, *The Scottish Hospital, of the Foundation of* CHARLES *the Second:* and instead of a Government vested in a Master, with a limited number of Governors and Assistants, it is, by this last charter, vested in a President, six Vice-Presidents, and a Treasurer; to be elected annually on St. Andrew's day, or the day after, as the case may require, and in such a number of Governors, as by any future bye-law of the Corporation may be determined. In other words, the number of Governors is, with great wisdom and propriety, left unlimited.

Sanguine hopes were now entertained, by the friends of the Institution, that the era of complete renovation

and

and unbounded prosperity had arrived. It was expected that the GREAT would patronize it, and, by their presence, bounty, and recommendation, raise it at once to splendor, affluence, and extensive utility. In this confidence, persons of the first rank were elected into the higher offices of the Corporation, and their attendance was earnestly solicited. But the time was not yet come that these expectations were to be realized. The great personages elected into office could not be prevailed upon to attend in their places, either at the general Courts, or the annual Festival of the Corporation. Rank and Title are the attractive of the MANY : Rank and Title continued to withhold its presence and countenance ; and the multitude, of course, refused to assemble. St. ANDREW, the patron of Scotland, had the mortification of seeing his sons, from year to year, parcelled out into small private parties, in fifty different regions of the town, to celebrate his day, by mere conviviality ; instead of uniting in one great determined phalanx, embodied under a Chieftain of name and ability, disposed to co-operate with heart, hand, and purse, toward the relief of their *poor Brethren*, and to make one cause of Hilarity and Beneficence.

The Welsh had set an encouraging example of the good effect of a public parade, and of an annual Sermon, on St. David's day. The latter of these expedients was suggested, as likely to be productive of some additional supply to the poor sons and daughters of St. Andrew

Andrew. It was attempted*, but with little effect; and therefore, after a second experiment, was discontinued.

And thus, with all the brilliancy of a NEW CHARTER, obtained at the expence of more than £600. the cause of the Corporation languished on for seven melancholy, heartless years, and seemed ready to expire of a lingering, consumptive indisposition. The number of Governors who assembled on the 30th of November, in honour of the Saint, and out of compassion to the wretched, gradually diminished; while many numerous private and public parties were passing the day in conviviality and joy, but contributing nothing toward the comfort of the poor and hungry, of the sick and naked.

In addition to this distressful situation, it was found, that the Hall and premises in Black-Friars were fallen into such a state of decay, as to threaten approaching ruin; and in that ruin the dissolution of the Corporation, and the misery of a multitude of helpless wretches, seemed to be unavoidably involved. But out of this almost desperate state, a dawn of hope arose. The great improvements carrying on in the vicinity of Black-Friars Bridge, had greatly enhanced the value of property in that quarter of the Town; and, consequently, the Hall and its appurtenances, though in a ruinous condition, had become a very considerable
object

‡ The preceding discourse was the first of two delivered on that occasion, and the only one that was printed.

object, from the quantity, and increased value, of the ground which they covered. The Corporation availed itself of these favourable circumstances, and in the year 1782, concluded an advantageous sale of their property at Black-Friars, with the Corporation of the City of London. Part of the money arising from this sale was immediately laid out on the purchase of the commodious Freehold Premises in Crane-Court, Fleet-Street, now in the occupancy of the Corporation, formerly the property of the Royal Society of Antiquarians. The surplus was a seasonable increase of their almost exhausted funds.

The year 1782 was destined of Providence to be a propitious epoch in the History of the Corporation; for, in a fortunate hour, the eyes of all were turned toward a young Nobleman, who happily possessed all the qualities requisite to the character of PRESIDENT of such an Institution, in such circumstances: a Nobleman who united to the highest rank, a most engaging urbanity of manners, and a very uncommon capacity for business; and who particularly excelled in conducting that style of public conviviality which is the just medium between sullen dignity and reserve, on the one hand, and noisy familiarity, on the other. JAMES, then MARQUIS OF GRAHAM, now his Grace the DUKE OF MONTROSE, the Nobleman in question, was unanimously called to the President's chair, on St. Andrew's day of this auspicious year. The face of affairs quickly changed for the better. The influence

of

of *one* Man was presently felt. Whenever the business of the Corporation rendered his presence necessary or of importance, the President was punctually in his place. He examined every thing with minute attention. He suggested plans of improvement with the sagacity of a man conversant in affairs, and with a considerateness that marked the man of humanity. On the day of the annual Festival, when the great exertion was to be made in behalf of the Charity, the President came generally attended by Persons of rank and fortune, who graced the cause by their presence, and supported it by their munificence. The apartments of the Corporation could no longer contain the flux of company, disposed, to a man, to cast his mite into the treasury, for relieving the miserable. Indifference kindled into zeal. Many of the parties which celebrated the Festival in separate bands, were induced to change their day, that they might not interfere with, and so impede, the work of mercy. Gentlemen of the highest rank and respectability accepted and executed the office of Steward, greatly to their own credit, and greatly to the advantage of the Charity. A correspondence, to the same effect, was opened with friends in both the East and West Indies; and very liberal donations were made and remitted.

It ever has been a favourite object of the noble President to create a broad, permanent and productive CAPITAL, to secure the charity, as far as it can be done, against contingent desertion, neglect and decay; and he has largely contributed toward the attainment

ment of this defirable end. In conformity to a bye-law of the Corporation, it is accordingly the practice, in order to the formation of fuch Capital, to inveft, in fome one of the public Funds, one half of every donation of ten Guineas, and upwards, to twenty; and the whole of every donation of this laft amount, or beyond it. The annual fubfcriptions of one or two Guineas, which is the qualification that conftitutes an annual Governor, and the moiety of the lower donations are applied toward the regular monthly expenditure. Every perfon, therefore, qualifying himfelf as a Governor for life, by a payment of ten guineas, has the fatisfaction of being affured, that one half of his bounty is fo much added to a permanent fund of relief; and that every fhilling of a donation or bequeft amounting to twenty guineas and upward, is part of a provifion made for the miferable, not only of the prefent, but of future ages.

Every Governor, whether annual or for life, has the privilege of recommending one, and only one, diftreffed object to the Committee appointed for the painful, but humane and meritorious, fervice of receiving the petitions, and confidering the cafes of the unhappy fufferers who come before them. This Committee fits at the Hall of the Corporation, in Crane-court, Fleet-ftreet, on the fecond Wednefday of the month, all the year round, from fix in the evening, to generally a very late hour, according to the number of poor petitioners. All Governors have a right to attend thefe meetings

meetings of Committee, and to sit, deliberate, and vote as if they were specially nominated to that effect.

A Gentleman, whose name well deserves to be transmitted to posterity with every mark of respect, as the unwearied benefactor of mankind, General ROBERT MELVILL, suggested an idea for the extension and improvement of the funds of the Corporation, which was first adopted and executed, in the year 1790; and which has been followed up, ever since, with singular effect. It occurred to the General, that St. Andrew's day, (Nov. 30) to which the great operations of the Charter were directed, was by no means favourable to the collecting of a numerous and splendid assembly of North-Britons, in London. Parliament rarely meets so early. By far the greater part of the Nobility and Gentry were, therefore, still in the country, beyond that season; and it could not be expected that the bare name of St. Andrew should have attraction sufficient to overcome the love of home, with its employments, amusements, endearments. To compensate the loss of revenue occasioned by this absence, He proposed a Spring-Festival, at a season when public or private business having drawn all descriptions of persons to the Metropolis, it was reasonable to hope for the attendance of number, of grandeur, of affluence. That the business of Parliament might not interfere, it was farther proposed that the day of such meeting should be Saturday, when the Members of both houses are disengaged.

The

The experiment was made, and succeeded beyond expectation. The humane Proposer of the scheme exerted himself with a zeal, assiduity, and perseverance, which surmounted every difficulty. Age, blindness, infirmity, were all forgotten in the ardor of his benevolence. He wrote, he visited, he argued, he rallied, he persuaded, he prevailed. The meeting was crowded, brilliant, generous; and the good General had the reward of his labours of love, in contemplating the benefit which they had produced to Society.

The year 1791 was rendered memorable in the annals of the Corporation, by the accession, among many others of inferior rank, of three most illustrious Benefactors, His Royal Highness the PRINCE of WALES, and his two Brothers, the DUKES of YORK and CLARENCE.

With a restlessness of benevolence, which strongly marks General Melville's character, He has lately proposed another method of procuring an increase of fund to the Corporation; by establishing a correspondent Board or Boards at Edinburgh, and the other Cities and great Towns of Scotland, for the purpose of soliciting and receiving contributions to the Charity. The Corporation have reason to hope that this too may, in time, become productive, as in justice it ought; for the objects which they are incorporated to relieve, are, for the most part, natives of those very cities and towns. The proposal has been received and approved by two successive general Courts, and a Committee appointed to consider of the most probable

means

means of carrying it into effect. The Committee have reported, that this object appeared to them in a promising light, but that the times seemed unfavourable to making the attempt just now, recommending, however, to the Court, to keep it still in view, that it may be resumed when opportunity invites.

But after all these exertions, there is still a very great proportion of opulent, substantial, thriving Scotsmen, resident in London and the neighbourhood, who do not contribute any thing to this charitable purpose. Many do not so much as know of its existence, who need nothing but information, to be induced to stretch forth the hand to promote it. For their sake, chiefly, this narrative is compiled; and it will inform those into whose hands it may fall, that for 130 years last past, there has been, and there is, in London, a chartered Company of Scotsmen, and the descendants of Scotsmen; the end of whose incorporation is, by voluntary contributions, to create a fund for the relief and assistance of poor Scots people who have not acquired a right to any parochial provision in England: and who have survived the power of labouring, or are disabled by casualty and disease to earn a livelihood, or who, desirous to return to their native country, are destitute of the means.

The number of such objects is much greater than is generally apprehended, though by no means incredible to any one who reflects on the vast multitude of journeymen artificers in every branch, seamen, day-labourers the wives of soldiers, sailors and servants, and

and others, who are continually flocking to London, but never arrive at the means of making good a settlement. With its present slender funds, the Corporation has of late been called upon to consider the cases, one year with another, of near one thousand aged, infirm, diseased, mutilated, helpless creatures, who had no other resource, no other hope: and, hard necessity! the administrators of these funds have been often obliged, with bleeding hearts, to dismiss the necessitous wretches with a very inadequate supply.

It may be here necessary to vindicate the Institution from a calumny with which some have hardened their own hearts, and poisoned the ears of others; and thereby robbed it of part of its support. The whole has been represented as a mere eating and drinking business, in which the name of Charity is employed as a cover to gormandizing. This insinuation is illiberal, cruel and unjust. Not a penny of the money contributed to the relief of the poor is laid out on eating and drinking. The extra-expence of the Festivals is cheerfully discharged by the Stewards. The Corporation used formerly indeed to treat the Gentlemen of the monthly Committee with tea and coffee, when employed on actual service; but even this is discontinued, and the trifling expence of it saved. The Beadle's salary and little perquisites excepted, no officer of the Corporation converts a farthing of the public money to his own use; and the Beadle's office is far from being a sinecure. Even the Secretary,

whose

whose office is of all others, the most laborious and troublesome, has no compensation for his time and trouble, but the privilege of occupying the premises in Crane-Court, free of rent and taxes, and these premises are, at all times, subject to the call and accommodation of the Courts and Committees of the Corporation.

If there be Scotsmen of fashion and fortune who either statedly or occasionally visit the Metropolis, whom the Corporation has not yet the honour of reckoning as members, it is to be presumed, they have never had proper application made to them; for it were an insult to suppose it could be made in vain. Not one of the Scottish Peerage who has either an hereditary, or an elective, Seat in the British Parliament, could possibly reject a decent requisition of his countenance and support to such a cause. The whole forty-five Scottish Members of the House of Commons, would undoubtedly, to a man, deem themselves happy in adding to its respectability and permanency, were it properly represented to them. Of Scotsmen not in Parliament, there must be a very considerable number, of high birth, and great fortune, who regularly pass a part of the year in London, and who would receive with pleasure a solicitation in behalf of indigence and distress. The intermarriages of illustrious and affluent English, with Scottish Families, might surely be turned to good account, in favour of a Scottish Charity. And let it be acknowledged with gratitude, that many Gentlemen entirely English, and particularly a considerable proportion of the Court of ALDERMEN of the City of London, have been so favourably impressed with the meritoriousness of the object, as, at different times, to qualify themselves as Governors for life.

The number of substantial tradesmen from North-Britain, who have not yet become members either by donation or annual subscription, is undoubtedly very great. Men of this description are rising into notice every day; they would be flattered by an application; and, being nearer in condition to the objects which the institution proposes to relieve, are more likely to sympathize with them, and to contribute toward their comfort.

There are many opulent families, now naturalized in England, but of Scottish extraction, and that not remotely, who assuredly would esteem it an honour to contribute to the relief of the unfortunate Natives of the Land of their Ancestors. And why not put a mark of respect on such, by making an application that goes on a presumption of their generosity and attachment to country, as well as of their humanity?

There is still another source of revenue, which has indeed been in contemplation, but hitherto, not fairly put to the test; though were the experiment made, it could not possibly fail: It is, the generosity, compassion, and public spirit of the Scottish LADIES of rank, fortune, and influence. It would be gross injustice to suspect *Them* of coldness and indifference to such an object, were it fairly represented. Could one such

Lady but witnefs the diftribution of the Corporation's charity, for one evening, the bufinefs would be done. For what would her eyes behold? A miferable affemblage of haplefs, helplefs *Scotswomen*, crawling in, one after another to afk, and to receive, a poor pittance, to keep alive a little longer the wafted lamp of nature —Old women of fixty, feventy, nay up to fourfcore years, who are paft their labour, who have furvived all their friends, who have outlived themfelves: yet in decent apparel, and of modeft deportment, looking with an earneft, but an half-extinguifhed eye, for the quarterly or half-yearly Guinea, and departing with benedictions, on their quivering lips, to the hand which beftowed it—Young women lamenting the premature death of their earthly fupport, pleading with the pathetic dumb fhew of a child unborn, or the affecting eloquence of an infant at the breaft, for a little fupply to the widow and the orphan—Females, in a word, in every varied form of human wretchednefs. With the impreffion of a fcene like this, and it is a picture after nature, with the impreffion of a fcene like this, warm on the heart, how would the humane Woman of Condition plead, in the next gay circle fhe entered, how powerfully, and how fuccefsfully plead, the caufe of female diftrefs! How would the hallowed flame be tranfmitted from one gentle bofom to another! How would the pleafure and fplendor of high life be dignified, be fanctified, be fweetened, by fcattering a handful of its *fuperflux* among the daughters

daughters of want! And what an acceffion of male fupport would not this produce? What Gentleman could ftand aloof, after the Female World had declared itfelf? Honourable, truly honourable, will it be for the great Lady who fhall lead the fafhion in this inftance; and honourable, truly honourable, for all thofe who fhall follow it. They *shall be had in everlafting remembrance. Generations unborn fhall arife and call them bleffed. Wealth and riches fhall be in their houfe. Their pofterity fhall be mighty upon earth.* For, *They have difperfed, and given to the poor.* They fed the hungry, they refrefhed the thirfty, they received and protected the ftranger, they clothed the naked, they vifited the fick, they enlarged the prifoner—and the Friend of the miferable will glorioufly requite them.

SERMON

SERMON V.*

THE UNIVERSAL EXTENT, AND EVERLASTING DURATION OF THE REDEEMER's KINGDOM.

---

* Preached at Salters-Hall, April 8th. 1780, before the Correspondent Board, in London, of the Society in Scotland for propagating Christian Knowledge in the Highlands and Islands; and published at the request of the Society, and of the Correspondent Board.

LONDON, 8th April, 1780.

At a board of the Correspondent Members, in London, of the Society in Scotland for propagating Christian knowledge in the Highlands and Islands:

RESOLVED,

That the thanks of this Board be given to the Rev. HENRY HUNTER, *D. D. for his Sermon preached this day before the Board; and that he be desired to permit it to be printed for the use of the Society.*

J. MACKINTOSH, Secretary.

TO THE RIGHT HONOURABLE

THOMAS EARL OF KINNOULL,

PRESIDENT OF THE GENERAL COURT:

THE RIGHT HONOURABLE

DAVID EARL OF LEVEN AND MELVILL,

PRESES OF THE COMMITTEE OF DIRECTORS;

THE CORRESPONDENT BOARD IN LONDON,

AND

THE OTHER MEMBERS AND BENEFACTORS,

OF THE

SOCIETY IN SCOTLAND,

FOR

PROPAGATING CHRISTIAN KNOWLEDGE;

THIS DISCOURSE

IS RESPECTFULLY INSCRIBED, BY

HENRY HUNTER

THE UNIVERSAL EXTENT, AND EVERLASTING DURATION OF THE REDEEMER'S KINGDOM.

REVELATIONS XI. 15.

And the seventh Angel sounded; and there were great voices in Heaven, saying, The Kingdoms of this world are become the Kingdoms of our Lord, and of his Christ; and he shall reign for ever and ever.

EIGHTEEN hundred years, almost, have elapsed, since Christianity was first planted in the world. During that extensive period, it has pervaded a very considerable part of the habitable globe. In some regions, it has fixed a more permanent residence; on others it has but just glanced: and such is the will of Providence, the splendor of " the Sun of Righteousness" has suddenly given place to the sullen gloom of the Prince of Darkness. The state of Christianity, at any given era, affords a prospect at once mournful and pleasing. It is always mournful to reflect on the extent and prevalency of ignorance, and vice, and misery, compared with

with the influence and effect of the Gospel of peace. It is ever pleasing to observe the progress which that gospel is making, and the triumphs which it is daily obtaining.

Of those parts of the terrestrial globe wherein this divine religion has acquired a lasting establishment, our own Country is one of the most distinguished. Great Britain has obtained an illustrious name among the nations. And what has principally procured, and supported, her reputation? Political wisdom, martial prowess, commercial skill; or Christian wisdom, moderation and liberality? Probably their combined force. It will, however, I doubt not, be readily admitted, that this last always has had, and ever will have, a commanding influence over all the rest. Can it ever, then, be deemed of little importance by any man who really wishes his country well? But, Does the present state of religion in Britain present a very encouraging prospect? I pretend not to exhibit an accurate, and complete, estimate of the times, in this respect. Infidelity abounds. "The love of many has waxed cold:" But even the prevalency of infidelity is not so discouraging, as at first sight it might appear; for infidelity has, of late years, totally changed its nature and its complexion. The infidelity of the day, is not that which attempts to support itself by argument

ment, which employs the powers of the understanding, and which, perhaps, in some, might possibly consist with virtue. No; modern infidelity is the child of ignorance and idleness; and its issue, is not elaborate, candid and ingenious essays, levelled at the Gospel, but dissipation, criminal indulgence, and every evil work. One evident advantage results from this state of things. The friend of Christianity is left entirely at leisure to pursue his plans for its propagation and success. Unbelievers now acquire their creed too easily, to think of disturbing others in spreading the knowledge of theirs. Let Christians be as zealous and diligent as they will, in diffusing their Master's, doctrine, their adversaries are too indolent, or too much engaged in other pursuits, to give them much, if any interruption.

And wherefore, men and brethren, should we not take advantage of the carelessness of the foe? Shall we always stand on the defensive? No; let us rise at once, and armed, not with sword and faggot, but with truth and meekness; with love to God, and compassion to men, carry the banner of the Gospel into the dark regions of ignorance and error and barbarism.

I mean not to consider the words of the text in connection with the circumstances wherein they appear, as uttered by a grand chorus of celestial voices, when

when the feventh Angel had founded his trumpet; but fimply, as containing a glorious and ftriking prophecy of the univerfal extent and everlafting duration of the Redeemer's kingdom. "Rapt into future times," the fpirit of prophecy defcribes that as already come to pafs, which was not yet done. *The kingdoms of this world are become the kingodms of our Lord, and of his Chrift.—This is of the Lord of hofts, who is wonderful in counfel and excellent in working,—who feeth the end from the beginning, faying, my counfel fhall ftand, and I will do all my pleafure.*

In difcourfing on this fubject, I propofe,

I. To confider the import of this expreffion, which is the burden of the fong of the heavenly choir, *The kingdoms of this world are become the kingdoms of our* LORD, *and of his* CHRIST : *and he fhall reign for ever and ever.*

II. We fhall enquire, What is the ground of belief and hope, that fuch a period, and fuch an event, as thofe predicted in the text, fhall indeed take place?

III. It may be enquired, *By what means* is a revolution fo great, and fo important, likely to be effected? and *what is our duty* in the contemplation of it?

1ft. Let

SERMON 5. THE REDEEMER'S KINGDOM.

1st. Let us consider the import of the expression, *The kingdoms of this world are become the kingdoms of our* LORD, *and of his* CHRIST; *and he shall reign for ever and ever.*

The same arguments which evince the existence of one living and true God, demonstrate also his care of, and his sovereignty over, the worlds which he has made. History and daily experience confirm the conclusions of reason; and Scripture, in every page, ascribes to God, the kingdom, the power, and the glory. Thus, *at the end of the days, I Nebuchadnezzar lifted up mine eyes unto Heaven, and mine understanding returned unto me, and I blessed the Most High, and I praised and honoured Him that liveth for ever, whose dominion is an everlasting dominion, and his kingdom is from generation to generation. And all the inhabitants of the earth are reputed as nothing: and he doeth according to his will in the Army of Heaven, and among the inhabitants of the earth: and none can stay his hand, or say unto him, what doest thou** ? *Blessed be the name of God for ever and ever: for wisdom and might are his: and he changeth the times and the seasons: he removeth Kings, and setteth up Kings: he giveth wisdom unto the wise, and knowledge to them that know understanding*‡. But the voices of the heavenly

* Dan. iv. 34, 35.   ‡ Dan. ii. 20, 21.

heavenly hoft, in the text, are evidently afcribing unto God a dominion over, and a propriety in, the kingdoms of the world, very different from that which he poffeffes and exercifes, as the great Creator and Ruler of all. *His Chrift* is joined with *our Lord* in this fupremacy; and therefore the dominion of grace muft be fuppofed to blend itfelf, in the government of this vaft Kingdom, with that which regulates the courfe of nature, and the temporal affairs of ftates and nations. " My kingdom," faid Chrift, " is not of this world;" intimating, as the context inftructs us, that it fhould not appear in worldly fplendor, nor fupport itfelf by the arm of flefh. But the prophecy under our confideration looks forward to a period, when the fpirit of this world fhall be fubdued, and brought into captivity, to the will of Chrift; when even the temporal interefts of kingdoms fhall be fubjected to the law of the gofpel. The words then, at the leaft, fignify, that, in procefs of time, the profeffion of Chriftianity fhall become univerfal; that the knowledge of the Lord fhall at length " fill the whole earth, as the waters cover the fea."

When we confider the extent of Chriftian knowledge at any former period, with refpect either to extent of territory, or to the numbers

of

of mankind, the calculation is diſtreſſing, and preſents us with one of thoſe myſteries of Providence whoſe intricacies and difficulty human underſtanding in vain attempts to unfold. Why the goſpel diſpenſation ſhould have been deferred ſo long, and then diffuſed ſo partially, are queſtions of no eaſy ſolution. To this we muſt, after all our reaſonings, and all our reſearches, at laſt reſort, God's time and method muſt needs in all things be the beſt: And, whenever the goſpel ſhall become the religion of the globe, as muſt be the caſe at length, it will infallibly appear that the delay itſelf promoted the deſign of the Eternal Mind, and powerfully contributed to the univerſality of its reception; juſt as the firſt introduction of Chriſtianity into the world, four thouſand years after the Creation, at a period when Grecian literature and the Roman arms had formed a communication between the inhabitants of half the globe, facilitated and quickened its progreſs, by opening a thouſand channels of intercourſe among mankind, which were unknown, untried, at any former period.

But little cauſe would Chriſtianity have to boaſt of its triumphs, were the univerſality of its profeſſion, at this promiſed era, connected with that coldneſs and formality which prevail in those nations where it has been already received and established. It has long been the nominal religion of almost all the states of Europe. But its spirit, alas! enters not into the government of so much as one single state. If the seriousness of the subject permitted, who could refrain from smiling at the idea, of his *Most Christian Majesty*, at the head of a Nation of Infidels! and of the Protestant Sovereign of our own country continuing to wear, among his other titles, that conferred by the bishop of Rome on one of his predecessors, as a reward (and it was all that the service or the design merited) for his maintaining one of the absurdities of Popery! The political state of Europe, at this day, is proof sufficient, that the councils of its princes are not directed by the Prince of Peace. Can there be joy and gratulation in heaven, at beholding " a form of godliness," while " the power is denied;" in surveying a generation of men, who " have a name to live, but they are dead;" baptized in the name of Christ, but devoted to the pursuits of this world?

If the prophecy in the text, then, has any meaning, it predicts a time, when the power of Christianity shall be universally felt, as well as its spirit understood; when all men shall become Christians,

Chriſtians, not merely in name, but in reality; when the angry paſſions ſhall ſubſide; ſelfiſhneſs ſhall flow out into univerſal benevolence, charity, "the bond of perfectneſs," ſhall every where prevail, and the will of God, in all things, ſhall be done on earth as it is in heaven.

Glorious and bleſſed day! when the fictions of the golden age ſhall be more than realized—when wiſdom ſhall illuminate, devotion exalt, and love inſpire every human breaſt—when relations ſhall be all dutiful and affectionate—neighbours benevolent and juſt—when princes ſhall be wiſe, and ſubjects happy—and neighbouring nations, free from jealouſy and free from fear, ſhall ſtudy each other's welfare, and promote each other's proſperity, as the children of one Father, and the diſciples of the ſame Maſter.

II. It may be enquired, What is the ground of belief, and hope, that ſuch a period, and ſuch an event, as thoſe predicted in the text, ſhall indeed take place?

It will be alleged, that the character of the preſent times, and the preſent aſpect of things, afford no very flattering ſymptoms of the flouriſhing, revived and prevailing ſtate of Chriſtianity, in the proſpect of which we have been now ſolacing ourſelves.

selves. It will be alleged, that, on the contrary, there are many and unequivocal tokens of decay, and of approaching diſſolution. The allegations are, alas! but too well founded. But admitting their weight, they only prove, that in our age, and in the place of the world with which we are acquainted, there is an apparent decline; and that there is little probability of a revival from the education, the manners, and the ſpirit of the riſing generation. For the chaſtiſement of a guilty land, who can tell but God may be about to extinguiſh the precious light, which ſo few are diſpoſed to improve. This has happened in other ages, and to other nations. But the hiſtory of other ages and nations conſtantly exhibits to us the riſing of the " Sun of Righteouſneſs" upon one region, as he ſets upon another, and the brighteſt periods of the Goſpel have generally been preceded by the deepeſt ſhades of ignorance and vice. In this, as in all things elſe, *God's ways are not as our ways, nor his thoughts as our thoughts.* If we look back to the infancy of Chriſtianity, and form our judgment of its future growth, from obvious appearances, we ſhall be ſanguine indeed, if we give it not up as a loſt cauſe. *Go and teach all nations,* ſays Chriſt to his Diſciples, *baptizing them in the name of the Father, and of*

the

the Son, and of the Holy Ghost: teaching them to observe all things whatsoever I have commanded you: and lo, I am with you alway; even to the end of the world*.

If we attend *only* to external circumstances, at the time when these words were spoken, nothing seemed more improbable than the existence of Christianity beyond the short and uncertain lives of its then professors. The world was, at that period, either buried in the grossest ignorance, or bewildered in a maze of vain philosophy, and " science falsly so called." And full well was the prediction of the Psalmist verified, in the early, the obstinate, and rancorous opposition which was made to the religion of the blessed Jesus. *The kings of the earth set themselves, and the rulers take counsel together against the Lord, and against his anointed.* The improbability of success was greatly increased by the internal character and spirit of the Gospel, and by the condition and character of its first ministers. For the genius of Christianity contradicted and exposed the most favourite maxims, disallowed and condemned the most prevailing practices of the world. To a mind engrossed by the wisdom, or the pleasures, the riches or the honours, which men naturally affect and pursue, nothing could be more

* Matt. xxviii. 19. 20.

more ungainly or forbidding, than the afpect of a doctrine which taught, which enjoined, which impofed the crofs; which profeffed to level every high mountain of pride, to dry up the very fountain of carnal joy, to lay the axe to the root of ambition, and which propofed to the covetous, treafures, but not on earth, treafures in heaven. And by what inftruments were purpofes of fuch hazardous and difficult enterprife to be effected? By men deftitute of authority, of influence, of addrefs: By men, whofe natural abilities, whofe country and parentage, whofe perfons and employments, were objects of derifion and contempt; not of refpect, or jealoufy, or fear.

An infidel of thofe days might have found plentiful food for ridicule, in the idea of *the end of the world*, and of the eftablifhment and continuance of a fect, till then, at the head of which ftood a few illiterate fifhermen, of no eftimation in the eyes of the world. But we have the advantage, my Chriftian friends, of reafoning, at this day, upon the matter of fact, which no argument can invalidate, and no ridicule expofe. The hated doctrine, and the defpifed minifters of a crucified Jefus, conquered oppofition, trumphed over the malice of earth and hell; and, without the aid of power, or guile, or gold; nay,

againft

againſt the weight of all theſe in the oppoſite ſcale, conſtrained men to embrace the Croſs, which is by nature the object of their averſion and diſdain. When this is conſidered, ſurely it cannot be deemed credulity, or the mere fondneſs of party and ſyſtem, to infer, that the power which has given ſtability to the Chriſtian church during ſuch a lengthened ſeries of years, both can, and will, give it an eſtabliſhment in the world, till time ſhall expire. It *may* indeed change, it *has* changed ſomewhat of its outward form, ſhifted its place of reſidence; has been variouſly reported of, and reſpected: but its being, nature, and foundation remain unalterable, immoveable.

Our ground of belief, then, is the matter of fact; namely the hiſtory of the world for near two thouſand years paſt, and the preſent footing which Chriſtianity has in it. In every other inſtance, relating to this all-important ſubject, we have found prediction uniformly juſtified by the event; and the divine veracity and foreknowledge eſtabliſhed beyond the power of contradiction. If, then, we admire and approve the faith of Abraham, and of the reſt, who "believed God" who "ſaw the Redeemer's day afar off" and rejoiced; who were perſuaded of the truth of the promiſes, and embraced them; ſhall we not exhibit an example

ample of the same humble trust and confidence, patiently waiting the fulfilling of the Scriptures, which shall have their accomplishment in their season.

All things are hastening to their final period. The world is waxing old, and falling into decay; and even the Christian Dispensation approaches to its consummation. And is it possible to conceive an issue more glorious, more worthy of God, more consonant to the genius and tendency of Christianity, than that which is here described? Actuated by hope, warranted by Scripture, prompted by the assenting voice of reason, and impelled by the warmer and better emotions of the heart, may we not conclude, that, as the origin of the world, presents us with the purity and perfection of human nature, in the persons of the first parents of mankind, during the short period of paradisiacal felicity, so its last, great, finishing scene may exhibit, not a garden, but a globe, peopled with their descendants, restored, through the mediation of their spiritual Head, to greater glory than their temporal father lost; the whole earth changed into a paradise, and that paradise changing into *new heavens, and a new earth, wherein dwelleth righteousness?*"

III. By

III. By WHAT MEANS is a revolution so great and so important, likely to be effected? and what is OUR DUTY in contemplation of it?

To the first of these questions, the general reply must be, "O Lord, thou knowest."—But without presumption, we may subjoin, By the spreading of useful knowledge: Christian men working under, and together with, God, for this end.—Great revolutions, to those who consider them at a distance, seem produced by extraordinary means, and are to be accounted for only by the interposition of a supernatural agency: while those who are placed nearer, can clearly discern the natural and necessary connection betwixt cause and effect. In some of the events which have been produced by a miraculous power, we stand astonished, not at the greatness, but at the meanness, and weakness, of the instruments which were employed. And when this greatest of all revolutions shall have taken place, is it unlikely that the improbability and inaptitude of the means, the feebleness and incongruity of the instruments, shall be one of the chief sources of admiration?

Again, in the great changes which have already taken place in the affairs of men, it is observable, that the human agents were often fulfilling the designs of Providence, not only without their own knowledge,

knowledge, but in direct contradiction to their own intention and inclinations, *For of a truth, against thy holy child Jesus, whom thou hast anointed, both Herod and Pontius Pilate, with the Gentiles, and the People of Israel, were gathered together for to do whatsoever thy hand, and thy counsel determined before to be done.* Who then can tell, but that the prevailing indifference about religion, which is the marking feature of our age; the rancorous opposition of some, and the treacherous friendship of others, may, in the wisdom, and under the power of God, be co-operating with the pious zeal and humble efforts of the serious Christian, toward the speedy accomplishment of the gracious purposes of Heaven? Will any one dare to say, that the period in question, however certain, is too remote, sensibly to affect, or eagerly to engage us, who are placed at such a distance? Livest thou, then, O man, to thyself alone? Hast thou, then, an interest in nothing but what thou art to see with thine eyes, and to be a partaker of? Is the restoration of human nature, to its original perfection; are the triumphs of the Redeemer, and the restitution of all things, indifferent to thee, because thy head may be laid low before the dawning of that blessed day shall arise? How wretched, how contemptible, is the selfish-

ness

ness which forbears to sow the seed, unless the enjoyment of the crop be secured! If ancestry had acted on such a narrow principle, how few, my friend, had this day been thy comforts!

What, then, is our present duty, believing, as I trust we do, that thus the Kingdom of Christ shall come; feeling that we have an interest in its approach, and persuaded that, by the blessing of God, our feeble efforts may contribute to its advancement? We have, first to consider what things chiefly retard the progress of Christianity, and to do our utmost toward removing such obstructions. And, secondly, we have carefully to cultivate in ourselves, and forcibly to recommend to others, those tempers and principles, and that conduct, which are suitable to the state of human nature exhibited in the prophecy.

Two things, chiefly, check the progress of Christianity—ignorance, and false notions of religion. Ignorance exposes human nature in its most humbling, degraded and disgustful point of view. Brutish ignorance, and detestable vice, are ever found wallowing in the same abominable cave. Light is the first-born offspring of God, both in the material and intellectual world. The gospel of Christ is the perfection of intellectual light. To diffuse that light, is to clear the way for the perception,

and

and the enjoyment, of every other bleſſing. Now it is the grand object of the Society in Scotland for propagating Chriſtian Knowledge, to ſcatter the light of truth, eſpecially where it is moſt likely to be received, and to do good. Senſible that inveterate habits are not eaſily ſubdued; that ignorance, conſolidated with the conſtitution by length of time, is hardly to be eradicated; they bend their chief care toward inſtilling religious knowledge at an early period of life, toward ſuckling babes with " the ſincere milk of the word," that the heavenly wiſdom drawn in by tender minds, may " grow with their growth, and ſtrengthen with their ſtrength." Inſtead of waiting till the monſter ignorance gather ſtrength, and become formidable through age, and then turning the world upſide down to deſtroy it, we betimes advance to its den and try to ſtrangle it in infancy. And inaſmuch as to prevent evil, is eaſier than to cure, and much better than to puniſh it, by ſo much is the plan of this noble Charity, in making early youth its object, preferable to thoſe which aim at the inſtruction, the correction, or amendment of advanced age.

Another great obſtruction to the progreſs of Chriſtian knowledge is, wrong notions of religion. This is an evil more alarming, more formidable, and

and more diligently to be watched, than the other. If ignorance degrades men into brutes, a corrupted fyftem of religion converts them into devils. Ignorance is a wild beaft of the night, which hates the light and fhuns the haunts of men; but bigotry is a ravening wolf of the day, which ftalks abroad, and feeks men to devour them. Now of all the corruptions in religion, that which profeffes to do God fervice by deftroying men, which expreffes love to the foul by practifing cruelty on the body, and which would turn the mild and healing doctrine of the compaffionate Jefus into an engine of torture and death; this furely is one of the moft grievous and intolerable. And this is the fpirit, this the practice of Popery. This way, therefore, the wifdom of the Society in Scotland for propagating Chriftian Knowledge, alfo bends its moft ftrenuous efforts; but in this, too, preferves that fpirit of difcretion, gentlenefs, and Chriftian moderation, by which all its proceedings are diftinguifhed. Inftead of idly declaiming againft Popery, where the danger of it is only a fubject of converfation, it ftrives to prevent Popery where it is a real evil. Inftead of attacking the enemy in the metropolis, where men are all eyes, all attention, all jealoufy; we purfue it to the bleak regions of the North, where,

where, immured with ignorance and barbarism, and confiding in the distance of legal power and authority, it keeps protestants in awe, and prevails by terror. Instead of hunting down old papists, we aim at rearing up young protestants; and, abhorring to imitate popery in one of its worst qualities, a spirit of persecution, we disdain not the example of its zeal, and humbly strive to oppose vigorous and persevering efforts in propagating the simplicity of "the truth as it is in Jesus," to its unremitting endeavours to scatter and cherish the seeds of its pernicious system. Whilst others, in their just detestation of this plague and destroyer of the human race, are desirous of extirpating it, we, with equal jealousy and detestation, wish to prevent its growth. Great is the victory of truth! pleasing is the triumph of diligence, of moderation, of zeal tempered with knowledge!

As we would accelerate the happy period when *the kingdoms of this world shall become the kingdoms of our Lord and of his Christ*, it must be our constant study, through the grace of God, to cultivate in ourselves, and to recommend earnestly to others, those principles and dispositions, and that conduct, which are suitable to such a glorious state of things. Suppose it to have arrived: What a wonderful

wonderful change muſt firſt have paſſed upon ourſelves! The kingdom of God muſt be within us, as well as round about us; for it is a kingdom of " righteouſneſs, and peace, and joy in the Holy Ghoſt." The kingdom of glory cannot come, till the kingdom of grace be advanced and perfected. The ruling principles of the kingdom of grace, are, faith, which *is the ſubſtance of things hoped for, the evidence of things not ſeen*; and hope, *the anchor of the ſoul*; and charity, which is *the bond of perfectneſs*. But this laſt is common to both kingdoms; it is therefore the greateſt of the three; and to the exerciſe of a particular branch of it, you are now called as Men, Britons, and Chriſtians, as the citizens of no mean ſtate in this world, and the expectants of another, a better, a heavenly country.

I am now to apply to your philanthropy, your generoſity, your patriotiſm. And you came hither for the very purpoſe of exerciſing theſe, ſpontaneouſly—cheerfully—unſolicited. I have only therefore, to place the object before you, as it is portrayed in the printed notice, which has brought us together this day.

" This ſociety have now in their ſeveral ſchools
" near eight thouſand children of both ſexes, who
" are inſtructed in the principles of the Proteſtant
" Religion,

" Religion, refcued from popery, barbarifm, and
" ignorance, and trained up to induftry, agriculture
" manufactures, and handicrafts; that they may
" be ufeful members of fociety, loyal fubjects to
" government, formed to virtue, and fitted for
" happinefs."

If ever there was a caufe which fpoke for itfelf, it is this. What father's heart but fwells at the fight of a numerous offspring, in the full enjoyment of health, and youthful vivacity, and cheerfulnefs, eating at the fame table, of the fame wholefome food, which his paternal care has provided! Chriftian, enjoy now that moft delicious of banquets. What a family have we here! Eight thoufand little ones, through Chriftian patronage and munificence, feeding on the bread of life! Ye who have children of your own, grudge not to increafe your family by extending your pious care to thefe young ones. Ye who have none, adopt this beautiful offspring, make to yourfelves heirs, whilft you live; difpenfe to their neceffities, make yourfelves rich. Their provifion muft be made from day to day: can you refufe to contribute toward to-morrow's repaft? Upheld by your foftering hand, they fhall " increafe in ftature, and in favour with God and man."

We

We live in an age of luxury of the most extravagant and expensive kind. Let me present you with an article of this sort—with a delicacy which the sensual and the vain know nothing of; with a feast, of which the understanding, the heart, and the conscience at once partake; and the value of the purchase you yourselves shall determine; it is that most satisfying of all entertainments, the making others happy, happy in time,—happy for ever. Have you prospered in the world? sanctify your gains by an offering unto the Lord. Whilst the prosperity of fools is destroying them, inflaming their pride, dissolving their principles, and corrupting their morals, let your success be adorned with piety, and charity, and condescension.

Ye generous English! we have adventured to transplant a scion from a noble stock of North British extraction, into your hospitable soil. Give it room, give it shelter, give it protection. You are far above the prejudices of the vulgar and illiberal. You will not stand enquiring, concerning the object of this charity, Whence comes it? but Is it worthy? Its worth and importance we cheerfully submit to your discernment. Scotsmen are proud to reckon so many of their English Christian brethren among the avowed supporters of this truly Christian

Chriftian, Proteftant, Britifh inftitution—and they rejoice to fee an union cemented, for the nobleft purpofes, by more than acts of the legiflature; by the unchanging, efficacious, and everlafting enactments, of mercy, and truth, and piety—an union in imitating our common Saviour,—an union in ferving the beft interefts of our country;—union in cultivating the worthieft principles in our nature,—union in purfuing the end of our common faith, the falvation of our fouls;—union in furthering the interefts of *the kingdom of our Lord and of his Chrift; and he fhall reign for ever and ever.* Amen.

END OF SERMON V*.

---

* As this volume contains another Sermon, preached before the Society for propagating Chriftian Knowledge, in the year 1789, the Reader will be prefented, as an addition to that Sermon, with a concife hiftory of the rife, progrefs and prefent ftate of the Society. This fuperfedes the neceffity of any farther addition here.

SERMON VI.[*]

THE BELIEF OF THE GOSPEL A SOURCE OF JOY AND PEACE.

---

[*] Preached at the Meeting-house in Monkwell-Street, the 21st of May 1783, at the ordination of the Rev. JAMES LINDSAY, A.M. to the pastoral office in that place.

To which is added, with the Author's permission, The CHARGE, delivered on that occasion, to Mr. LINDSAY, by the Rev. JAMES FORDYCE.

THE BELIEF OF THE GOSPEL A SOURCE OF JOY AND PEACE.

―――

Romans xv. 13.

Now the God of hope fill you with all joy and peace in believing, that ye may abound in hope, through the power of the Holy Ghost.

THE great ends for which the Gospel was written, and for which it is preached, are, that the professors of Christianity may be, from time to time, instructed in the grounds of their belief, and that they may enjoy the consolations which flow from a well established faith. The reason assigned by Luke, the beloved physician, for his writing the history of Jesus Christ, is, that Theophilus might "know the certainty of those things, wherein he had been instructed." There is one great disadvantage attending a civil establishment of Christianity, namely, the reception of it from fashion, rather than from a persuasion of its truth and importance. In such a state, as many are offended with the Gospel for no cause, so, many embrace

embrace it they know not why, and hence are utterly unqualified to give an anfwer; to any man " who afketh a reafon of the hope that is in them." One cannot help wifhing, my beloved friends, that it were otherwife; it were to be wifhed that profeffing Chriftians fhould not only have comfort in the exercife and enjoyment of their privileges, but alfo, that their comfort fhould be built on the folid foundation of knowledge and conviction; that they fhould not only be filled with " peace and joy in believing," but that they fhould, at the fame time, know in *whom*, and *why* they have believed. I have therefore chofen the words juft now read, and the folemnity of the ordination fervice of a Gofpel Minifter, as affording a fit fubject of difcourfing to you, in as plain and perfuafive terms as God fhall be pleafed to enable me, of the grounds and evidences of your holy faith, that, through the bleffing of heaven, it may adminifter to you, " everlafting confolation and good hope, through grace."

The Apoftle fuggefts, verfe 4th, that Scripture is the fource, and the repofitory, of ufeful knowledge; and that the reafons why divine truth was committed to writing, were, our information, our hope, and our joy: " For whatfoever things were written aforetime were written for our learning, that

that we through patience and comfort of the scriptures might have hope." At the 8th verse, he considers the salvation of a lost world, as the grand object of the Most High, under the Jewish, as well as under the Christian dispensation, which are indeed not two, but one, in two different forms. "Now I say, that Jesus Christ was a minister of the circumcision for the truth of God, to confirm the promises made unto the fathers: And that the Gentiles might glorify God for his mercy, as it is written, For this cause I will confess to thee among the Gentiles, and sing unto thy name. And again he saith, rejoice ye Gentiles, with his people. And again, Praise ye the Lord, all ye Gentiles, and laud him all ye people. And again, Esaias saith, "There shall be a root of Jesse; and he that shall rise to reign over the Gentiles, in him shall the Gentiles trust." The passages which he here quotes, from Moses, from David, from Isaiah, clearly prove that, at three very different and distant periods of the Jewish Church, full and explicit intimations were given of an approaching deliverance, not to the Jews only, but to the Gentiles also; and it cannot admit of a doubt, that the deliverance, to which they refer, at least in Paul's apprehension, was that which Jesus Christ effected by his incarnation, life, death, and resurrection. Here, then, God has laid the foundation

dation of one pillar of the Christian faith, namely, in the concurring and express declarations which He " at sundry times, and in divers manners," made to the world, concerning this great event.

Not to insist on that first and general prediction, concerning the seed of the woman, who was to be the bruiser of the serpent's head, let us advance to the period when God began to reduce into a particular form and system his purpose of good will. to men; that is, when Abraham, at the age of seventy-five years, was called of God from his kindred and habitation; separated not only from his idolatrous neighbours, but from his own nearest relations; sent into a state of perpetual banishment, childless, and beyond all hope or probability of progeny; and yet, under all these disadvantages, constituted and declared the heir of the promise, the progenitor of that illustrious Saviour, in whom at length, " all the families of the earth should be blessed."

From that moment, we see a fence planted around him and his family, which the violence of hostile surrounding states was not able to break through, nor the revolutions of neighbouring kingdoms, to pluck up, nor the wastes of all-devouring time to impair, till the designs of Heaven were accomplished.

In

In all the subsequent events which affected this family and their descendants—their various conditions and places of residence—the declarations made of them—the observances enjoined them—the changes of their government, from its establishment to its annihilation—all kept in view the object presented to their venerable ancestor—the MESSIAH or SHILOH, to whom " the gathering of the people should be." That men, living so remote from each other in point of time, and under such various aspects of Providence, should be led to consider one and the same object as possessing a supereminent excellency and importance, and, however differing in other respects, in perfect union here, is not to be accounted for on the usual principles of human nature, and from the ordinary current of human affairs; and therefore can proceed only from the Lord, who is " wonderful in counsel, and excellent in working."

If it be asked, Wherein consists the credibility of that record, which conveys the knowledge of these things to us? It may be answered, That this very harmony and consistency will be admitted as no inconclusive argument, by the candid and unprejudiced. To those who believe a superintending Providence, in the administration of the affairs of this world, the truth and importance of these sacred Oracles will be at once demonstrated, from
the

the care which that Providence has evidently exercifed over them, in guarding them not only from external danger, but alfo from internal corruption. To what remote antiquity muft we recur for the origin of the earlieft of thefe venerable books? Through what a long extended line, muft we purfue their progrefs, till they were completed? From how many accidents have they been preferved? How many generations of men have they outlived? How many revolutions of the world have they withftood and efcaped? The perfons who were divinely infpired to compofe them, are long fince departed. The men and the nations who often attempted to deftroy them, have many ages ago been cut off from the face of the earth. That nation which was once the guardian and repofitory of them, is now difperfed and fcattered abroad, and exhibits a ftriking and lafting monument, in its character and punifhment, of the eternal, immutable truth, of the Revelation of God to their forefathers. The languages, in which Scriptures were originally written, are gone into difufe, except among the learned few. Neverthelefs the word of JEHOVAH is an open treafure to every kindred, and people, and tongue. The wit of man has been employed againft it, and it maintains its ground. The malice and power of men have attempted to crufh it, and yet it remains in full vigor. The weaknefs of fuperftition, and the madnefs ness of enthusiasm have aimed at perverting it, but it still runs pure. The fury of successively contending parties, has tortured and wrested it to their several purposes, but, when their violence is extinguished and forgotten, it preserves an awful, steady, and unpliant dignity. And the experience of the past, leaves us no room to doubt of its future stability and progress. I shall add but one consideration more, under this part of my subject. The credibility of the Holy Scriptures of the Old Testament, as constituting a proof of the Gospel, will be put beyond a doubt, if we consider through what hands they have been transmitted to us. Can the Jews, the inveterate enemies of Christianity, the murderers of the Lord of glory, be suspected of a design of contributing toward the chief support of the Christian faith? Surely no!—But yet they have done it. Without seeing the end which God had in view by it, they carefully preserved the inspired books; they had them numbered to a line, nay to a single letter, to prevent all addition or diminution; and they have thereby, unknown to themselves, furnished the world with the clearest evidence of what they would willingly crush and destroy, and to this day, exhibit their own condemnation as the ground of their hope.

If

If it be asked, farther, Why the knowledge, and possession, of the Scriptures, a matter of universal concern, were so long limited to a peculiar spot and a particular people? It may be answered, that in the very act of calling Abraham and his family, to the high honour of being the guardians of the divine Revelation and the ancestors of our Saviour according to the flesh, an express intimation was given, that such distinction was not for their sake merely, but for the general good; that, at length, ALL Nations might be blessed in one who should descend from that particular family, and in consequence of promises and predictions which were, for a season, to be deposited with them, in behalf of the world at large. And the history, not only of that people, but of the surrounding and succeeding nations and empires, satisfyingly proves, how wisely, and how well, an end so benevolent was answered, by means, at first sight, so improbable.

That people " to whom pertained the adoption, and the glory, and the covenants, and the giving of the law, and the service of God, and the promises: Whose are the fathers, and of whom, as concerning the flesh, Christ came," were, for many ages, doomed to an unsettled, wandering state. They travelled from country to country

country. They were apparently fufpended of Providence, a fpectacle before the eyes of all the nations whither they went, to warn them of the folly and wickednefs of idolatry, and to call them to the living and true God.

The venerable patriarchs themfelves were early employed in this fervice. Abraham was fent to Egypt, and afterward fojourned among the Philiftines. Ifaac alfo lived all his life long in the midft of Idolaters: and Jacob was appointed to fojourn many years among the Affyrians, for the purpofe of conveying thither the knowledge and worfhip of the one Supreme. And when it pleafed God, at length, to eftablifh their pofterity in a country of their own, the fpot which He chofe was the very centre of the great and extenfive empires which then divided the known world. Thefe empires, unknown to each other, were, one after another, extending their conquefts and their boundaries, while the preparation of the Gofpel of peace, was haftening to its maturity in the hands of a few Hebrew fhepherds; till at length the promifed, the appointed, the expected, the feafonable hour, " the fulnefs of time" came, the Prince of peace appeared.

Permit me to mention fome ftriking circumftances in the ftate of the world, at that period, tending to evince the fpecial care which the divine

vine Providence exercifed over it, and to exhibit the evidence of Chriftianity which flows from it. While the arms of Greece, under Alexander the Great, as he is commonly ftyled, were reducing to fubjection the eaftern world, and adding the vaft empires of Affyria and Perfia to the Grecian ; Rome was, in the weft, by violent, though rapid ftrides, haftening to univerfal dominion in Europe. And the fierce difputes which enfued upon the death of Alexander, which armed his fucceffors one againft another, and difmembered the large and unwieldy fabric of his kingdom, paved the way for the Roman ftandard, till it advanced, from conqueft to conqueft, to plant itfelf in remoteft Afia. And thus, immediately previous to the Chriftian era, half the globe had become fubject to one power, and was combined in one mighty fyftem of government, beyond comparifon greater than the world ever faw before or fince. To increafe our wonder, in order to facilitate the introduction and diffufion of the Gofpel, the commotions of the nations fuddenly fubfided, the bloody portal of Janus was fhut, and all was hufhed into univerfal peace : and that, at a time when fcience fhone in all her fplendor, when philofophy was feated upon the throne. Here, then, was a field wider than ever opened at

any

any other time, in which truth was to expatiate, and a teſt was applied to it, which nothing but the truth could ſtand. And thus, He who *ſhakes the Heaven and the Earth, the Sea and the dry land, ſhook and ſettled all nations*, when the *deſire of all nations* was to *come*. And hence, we are inſtructed, that the truth of God was bounded for a time, to prepare the way for its more unlimited extent afterwards; it was laid up in Judea, that thence, as from a centre, its light might diffuſe itſelf over the whole Roman empire. " And all this is of God, who alone knoweth the end from the beginning, ſaying, My counſel ſhall ſtand, and I will fulfil all my pleaſure." For the eſtabliſhment of your faith, Chriſtians, Alexander fought and conquered; Socrates and Plato taught; Auguſtus made peace, and commanded the world to be taxed; Iſaiah and Daniel propheſied.

Such are the grounds of your faith and hope in Chriſt, ariſing from the ſtate of the world previous to, and at the time of, his appearance. We now advance to that period itſelf; and ſhall conſider, How far the perſon whom we call Lord and Maſter, anſwered the expectation formed of him, and fulfilled the predictions ſpoken concerning his perſon, character and office; and ſhall examine

amine the proofs which he personally exhibited of his being the Messiah.

It is an acknowledged principle of natural Religion, That, from the known wisdom and mercy of God, his creatures in distress have reason to expect relief; but, the time and manner of granting such relief, they must not take upon themselves to determine, but leave it to that Wisdom which is the ground of their hope. Previous, then, to an intimation from Heaven, who could have said, by whom, and in what manner, He was to work deliverance for his miserable and guilty creatures? Such an intimation He was graciously pleased early to give, as the encouragement of our hope; and now, that the great work of redemption is finished, we can discover a fitness and propriety in the means employed, though we durst not presume to say what these ought to have been, until they were discovered to us.

The person who came upon the merciful errand of salvation, was God's own eternal Son, humbled to our level, made a partaker of our meanness and misery, but totally free from our guilt. In such a deliverer, then, we behold One, who, we have reason to believe, would enter thoroughly into our case, from the near relation, which he bare to us, and who, at the same time, could suffer no impediment nor interruption in his benevolent

volent work, from any neceffary attention to his own private intereft; one, placed in a ftation where he could fet us a perfect example of all holinefs, and poffeffing a nature wherein he could, by death, make a full atonement for fin; and, at the fame time, in virtue of a fuperior nature, give value to that atonement, remove the curfe which was in full force againft his guilty brethren, whom he came to fave, and, through death, open to them the way which leads to eternal life. Then, and never till then, was fully underftood the meaning of thofe bloody facrifices which were, from time to time, offered up to appeafe divine juftice; and of that, and fuch like expreffions, " without " fhedding of blood there is no remiffion of fin." And here we alfo difcover the reafon why Chrift is in Scripture denominated " the Lamb *flain,* from the foundation of the world."

But again, the arrival of Jefus Chrift did not take the world by furprize. The fending of his Son into our world, was no new and fudden intention of the everlafting Father, in the four-thoufandth year from the creation; but was a deliberate purpofe, formed before all worlds, and declared to man, the inftant his condition required a Saviour. That declaration was repeated, and was rendered clearer and fuller, as time rolled on, till it became fo pointed and particular, as to leave candid minds, who were informed of it, no room to hefitate concerning the application, when the object of the heavenly Revelation actually appeared.

To adduce only one or two out of that cloud of witneffes, which prove Jefus Chrift to be He, of whom God fpake to the Fathers by his fervants the prophets, let me refer you to Ifrael's dying bed, and dying words, in the bleffing which he pronounced upon Judah his fourth fon: " The fceptre fhall not depart from Judah ; nor a law-giver from between his feet, until Shiloh come : and unto him fhall the gathering of the people be *:" Thefe words were fpoken as long *before* Chrift's day, as it is from it, down to the prefent period. Jacob's whole family confifted then of no more than feventy fouls, and thefe driven by famine, for fubfiftence, into a ftrange land ; and that land foon proved a houfe of bondage to them. Six hundred years, and more, elapfe, before a King is known at all in Ifrael ; and when one is at length chofen to reign, not the tribe of Judah but of Benjamin furnifhes the fovereign. When that tribe was, after fo long a delay, called at length to the regal dignity, the youngeft fon of a younger family is placed on the throne. In the third generation, the throne is fhaken to
the

* Gen. xlix. 10.

the very foundation, and a violent revolution ſtrips the crown of Judah of ten tribes, and erects a formidable rival kingdom. But this very revolution, inſtead of weakening or deſtroying the deſtined ſucceſſion, ſerves only to illuſtrate and aſcertain it. In proceſs of time, a hoſtile invaſion plucks up the kingdom by the very root; and both prince and people are carried captive into an enemy's country. But yet, in the very wreck of empire, in the almoſt neceſſary diſſolution which a ſeventy years captivity muſt produce, the exiſtence of the ſtate is preſerved, and the royal line is maintained unbroken; and Judah is again miraculouſly eſtabliſhed in his own land; till, at laſt, the kingdom changes a temporal for a ſpiritual head, in the perſon of the bleſſed Jeſus. And, after ſo long a period, the ſceptre at length departs from Judah, when the Jews themſelves give up the right of judging, to a foreign power, and acknowledge they have no King but Ceſar:—thus proving the truth of God, in the appointment of Him whom they were zealous to deny.

The noted prediction of Moſes, "a prophet ſhall the Lord your God raiſe up unto you of your brethren, like unto me; him ſhall ye hear in all things, whatſoever he ſhall ſay unto you" recorded in Deuteronomy xviii. 15. and applied by the Apoſtle to Chriſt, Acts iii. 22: The minute deſcription of the material and particular circumſtances of Chriſt's death, as delivered by David in the 22d Pſalm ; of his death and burial, by Iſaiah in the 53d. Chapter of his prophecy—and of the preciſe time and end of his ſufferings, defined by Daniel toward the end of Chapter 9th. of his book, conſtitute ſo many diſtinct and ſeparate proofs, in their exact correſpondence with the events which took place, in the land of Judea, under the adminiſtration of Pontius Pilate, that no one but our divine Maſter could be the object of theſe prophetical enunciations ; and, united, they form ſuch a weight of evidence, as nothing but inveterate and determined prejudice is able to withſtand.

But our bleſſed Lord did not remain merely paſſive, in furniſhing us with evidence whereon to build our faith. That we might place all confidence in him, as a Saviour, he claimed a divine original—he called himſelf the Son of God. And how was this claim ſupported? He did the works of God. He exerciſed an unlimited authority over the whole world of nature; over things viſible and inviſible. The prince of the power of the air fled at his command. The boiſterous elements

ments heard and obeyed his word. Difeafe, and death, and the grave, fulfilled his pleafure. To his penetrating eye the darkeft recefles of the human heart ftood unveiled, and hell itfelf could find no covering. To adduce proofs were fuperfluous to thofe who are accuftomed to read the Gofpel. And thefe things were not done in a corner, nor performed before perfons who were difpofed to believe. The difplays of this divine power were neither few nor doubtful, but were exhibited in the face of the fun, before multitudes of fpectators, and of thofe not a few who were mortified and provoked with what they faw; who were under every difpofition to detect and expofe an impofture, had it exifted, and who were not deftitute of ability, or opportunity, for making every enquiry neceffary to this purpofe.

It will be faid, That the evidence arifing from miracles is good only to thofe, who were eye and ear witneffes of them. This would be to reduce hiftorical evidence within a very narrow compafs. In what a deplorable ftate of ignorance and uncertainty would the human mind be involved, were nothing to be confidered as true and certain, but what falls under the cognizance of our own fenfes? In other cafes, and why not here? we reft, and act, on the evidence of credible witneffes who have undoubted

undoubted access to right information. Concerning the existence, the character, the life and death of Socrates, nobody pretends to entertain a doubt. The same may be said concerning the other sages, philosophers, moralists, and heroes of antiquity. And yet, I will appeal to the candor of the impartial Deist himself, whether the evidence, of which we are in possession, concerning Jesus of Nazareth, be not much more clear, full, direct, and unsuspicious, than that which respects any other name existing previous to, contemporary with, or even coming after, our Divine Master, down to the age which immediately precedes our own. Indeed the happy Revolution which wrought the temporal deliverance of these kingdoms, an hundred years ago, is an event not more clearly authenticated to me, than the decease which Christ accomplished at Jerusalem, for the salvation of a lost world, when Tiberius Cesar was Emperor of Rome, and Pontius Pilate governor of Judea. Unless, therefore, the ages past are to be reduced to an universal blank, unless dark oblivion is to draw her sable mantle over all preceding events, with her rude hand demolishing every venerable monument —with her malignant pencil blotting out each precious record; unless human knowledge is to be confined to the little circle in which every man expatiates,

expatiates, to the few fleeting years which he spends upon earth, and to the slender, unimportant facts, which fall under his own observation,—and who can bear to think of assenting to this? the truth, and the importance, of the Gospel, rest upon a rock, against which the folly, the madness, the desperate wickedness of man—against which *the gates of hell*, shall never prevail.

Such being the *nature* and *evidence* of the Christian faith, *hope*, and *joy* flow from it, as naturally as the stream does from the fountain. As no man however, can call Jesus Lord, but through the power of the Holy Ghost, and as it avails little to have the understanding enlightened, and the judgement convinced, if the heart remain insensible, alienated, rebellious; we must, if we would succeed, change the object of our address, and turn the word of exhortation to men, into earnest prayer to God, adopting the words of the Apostle in the text, " Now the God of hope fill you with all joy and peace in believing, that ye may abound in hope, through the power of the Holy Ghost," And oh! that I could with truth add, in Paul's words, respecting both you and myself, " And I myself also am persuaded of you, my brethren, that you are full of goodness, filled with all knowledge, able also to admonish one another

another. Nevertheless, brethren, I have *spoken* the more boldly unto you, in some sort, as putting you in mind, because of the grace that is given to me of God: That I should be the minister of Jesus Christ to the Gentiles, ministring the Gospel of God, that the offering up of the Gentiles might be acceptable, being sanctified by the Holy Ghost." From what hath been said, we discover,

1st. The necessary connection between divine knowledge and holy joy. As in the world of nature, God has inseparably united light and heat in the same body, so, in the world of grace, the shining, the useful, and the happy Christian, is a glorious compound of intelligence and zeal. What has the world not suffered through the separation of these! What havock of the human species has fervor founded in ignorance made! How many thousands have been misled, bewildered, lost —plunged into the abyss, precipitated from the rock, following that wandering fire, that glow-worm of the night—mere human reason! The lightless heat of Popish superstition has strewed the earth with multitudes of the slain. The frigid light of philosophic phlegm, would rob the human heart of its most precious cordial, and sacrilegiously pull down the last refuge of the miserable. What God has joined together, let not man endeavour to put asunder. Let us do our utmost

most to give the lie to that maxim of infidelity, " ignorance is the mother of devotion," and, with equal earnestness, exhibit a practical proof, that the knowledge of God, is the love of God;— and that the love of God is man's truest felicity.

2. We here discover the relation which God has been pleased to establish between the careful and diligent use of appointed means, and the interposition and agency of his spirit and grace. "By grace are ye saved, through faith, and that not of yourselves, it is the gift of God*:" Is preaching therefore useless and instruction vain? Surely no; for, leaning on the same authority, we affirm, " that faith cometh by hearing, and hearing by the word of God."—That God can, and may, by an immediate revelation of his will, fill an ignorant and guilty soul, totally excluded from the usual helps, with wisdom and with joy, and of a stone raise up a child to Abraham, who can take upon him to deny? But that He should thus condescend to indulge the indolence, or to humour the perverseness, or to prevent the cavils, of the lazy, the peevish, the froward, or the proud, who shall presume to expect? As if the Kingdom of Heaven were to be taken by storm, so are we to fight, to run, and to strive: as those whose " righteousness is filthy rags;" whose utmost

* Eph. ij. 8.

utmoſt efforts are abſolute feebleneſs, whoſe higheſt merit would expoſe to condemnation, ſo are we to look for the recompence of reward, not as a debt, but of grace.

3. Let me point out to you another all important connection, ſuggeſted from the ſubject—the connection of inſtruction and prayer. Had the Apoſtle of the Gentiles ſatisfied himſelf with writing and preaching to the Romans, he might have written the world full of Books, and ſpoken with a thouſand tongues, to no manner of purpoſe; he would have remained a mere *ſounding braſs, or tinkling cymbal.* Or, had he, on the other hand, ſpent a lifetime on his knees, to the petrefaction of the muſcles and ſinews, though he might have attained the character of the pious devotee, he muſt thereby have forfeited the much higher one, that of the diligent, zealous, and ſucceſsful Apoſtle. But we find him conſtantly blending the two together. "I beſeech you therefore, brethren, by the mercies of God, that ye preſent your bodies, a living ſacrifice, holy, acceptable unto God, which is your reaſonable ſervice." "Brethren, my heart's deſire and prayer to God for Iſrael is, that they might be ſaved." When we have delivered our Sermons, perhaps we have performed the leaſt part of our work; as he who has ſown the ſeed, has acquitted himſelf of only a

portion of his hufbandry. Would we have it to take root, and grow, and bring forth fruit, the influences of Heaven are to be regarded, expected, folicited. On the contrary, to expect a crop, through mere exterior influence, from a field, on which we have beftowed no labour, into which we have caft no feed—is to treafure up for ourfelves forrow and difappointment. Let us therefore watch and pray, labour and pray—and *continue inftant in prayer.*

It is with singular satisfaction I present to the Reader, as an Addition to this Sermon, a Composition on which I bestowed no labour; and which, though it totally eclipses my own, I am happy to give a second time to the world, in the confidence that I am conferring an unspeakable benefit on mankind, and particularly on my Brethren in the Ministry. Who, indeed, would not be vain to have it known, that his co-adjutors in the ordination Service of James Lindsay, *were such men as* James Fordyce, Andrew Kippis, Abraham Rees, Hugh Worthington?

Principibus *sociari* viris haud ultima laus est.

The CHARGE.

CONSIDERING the very important, intimate, and endearing relation, in which I had so long the pleasure of standing to this Christian Society, it would be unkind to them, and ungenerous to you, Sir, whom they have called to succeed me in that relation, if I did not take a particular interest in the present occasion, if I did not feel a more than common solicitude for your reputation, usefulness, and comfort. That you are duly sensible of the honour, which the Congregation in Monkwell street have conferred upon you, by their deliberate choice, and that you are properly affected by the solemnity with which you have thus publicly been set apart to your sacred office as their pastor, I entertain not a doubt. In consequence of both, and of the character you have hitherto maintained, I am satisfied that you will be earnestly disposed, with God's assistance, to give them every possible proof of your faithfulness and zeal.

But of these, perhaps, you cannot in effect give a better proof, than by imitating in the course of your

Miniftry the practice of St. Paul, as defcribed by himfelf in his fecond Epiftle to the Corinthians, the fourth Chapter and the Second verfe; where, after he had faid, " feeing therefore we have this " Miniftry, as we have received mercy, we faint " not, but have renounced the hidden things of " difhonefty, not walking in craftinefs, not " handling the word of God deceitfully," he adds, " but by manifeftation of the truth, com- " mending ourfelves to every man's confcience, " in the fight of God—" Mark his expreffions well— " by manifeftation of the truth, commend- " ing ourfelves to every man's confcience in the " fight of God."

Here, my reverend and worthy Brother, you will, if I miftake not, learn thefe three great points, peculiarly deferving your attention. Firft, at what kind of popularity you fhould aim, as a Minifter of the Gofpel; you are to commend yourfelf to every man's confcience: fecondly, By what means you muft do this; by manifeftation of the truth: and in the third place, from what principle you fhould thus act; In the fight of God. I am fure it will not offend you, Sir, and I hope it may not be unedifying to this affembly, if I now offer to your candor, in their prefence, fuch imperfect hints on thefe topics, as I have been able to throw
together

together, in a ftate of indifpofition and pain, which I did not forefee when I undertook this part of the fervice.

As to the firft point, I need not fay, that you will naturally and juftly feek the approbation of your hearers in general, but efpecially of the people with whom you are connected as their Minifter. The Preacher, the Paftor, who can be indifferent about his reputation or acceptance, is a wretch and a fool; and will fooner or later incur the infamy and the mifery he merits. You, Sir, want not to be told, that your peace, your honour, your utility, will all depend, under God, on the character you fhall be found to deferve in your function; and I am certain, you have too much worth, as well as prudence, to flight interefts like thefe.

But obferve, I befeech you, the practice of our Apoftle. He commended himfelf to every man's confcience—to his *confcience*, not to his caprice, or prejudice, or finful paffions, or foolifh humours, or " itching ears," or love of flattery, or fond conceits of any kind. Popularity gained, by foothing or gratifying any of thefe, is poor, contemptible, wicked, impious; below the wifh of an honeft man, odious in the eftimation of a faithful Minifter. You, my friend, will difdain and deteft it, by whomfoever it is acquired. " If,"

fays

says the same Apostle, " I seek to please men, then am I not the servant of Jesus Christ." If he sought the favour of his fellow creatures, at the expence of his integrity, to the derogation of his office, or yet from any view ending merely in his own person, as separate from the cause he espoused, he should in that case deem himself ingrateful to the compassionate Saviour, from whom he had received such singular mercy, and, unfaithful to the holy Master, who had in so extraordinary a manner called him to be an Apostle, and had during his own ministry preached and laboured, not for applause or wealth, or worldly objects of any sort, but " to seek and save them that were lost;" to cure instead of inflaming the disorders of his hearers; to renew, and in renewing to comfort, the hearts of men, instead of filling their heads with vain notions and delusive hopes.

But does not the very man, whose example I am holding up, declare of himself, " he pleased all men in all things, and that he became all things to all men?" Most true; and for this spirit of accommodation he has been reproached, with a triumphant air, by those who had not the candor to study his history, nor the soul to comprehend his character. It is evident, from a fair consideration of his words, and of his conduct, that

in

in adapting himself to persons of different sects and parties, of different opinions and modes in religion and in life, he acted from motives equally pure and benevolent. It was that he might " gain some" to the love and obedience of the truth, to the laws and privileges of the Kingdom of God; of that Kingdom, which, as he nobly expresses it, " is not meats and drinks," consists not in forms and ceremonies, or rules and observances of a ritual nature, " but righteousness, and peace, and joy in the Holy Ghost." As to himself, he utterly disclaims any desire of partial attachment, or undue respect from his followers, of whatever denomination, with every idea of dominion over their faith. " He preached not himself, but Christ Jesus the Lord, and himself their servant for Christ's sake." He reprobates those " who held the persons of men in admiration," whilst they overlooked their doctrine, or neglected their advice. With an enlargement of heart, which self-denial alone could teach him, he condemns the unreasonable prepossessions that made one say, " I am of Paul," and another, " I am of Apollos." With a warmth of style that arose from the generous ardour of his soul; full of piety and humility at the same time, he adds, " Who then is Paul, and who is Apollos,

but

but Ministers by whom ye believed, even as the Lord gave to every man? I have planted; Apollos watered: but God gave the increase. So then, neither is he that planteth any thing, neither he that watereth, but God that giveth the increase." Possessed by the same self-denying spirit, he asks on a similar occasion, " Was Paul crucified for you, or were ye baptized in the name of Paul?" What shall we say more? Wherever this exalted man could accommodate his instructions or his deportment to the various conceptions, respective situations, or innocent weaknesses of his hearers, without sacrificing his sincerity, or debasing his function, there he was ready to shew all the meekness and pliancy of the sweetest child, with all the courteousness and liberality of the most accomplished man. He knew that affection was not to be forced, but conciliated; that characters and occasions must be studied; that too strong a light must not be thrown into distempered eyes; that every generous allowance was to be made for the errors of education, and the circumstances of men, for their degrees of understanding, and their diversities of temper; and he considered, that the Preacher who would be " wise to win souls" must be careful not to shock them without necessity—I said, without necessity.

neceffity. For there are cafes, in which it may be abfolutely unavoidable to give charitable pain; where lenity to the offender would, as in a magiftrate, be cruelty to the public, and palliating the fore, would, as in a furgeon, be treachery to the patient. In fhort, St. Paul commended himfelf to every man's confcience, when he could do fo without violating his own. But when the honour of his Mafter, the dignity of his office as connected with that honour, and the interefts of truth and righteoufnefs as infeparable from both, demanded a bold defiance of obftinate adverfaries, or an open rebuke of erroneous friends, no one could difplay a firmer mind, or a more intrepid zeal. He feared no refentment; he regarded no calumny. His principles inclined him, " to pleafe men for their good to edification," as he has expreffed it with a happy precifion: but his principles likewife raifed him above every bafe and every mean compliance.

However defirable it may be to convey wifdom through the vehicle of delight; and though you, Sir, will practife this method as often as you can, (what prudent or good-natured preacher would not wifh to practife it?) yet there are times when you may find it impoffible; as when you are obliged by faithfulnefs to expofe popular follies and fashionable sins, to use the language of undisguised reproof, to assume the tone of virtuous indignation, or inculcate rules of discipline and strictness to which the licence of the age is totally adverse.

He that cannot flatter will often displease. So did St. Paul. " Am I then your enemy, because I tell you the truth?" So did St. Paul's Master. These are hard sayings : who can bear them? exclaimed many of his Disciples; " and from that time they walked no more with him :" not to speak of the persecution he endured from the worst men, because he rebuked them with freedom. If, for doing your duty, you should meet with similar treatment from some, you may regret it, chiefly on their account who betray so bad a spirit : but still you will enjoy the consciousness of your own rectitude; you will triumph in the thought, that you are " a partaker of Christ's sufferings :" you will rise in the esteem of the best people and the soundest judges; and perhaps at the very instant that others are provoked by the liberty, with which you have reproved their vices, or opposed their errors, they will feel in spite of both, that you have commended yourself to their conscience, and be forced in the secret of their hearts to confess the truth, and to respect the preacher.

preacher. " When Paul," says the history, " reasoned concerning righteousness, temperance, " and judgment to come, Felix trembled." The unhappy man, though armed with power, elated with flattery, and attended by the guards of his person and the ministers of his luxury, was nevertheless alarmed, confounded, and shaken through all his frame, by the thunder and lightening of the arguments, which the home-felt horror of a guilty mind could not help applying where they were intended.

I trust, Mr. Lindsay, you will never satisfy yourself with vague harangues, or visionary speculations, in the pulpit; such as carry no conviction, touch no heart, tend to make no one present better or wiser, however they may, for a moment, amuse the gaping multitude, or excite even the loudest applause from the half-judging. I trust, you are of opinion, that one soul awakened, one sinner converted, one believer confirmed, a single hearer thrown back upon himself, and sent away silent, thoughtful, and anxious about his salvation, will be truer praise, and a greater victory, than if crowds, turning to one another, should cry out, " What elegance! What learning! " How wonderful! What an orator!" In reality, so few are qualified to pronounce on the

critical

critical merits of a sermon, or the comparative talents of the preacher, that those acclamations from the many, are of no value in themselves, and will not be the object of a conscientious Minister. On the other hand, perhaps, our places of worship are seldom attended by persons so very ignorant or frivolous, that they may not, by the blessing of God, be made to feel, some time or other, the impression of a pertinent, serious, and animated discourse, addressed to their native sense of right and wrong, or to the hopes and fears of eternity implanted within them. But surely an unmeaning and undiscriminating noise of vulgar popularity, first raised by individuals, who affect to judge and to lead in those matters, however unfit for either, and then joined by the sequacious herd, is a very different thing from the internal attestation I described. Leave those who court to obtain and boast so small a prize. It has been obtained and boasted by coxcombs, by dunces, by bigots, by hypocrites. " Come not thou into their secret : unto their assembly," my brother, " be not thou united." They sacrifice the honour and end of their function to the sordid idol of self-love, in the very name and temple of the Most High.

If

If some better men of the profession have, by capacity, zeal, and assiduity, acquired a better fame, envy not their success, detract not from their reputation, do them justice on all occasions, and " bid them God speed." If, on the other side, men possessed of equal merit, are not held in equal esteem, let them not, on that account, be less the objects of your respect and approbation. With regard to yourself, be assured the only popularity that will give you solid satisfaction in youth and age, in life and death, must be derived from the hearts of those who know you best, bearing witness to the truth, importance, and usefulness of your instructions, to the affection and earnestness with which you enforce them, and to the corespondence of your conversation and deportment with all the rest. Amongst other passages of our Apostle on this subject, beside that under consideration, read and meditate his farewell discourse to the Elders of Ephesus. What magnanimity, dignity, triumph, does he there express, in a review of his Ministry, of the principles by which he was actuated, and of the fidelity with which he had commended himself to every man's conscience!

Observe again these significant words. He does not say, to every man's understanding, or fancy,

fancy, or paffions, but to every man's Confcience. Were the others then to be neglected or overlooked? By no means. If the underftanding were left out, or little regarded, where were fober thought, juft conclufion, genuine principle, or rational conduct? If the fancy were defpifed or forgotten, how was attention to be effectually engaged from the generality of hearers? how was fenfibility to be called forth, or kept alive, in any tolerable degree? And if there were no application to the paffions, what was to intereft the foul, to roufe her from her floth in matters of fpiritual concern, or to ftimulate her intellectual exertions? The powers I fpeak of were all formed by the hand of God: they are all effential to the compofition of man: they ought all therefore to be addreffed in their turn, and made fubfervient to his improvement. They are all accordingly addreffed in Scripture, with equal wifdom and energy; and to fay, that any one of them fhould be flighted by a preacher, were petulance and futility, or ignorance and dullnefs in the extreme. But ftill I muft think, that it is not fufficient to inform or fatisfy the judgment, that it is not fufficient to entertain or delight the imagination; that it is not fufficient to excite fome temporary movements in the affections, however pleafing or

promifing

promising these may appear at the instant; since all this may be done, and yet the conscience remain untouched, and the heart uninfluenced to any valuable purpose, as before. Mere assent does not constitute vital faith. Brilliant conceptions will not make any man truly wise, and strong emotions have no necessary connexion with the duties of religion, or the offices of life. A representation on the theatre may amuse, may strike, may agitate, while it lasts, but is no sooner over than it fades from the mind, without leaving there one noble sensation or one virtuous resolve. And a discourse from the pulpit may be full of argument, or description, or fervour of a certain kind, or all these together, and yet do no good—Why?—Because it may only prove what is already admitted, or please the injudicious with glittering conceits and gaudy phantoms, or raise at the moment some mechanical feelings, wonderfully flattering, and easily mistaken for devotion or benevolence; or peradventure it may unite these several effects; whilst, in reality, nothing shall come home to men's business or bosoms, to the most important interests of society, or to the mighty concerns of an everlasting existence; and the hearer is left to go away remarking on the preacher, perhaps extolling him, without being prompted to pause and

and reflect upon himself. As we formerly mentioned, our Apostle reasoned before Felix, till he trembled. But why did he tremble? Because the topics on which the reasoning of the preacher turned, were " righteousness, temperance, and " judgment to come," that is, the topics of all others most directly calculated to lay hold, in that alarming manner, on the conscience of a proud sensual and iniquitous governor, such as his auditor then was.

While it is your study, Sir, to let your hearers see themselves as in a mirror, take care it do not flatter. It should indeed neither magnify, nor diminish, nor exhibit any object different from the reality. Let it still " shew virtue her own feature, " vice her own image, the very age and body of " the time their form and pressure." If those, to whom you hold it up with a steady determined hand, should, after viewing themselves truly reflected there, fail to profit by the discovery, like the man St. James describes, " who, beholding " his natural face in a glass, goeth away and forget- " teth what manner of person he is," what blemishes he should remove or lessen, what advantages he should preserve and improve, the fault is not yours: you have done what became you; and
though

though, in that inftance, your hearers fhall have neglected your admonition, their hearts muft atteft your faithfulnefs.

Permit me, Sir, on this occafion, earneftly to recommend what our good old divines called Experimental preaching, in which I cannot but think the more enlightened part of them excelled; and that which I conceive fhould be joined with it, if indeed they are not one and the fame, Characteriftic preaching, as I would take the liberty to ftyle it. Avoiding offenfive perfonalities, invidious applications, illiberal cenfures, with all ludicrous and trivial particulars, its aim is to delineate, as opportunity ferves, the principles and views, the ruling paffions and incidental propenfities, the different conduct, difcourfe, purfuits and taftes of good and bad men, through their various modifications and conditions, with the different ways in which they are affected by the events of providence, by the claims of religion, and by the operations of Heaven on their refpective minds.

Give me the preacher, who has not formed his fyftem merely in the fchool or in the clofet, but has ftudied Chriftianity in the writings of the New Teftament, and mankind on the theatre of the world; who is acquainted with the rules of a found and liberal cafuiftry, equally removed from

rigour

rigour and laxnefs; who avoids alike the extremes of elating his hearers into prefumption, or finking them into defpair; who, with a generous freedom, unfolds the grace and mercy of the evangelical covenant on the one hand, and, on the other, ftates its facred and indifpenfable terms with the greateft clearnefs and firmnefs, not daring to explain away or foften down a fingle precept of Chrift, in favour to the corruptions of men, nor yet to reprefent his fervice as gloomy or fevere. Give me the preacher who probes the wounded fpirit to the bottom, not to irritate but to heal it, to heal it radically, not to palliate the fore; who is folicitous to relieve the doubting yet honeft mind, to ftrengthen the virtuous yet feeble refolution, to recal the unhappy wanderer from the road of truth or duty, and " to comfort the mourner in " Zion;" but who at the fame time is too fincere " to fpeak peace where God has fpoken no peace;" who on the contrary bears down upon the felf-righteous and felf-deluded finner with a torrent of conviction, that " fhall fweep away the refuge " of lies." Give me the preacher who knows how to paint the fhades and gradations of vice and impiety, to expofe the guilt and mifery of both, to contraft the oppofite ftates of fin and holinefs, to diftinguifh between wilful tranfgreffion and involuntary

voluntary frailty, between growth and decay, between ſtrength and weakneſs, in the ſpiritual life; above all, to deſcribe, with ſkill, and with feeling, the nature and excellence, the riſe and progreſs, the workings, conflicts, and victories of the divine principle in the ſoul of a ſincere believer, till it arrives at perfection in the regions of immortality —give me ſuch a preacher, and I will embrace him with love and veneration, to whatever communion he belongs, I will honour and applaud him as " a Maſter in Iſrael," and " a workman " that needeth not to be aſhamed, rightly divid- " ing the word of truth."

Obſerve once more on this head, that the Apoſtle ſpeaks, not of commending himſelf to the conſcience of any particular man or claſs of men, but to Every man's conſcience without exception. He was, in the beſt ſenſe of the phraſe, a Catholic preacher. He no ſooner ſhook off the fetters of Jewiſh prejudice, than his affections expanded to the whole human race: from a furious bigot he became an ardent philanthropiſt. The ſpirit of Chriſtianity, like the light of the ſun that animates all nature, kindled in his boſom a flame of univerſal benevolence. He conſidered his labours as a kind of general property. " I am a debtor," cries he, " both to the Greeks and to the
" Barbarians,

"Barbarians, both to the wife and to the unwife." How liberal a sentiment! How different from that which seems to have possessed those pagan philosophers, who confined their doctrines to the rich, the learned, and the great, looking on the rest of mankind as beneath their notice; perhaps from a supposition, that they could add but little to their consequence, or their fame!

St. Paul proceeded on higher grounds. He knew that his Master had preached the Gospel to the poor, to the illiterate, to the despised of this world; and had commanded it to be preached, by his Apostles and Ministers "to all nations;" that "with God there was no respect of persons;" that "he would have all men every where to re-"pent, and come to the knowledge of the truth;" that as salvation was equally designed for all, who were willing to accept of it on the terms proposed, so it should be equally offered to all; that the soul of every man was infinitely precious, in the estimation of his Maker and Redeemer; and that every man's conscience was formed with a power of enjoying the most exalted satisfaction, or of suffering the deepest anguish, both here and hereafter, "according to the deeds done in the body "whether they be good or evil." Such considerations will help us to account for the comprehensive and

and impartial zeal of our Apoſtle; and ſuch conſiderations will prevent you, Sir, from ever intentionally neglecting any part of your audience, be their capacity, condition, or character, what it may. Impreſſed with ſuch conſiderations, you will be far from ſtudying the taſte, or ſeeking the approbation, of your more enlightened, and refined, or critical hearers only, without regard to the bulk of the people: you will be far from palliating the vices of the wealthy, any more than thoſe of the neceſſitous: you will readily "condeſcend to men of low eſtate;" as, without flattering, you will ſhew due reſpect to better rank. Let me obſerve by the way, that your attention to virtuous obſcurity will be amply rewarded in the very act. Amongſt perſons of humble ſtation in this place, you will find thoſe who are entitled to much eſteem for their native ſenſe, modeſt worth, and ſober unpretending piety. I ſhall always remember them with affection, and reflect with pleaſure on the agreeable and edifying hours I paſt in their company. The world knows them not, nor are they ambitious of its knowing them. But the moſt valuable metals have been frequently diſcovered, where they were leaſt expected.

With

With many preachers it is but too common to forget the grand diftinction of righteous and wicked, that divides mankind; compared to which all other diftinctions are trifling and vain. Of courfe they addrefs themfelves to their hearers without difcrimination, and confequently without effect. Many too feem to think only of the Saints, and to dwell exclufively on their peculiar privileges, as if they alone were prefent; or as if the Sinners that mixed with them deferved no regard; or as if the former were fubject to no fnares, no deviations, or felf-deceit. Of many likewife it may be remarked, when they fpeak of the latter, that by exaggerating their guilt, confounding their characters, and not allowing them any degree of virtue or of praife, they either fill them with defpair of amendment, or lead them to harden their hearts againft reprefentations which appear fo unjuft.

Let impartiality, my dear Sir, be your conftant rule. Confider the word of the Lord to the Prophet as directed to you; " Cry aloud, fpare " not, lift up thy voice like a trumpet, and " fhew my people their tranfgreffion, and the " houfe of Jacob their fins." Boldly remind the profeffors of religion, that neither foundnefs of belief, not ftrictnefs of appearance, nor folemnity

of

of discourse, nor the most numerous or specious forms of devotion, nor the warmest attachment to any particular system or sect, nor yet the highest pretensions to I know not what extraordinary emotions and extacies, can ever sanctify falsehood, or fraud, malignity, arrogance, or selfishness. Boldly remind them, that if they are guilty of these things, all the rest will only serve to encrease their condemnation tenfold, and to cast the foulest reproach on " that worthy name" which they most unworthily assume. With equal boldness on the other hand, tell the men of the world, that the parade of sentiment, the punctilio of honour, or even the frequent display of what they call Goodnature, will but ill atone for vice and prophaneness. Nor fail to warn, with unreserved freedom, the idle and the giddy, against trusting to their supposed innocence, because " they run not to the " same excess of riot" with the debauched and the profligate. Inculcate upon them again and again, that an insignificant life is utterly unbecoming reasonable beings; and that no conduct, which has not principle for its guide, will avail in the hour of sorrow, on the bed of death, or at the last tribunal.

But whilst you are firm and courageous in admonishing all, see that you be candid too and discreet

creet; tempering the fervour of zeal, " with the " meeknefs of wifdom ;" and be affured, that fo long as you thus hold up the ftandard of a folid, unaffected, and noble piety, there are few, very few, of any defcription within the reach of your voice, who will not be convinced at their hearts, that your caufe is good, and that, in maintaining it without fear, and without partiality, you act a manly and an honourable part.

Which brings us to confider more directly, in the next place, by what means you fhall commend yourfelf to every man's confcience. And this we learn at once, from the practice of our Apoftle. It is " by manifeftation of the truth"—not of truth in general: your bufinefs here is not to make men fcholars, but Chriftians—not of this, or that, or the other particular truth of religion, in exclufion of the reft : you are to " declare the whole " counfel of God," as far as you underftand it; and " to keep back nothing that is profitable." Your concern is with the truth at large, with the " truth," fo called by way of eminence, that is, with " the word of God" mentioned immediately before our text ; but more efpecially with " the truth " as it is in Jefus, the faithful and the true wit- " nefs," who came from the God of truth, to reveal his will for the falvation of man. Your concern is with that truth which was publifhed by

Chrift

Christ and his Apostles, confirmed by prophecies and miracles, above all, by the resurrection of its Author from the dead, agreeably to his own predictions; with that truth which has stood the test of seventeen hundred years and upwards, maintaining its ground in the most enlightened ages and countries; after the fullest and freest enquiries, against the scoffs of infidelity, and the flames of persecution, amidst the blindness of bigots, and the wrangling of artful or ignorant priests—what shall I say more?—with that truth which has made innumerable souls free, by delivering them from the bondage of error and corruption, " into " the glorious liberty of the sons of God." In a word, your concern is with the whole extensive system of leading facts, divine doctrines, moral precepts, evangelical ordinances, precious promises, and tremendous threatenings, contained in the New Testament, and constituting altogether that admirable superstructure which Christianity has raised, partly on the foundation of the Old, as predicting and prefiguring it, and partly on that of Natural Religion, whose principles it corroborates, and whose defects it supplies. Such, my reverend Brother, is in substance the truth you are called to manifest fairly and openly, without prevarication or disguise, but not without distinction,

tinction, or a proper regard to the matter, the composition, the style, and the delivery, of your discourses.

1. With respect to the Matter; it should certainly be comprehensive and diversified, as the field that lies before you. Survey it for a moment. Does it not present to view whatever can be conceived most amiable or awful in the attributes, will, and counsels of the Supreme, or most wonderful, affecting, and instructive in the dispensations of his Providence, or most interesting to man in his single or social capacity, as a mortal or immortal, a fallen or redeemed, a guilty or pardoned, a sinful or sanctified creature, as a rational, moral, and accountable agent? Does it not lay open his origin, his frame, his wishes, and his wants, with his total insufficiency for his own happiness? Does it not discover the errors of his understanding, the wanderings of his imagination, the tyranny of his passions, the disorders of his heart, and his utter inability to recover himself, without a superior interposition, and heavenly aid? Does it not set forth the deformity of vice, and the beauty of holiness, with their respective fruits, both present and future, the vanity of the world, the shortness of life, the certainty of death, the solemnities of judgment, and the infinite magnitude

nitude of eternal things? In fine, does it not display " the excellency of the knowledge of " Chrift," the divine perfections of his character, the facred fimplicity of his doctrines, the purity and benignity of his laws, the fublime and beautiful graces of his converfation and demeanour, his aftonifhing humiliation, meritorious fufferings, and triumphant refurrection, with the greatnefs of his confequent exaltation, the power of his almighty fpirit, the wifdom and mildnefs of his adminiftration, the conftitution, order, privileges, and extent of his church, the glories of his fecond coming, and, to fay the whole at once, his all-fufficiency to fave a lapfed creation?—What a field for the Chriftian Preacher! How vaft, how various, and magnificent! Where, alas, is the man that can do it juftice? But are not they to be pitied, who for want of talents, or tafte, or liberality, or feeling, or induftry, or zeal, circumfcribe their views to a few particular fpots, which they go over and over perpetually, without variation, and without end; inftead of—what?—inftead of expatiating delightfully amidft its treafures, and improving them by turns, for their own benefit, and that of others? Would you call fuch men " faithful ftewards of " the manifold grace of God?" Would you call fuch men " able Minifters of the New Teftament?

" ment?" Is this that "manifestation of the truth," by which the Apostle Paul commended himself to every man's conscience? You will not, you cannot think it.

. Surely, Sir, you are better acquainted with that complex instrument, the human mind, than to suppose you should strike only some of it's strings; when by a larger compass, and greater command, you may bring out so much more expression and harmony. And for your Bible, you know and love it too well, to forget, that " all Scripture is " given by inspiration of God, and is profitable " for doctrine, for reproof, for correction, for in- " struction in righteousness ; that the man of God " may be perfect, thoroughly furnished unto all " good works."

Those preachers appear to me both defective, who dwell incessantly on the depravity of nature, and our justification by faith, or on the dignity of man, and the sufficiency of virtue; treating of either in a loose and declamatory, or in a dry and metaphysical, manner; so as to leave the boundaries of truth, and the obligations of morality, undetermined ; or what is worse, to set the doctrines and duties of religion at variance. Of all heresies, indeed, the most dangerous and pernicious seems to be, that of crying up it's doctrines,

trines, in prejudice to it's duties, or in neglect of them; that of depreciating the importance of a holy life, or touching on it in a feeble, reluctant, and transient manner. Thus in effect, " Christ is " made the minister of sin," the grace of God, offered in the gospel, is perverted into an engine of corruption, and bad men are buoyed up with a groundless confidence into fatal security. If Christianity be not calculated to render it's disciples virtuous and happy, what valuable end can it serve?" But if it be, as it doubtless is, calculated to do both at the same time, what shall we say of those whose doctrine tends to represent it as an encouragement to live in vice, and yet to hope for Heaven? They must be horribly depraved, or strangely deluded. On the other side, it argues very little acquaintance with the heart, or the history of man, to imagine that he may be effectually reformed by mere precepts, however just, or by moral harangues, however fine, independently of those great principles and motives, which must lead him from himself to God, for pardon, assistance, and eternal life, in the road of an unfeigned repentance, an humble trust, and an unreserved obedience.—But why insist on a point so plain? You, Sir, will never wish to " put a-" sunder what God hath joined." You will
" preach

" preach faith, without which it is impossible to pleafe him;" but what faith? That only which worketh by love, purifieth the heart, overcometh the world, and keepeth the commandments." And you will preach morality; but what morality? That alone which I have now mentioned, as the fruit and operation of genuine faith; that alone which makes men fincerely and uniformly good, from choice, from principle, from a fenfe of duty, from the infpiring profpect of God's approbation through a bleffed immortality.

In this kind of preaching you will be confirmed, not only by St. Paul's own practice, which I need not defcribe to you, but by his emphatical charge to his beloved pupil, the young Evangelift Timothy. His words are indeed remarkable, and never to be forgotten: " ·This is a faithful faying; and thefe things I will that thou affirm conftantly, that they who believe in God be careful to maintain good works."

Truft me, Sir, this practical manifeftation of the truth will do more to convince the confcience, and to warm the heart, than all the fcholaftic notions, and philofophical refinements, in the world. They are too remote from life, from action, from affection, from the defign of God in forming the foul

for

for the love and enjoyment of that which is his image and his glory, divine truth. From this bright ineftimable object the foul, indeed, is prone to be feduced, by appetite, paffion and deceit: fhe then wanders in darknefs and wretchednefs, purfuing phantoms that flatter, difappoint, and diftract her; till it pleafes God to open her eyes and fhow her again her firft companion and original friend. Happy, if yet difpofed to return! For though fhe muft expect to be reproached, for having relinquifhed fo wife and fo venerable an affociate, ftill if it is not her own fault, an everlafting union may take place; and oh, what tranquility and joy will be the refult!—How honourable for you, dear Sir, if you are often made the inftrument of bringing about this bleffed correfpondence!—Shall I tell you what I efteem the very triumph of the pulpit? Suppofe that you addrefs your audience on topics of the greateft utility and moment; fuch, for example, as draw deep into the deceitfulnefs of fin, the emptinefs of the world, the maladies of the heart, the remedies provided by the Gofpel, the manner of applying them, the neceffity of a new nature and a divine life, the worth of the foul, the need of falvation, and the importance of eternity, with many others which might be named. And now, fuppofe, suppose, that whilst you are thus engaged, time after time, your hearers are arrested, suspended, fixed, turned inward upon their own minds, and irresistably led to say, every one for himself, " I am the man concerned in these " things: these things demand my profound- " est regard, my most solemn consideration, " my immediate improvement: they are the " words of truth and soberness: by the blessing " of God, I will ponder and apply them, with- " out a moment's delay."—I call this the triumph of the pulpit.

If this triumph is not instantly followed with all the visible effects, which might be wished or hoped, deem it not, therefore of no consequence. Persevere, and repeat it as frequently as you can. Though it is not your province to change the heart, still it may be of use to alarm the conscience. Though the liveliest fears of that apprehensive power are not always productive of amendment, they often contribute to it; and where they do not operate a thorough conversion, there is reason to believe they, notwithstanding, in many cases, check the progress of vice, and incite a. variety of actions, which, though not directly virtuous, are yet profitable to men, and as such, deserving of praise. It is remarkable, that where

the

the truth is manifested with fidelity, the hearer shall often apply to himself, as aimed at him in particular, descriptions and admonitions, by no means pointed to any one individual, but only thrown out by way of general reproof or illustration, from the preacher's knowledge of life and manners. " A word spoken in season," without any peculiar direction by the speaker, like " a " bow drawn at a venture," shall pierce to the soul some conscious sinner, with a wound that nothing can heal, but the salutary influence of religion. To change the metaphor, the sparks of conviction, which have lain, perhaps, for many years latent in the transgressor's bosom, shall on some unsuspected occasion, by the powerful coruscations of divine truth, like lightening from Heaven, be kindled into a fire, that no pride or depravity can extinguish, but that will continue to burn inwardly, 'till it has either wholly consumed " the old man which is corrupt," or at least destroyed some of those " deceitful lusts" or bad passions, that were hurtful to society, or would have led into deeper ruin.

In thus recommending to you more immediately " the manifestation of the truth" with plainness, as it is contained in the sacred writings, or connected with them, do I mean, that you may

may neglect any advantages or aids to be derived from general knowledge, polite literature, or the the rules of rhetoric ? Far otherwife. I wifh you, Sir, to ftudy all thefe very diligently. St. Paul was himfelf knowing, polite, and eloquent : nor did that Chriftian Apoftle fcruple to quote heathen poets; neither can I at times help fuppofing, that he caught a portion of his fire from fome of the ancient orators, a Pericles, perhaps, or a Demofthenes ; fo ftrongly does he refemble them in their ardent ftyle, and impetuous manner! You cannot cultivate too carefully your acquaintance with the beft authors of antiquity, thofe juftly approved models of good fenfe, fine writing, and genuine tafte. If, befide them, you are converfant with the moft valuable writings of the moderns, in hiftory, poetry, morals, philofophy, fciences, and arts, your mind will be more and more opened and enriched ; you will acquire a greater compafs and variety of ideas, with a larger ftore of images and allufions, to illuftrate, enliven, and adorn them. Still, however, let " the men " of your council" be Mofes and the Prophets, the Evangelifts and Apoftles, with thofe pious and learned perfons of different ages, who have entered moft fully into their meaning and fpirit. When it is faid, that " Apollos was an eloquent man,"

it

it is added, " and mighty in the Scriptures." But whilst for every reason you search them with peculiar attention, fail not to join a close observation of the world, of the age you live in, and especially of the people with whom you are personally concerned. If to all you add a strict examination of your own heart, and an intimate experience of the power and sweetness of religion, as a vital principle within you, need I say, that you will possess " a treasure, from whence " to bring forth things new and old," adapted to every case and capacity; that you will be qualified to set the most important points in the most striking lights, and impress them on your hearers with the deepest feeling?

So much for the matter of your instructions. It is to be comprehensive and various: but they are to turn chiefly on those views that are at once evidently scriptural and rational, alike serious and practical, pointed to the conscience, applicable to life, and connected with salvation.

2. Let us now say something of their Style. If manifestation of the truth be your object, you will consider perspicuity of style as of the first importance. But clear language will chiefly depend on clear conceptions. At least, accuracy of thinking will contribute to accuracy of writing and of speaking

speaking. You will not, however, stop here. The present age demands elegance as well as correctness; and you have some hearers that will not be satisfied without it. As to those miserable bunglers in the pulpit, and their miserable admirers, who with no less ignorance than petulance, decry the beauties of diction, and the graces of elocution, they only merit contempt mingled with pity. The Preacher from the throne " sought to find out acceptable words," and compares the sayings of the wise to " apples of gold in " pictures of silver." The graceful and pointed words of him who " spake as never man spake," astonished his hearers, and disarmed his adversaries. Apollos, we have seen, is celebrated in Scripture as " an eloquent man ;" and as to St. Paul, what person of any taste does not know, that however he disclaimed, as became an Apostle of Christ, what he calls, " the words of man's wisdom," that is, the vain philosophy, and artful sophistry, so prevalent in his days, he was himself an orator of the first rank, full of force and elevation, with a marvellous career of mind, and torrent of style, by which he confounded and overwhelmed the enemies of the truth, but which he could restrain and moderate when he thought proper, in such a manner as to temper the whole into the sweetest persuasion. It were easy

easy indeed to shew, that the Scriptures in general exhibit all the diversified figures and energies of the truest eloquence, I mean that, which not only satisfies the judgment, and delights the imagination, but penetrates the conscience and goes home to the heart. There is undoubtedly, as there ought to be, great simplicity in many parts of the inspired volumes. But what then? It is a beautiful simplicity, that has nothing in it silly, flat, or tame. It is always natural, often tender and affecting, often too the companion of sublimity, and not seldom it's parent. Religious truth is indeed a venerable form. They disgrace her dignity who cover her with tatters, or clothe her in a mean garb; as those prophane her purity who trick her up in a flaunting attire, or disguise her chaste and serious countenance with artificial colouring, and frivolous airs. In both ways it must be owned, the Ministry has been often brought into contempt, and the cause of piety exposed by those who profess to plead it. But, perhaps, nothing degrades the pulpit so much as low phrases, little witticisms, trifling stories, childish conceits, and gross vulgarisms. I am sure you will carefully avoid them. You find nothing of this sort in the sermons of Christ or his Apostles. Let none pretend, that it it is necessary by way of accommodation

accommodation to the inferior orders of the people. Chrift and his Apoftles, in addreffing men of the fame condition, did not judge it neceffary, or they would have practifed it. Are the preachers I fpeak of, more wife or compaffionate than our great Mafter, and his infpired Minifters? That the people, even of the moft common claffes, if accuftomed to a good ftyle, and decent manner, would be more thoroughly pleafed, more foundly inftructed, and more truly edified, I have not the leaft doubt.

Happily for you, Sir, your mind was early tinctured by a claffical education, which you cannot have failed to improve, by being employed for a courfe of years in communicating the fame advantage to others. When I mention this, I take it for granted, that from thofe ufeful labours you have brought with you habits of kind affection for youth in general, and benevolent folicitude for their culture in a higher fenfe. To you therefore, with peculiar propriety on that account I may recommend my dear young friends now committed to your paftoral care; and I do recommend them accordingly, with the warmeft wifhes for their improvement under your pious inftructions. Forgive me, if, in the fervour of my heart on a fubject that always lay near it, " I even charge
" you

" you before God, and the Lord Jesus Christ,
" who shall judge the quick and the dead at his
" appearing and his kingdom," to watch over so precious a charge with unwearied vigilance, beset as they are by such temptations, at such an age, in such a metropolis! Feed these lambs of the flock with knowledge. Conduct them to that Shepherd, who will carry them in his bosom. Caution them against trusting in themselves, or in the world, wherever their best interests are at stake. Point out to them their danger and their duty. Teach them in what way they may escape the one, and by what strength they may perform the other; whilst you cherish in them, by every gentle and engaging method, those sacred principles of truth, which alone can make them wise, or keep them virtuous. As yet their consciences are tender and awake. Their parents will bless you for your friendly endeavours; and when their parents are laid in the dust, they will stand up in their places to adorn religion, and support it's interests. They will be an honour to your Ministry; and peradventure—they may still remember him, who first shewed them the path to Heaven.—But to return from this digression, shall I presume,

3. To offer a few hints respecting the Composition of your discourses? First of all then, aim

not

not at crouding into any fingle fermon, fuch an extent or variety of matter, as would hinder your giving the feveral particulars their due weight or neceffary illuftration ; as would perplex the minds, or burden the memories, of more common hearers, and fo hurry their attention from one part to another, as to prevent their comprehending clearly, or feeling fenfibly, any of the numerous topics that pafs in fuch rapid fucceffion. Sermons intended for the clofet, where they may be read at leifure, ftudied, and read again, will no doubt admit of more diverfity and compafs. But for general ufe, it may be beft to felect on each fubject a few important points, diftinct from one another, yet fo connected as to form a whole, and to be fo managed that they may throw reciprocal and growing light on the leading truth, or truths, meant to be explained, inculcated, and left with full impreffion upon the audience. In doing this, avoid too many fubdivifions. They look formal and fcholaftic. They are apt to run into each other. They fritter away the fubject. They break the force and current of the compofition. They embarrafs the hearer, and diftract his recollection.

The textual method of preaching, and likewife the practical expounding of Scripture, will often
be

be highly acceptable and inftructive. But how both may be practifed with moft advantage, or indeed any other mode of compofition for the pulpit, I pretend not particularly to direct. Different men will be moft fuccefsful in purfuing different modes, according to the apprehenfions of their refpective auditories, or their own peculiar manner of conceiving the fubjects that come before them.

But in religious addreffes, of whatever form, you, my friend, will probably be of opinion, that minute criticifms, nice diftinctions, fchool fubtleties, " queftions of doubtful difputation, and " oppofitions of fcience falfely fo called," minifter but little " to godly edifying," and muft appear, at beft, but ingenious trifling to judicious hearers, while they idly amufe the merely curious, and wafte thofe invaluable moments that fhould be devoted to fo much better purpofes. Nor will you deem a difplay of erudition very often neceffary, where the great point is not to make men learned, but good. Yet lefs will you think it right, to fcatter on every topic a profufion of flowers, which, in fact, would only overlay and obfcure it; to weaken or puzzle the belief of doctrines, fufficiently plain and acknowledged, by fuperfluous arguments, or laboured inveftigations; or, finally, to load your difcourfes with heaps of indigefted quotations

quotations from Scripture. With regard to the last of these, I need not tell you, it is by a very different application of " the word of God," that it will generally be found " quick, and powerful, " and sharper than any two-edged sword, piercing " even to the dividing asunder of soul and spirit, " and of the joints and marrow, and a discerner " of the thoughts and intents of the heart." Least of all will you be disposed to give your compositions the tone of what is called Religious Controversy; which, except on very particular occasions, when it may become necessary, could answer no other end, than to magnify the unessential difference of sects and parties, and to inflame them against one another, instead of removing their mutual prejudices, and uniting their hearts in the bond of peace.

But whilst, in composing your discourse, you exclude from them whatever would obstruct or impair their acceptance and utility, I would not have you lay any unnatural restraint on your imagination, if, as I hope, you are possessed of that power. I wish you to give it flight, on all proper occasions. Let it " mount up with wings, as eagles" gazing on the sun. Let the intellectual and immortal sun of divine truth, illuminate, warm, and guide you in your ascent. But left at any

any time you should be dazzled by an excess of splendour, in the more intense contemplation of that glorious luminary, and wander into visionary regions, beyond the sphere of life and nature, let judgment and taste be your inseparable companions. They will prevent you from losing yourself in wild conceits, and puerile fancies, wholly repugnant to the purposes of sound and manly instruction. But let not the saturnine remarks of cold or phlegmatic critics damp your spirit, or chill your ardour, so long as these are honest and well-directed. What, if on their account, you should undergo the charge of religious enthusiasm, so formidable and obnoxious in this sceptical age? You will remember, that without a glow in the mind, bordering on rapture, and an ambition to excel, which animates and fires the human faculties, nothing eminent or great is to be attained in any profession, in those professions especially, whose object is to delight, to persuade, to move. If this be enthusiasm, it is a laudable one, and no where more becoming than on subjects of religion, the most interesting and exalting of all others.

4. Permit me further to remind you, that were your matter ever so good and proper, your style and composition ever so admirable, the effect of all would be greatly counteracted by an unhappy Delivery.

Delivery. It is indeed piteous to reflect, how often difcourfes, the beft perhaps in every other refpect, have been enfeebled, not to fay marred, even to the moft willing and intelligent hearers, by a frigid look, or languid air, or ungracious manner, in the preacher; or elfe by a difagreeable hefitation, or a drawling tone, or a whining famenefs, or a flovenly pronunciation, or fomething unnatural, inelegant, aukward, or inexpreffive, I cannot tell what. For the defects in elocution are numberlefs, and though fometimes fcarce to be defcribed, yet fo unpleafant to the eyes, or ears, or feelings of the more difcerning, as, in fpite of their utmoft candour, to impede exceedingly the delight and edification that might have otherwife been received.—Let me caution you, likewife, againft too hafty an utterance; a fault very incident to lively fpeakers, but which does not well accord with the gravity and folemnity of the pulpit, is apt to leave the hearers behind, and fometimes to betray the moft accurate preachers, if not much on their guard, into miftakes that were better avoided, and would readily be prevented by a more deliberate enunciation.—Allow me to add on this occafion, that you cannot ftudy too diligently, the accent, emphafis, and idiom of the Englifh language. It is a piece of refpect you owe to
your

your Englifh auditors, and will contribute more to your appearing with advantage, and fpeaking with energy, than fome of our countrymen will eafily believe.—Much might be faid, if there were time for it, on the natural, fignificant, and graceful modulation of the voice in the pulpit; in other words, to fhow how the ideas and emotions of the preacher may be expreffed, by living founds, with truth and force, variety and harmony, gravity and fpirit at the fame inftant. In reality, the effects of fuch a modulation are incredible. In what relates to the exterior of eloquence, there is not perhaps any part of fo great importance, and yet fo little underftood in modern times. The ancient orators feem, above all others, to have ftudied the regulation of the voice, in public fpeaking, and to have afcribed peculiar power to this engine.

Without entering into particulars on the article of delivery, I am inclined to believe " the beft " rule for a preacher, is to feel what he fpeaks, " and to fpeak as he feels; like a man of fenfe " and probity, delivering his mind with clearnefs, " freedom, and earneftnefs, to thofe about him, " on a matter interefting both to himfelf and " to them."

With this view, Sir, let me advife you, before you enter the pulpit, to fteep your thoughts in your fubject, if fuch a phrafe may be allowed, till they are all over tinctured with it. Or if you like the allufion better, give yourfelf up to the impulfe of your theme. Let it take full poffeffion of your foul, and warm your nobleft affections. Then you will fpeak with true fimplicity, and native unftudied animation, as becomes "the lively " oracles of God :" you will " fpeak becaufe you believe," and becaufe you love the truths which you inculcate. What will be the confequence? Your hearers, feeing you in earneft, will be pleafed with your fincerity, touched by your fenfibility, and open to your arguments and advice. There is in pious fervour, if attended with difcretion, and fupported by fenfe, a power of perfuafion not eafily refifted : and I prefume it will generally, if not always, be found, that the moft ferious and affectionate Minifter is the moft beloved and the moft ufeful Minifter, though he may not be followed with the greateft numbers, or with the loudeft applaufe.

He whofe manner is cold or indifferent, has certainly but little room to expect, that his inftructions however good or important in themfelves, fhall often be heard with much attention, or

enter-

entertained with much regard. Whatever some foolish refiners may pretend, the more a preacher appears to feel what he says, the more he will affect his audience; and that preacher will commonly appear to feel most who actually does so. His voice, his countenance, his gesture, will concur in manifesting his sensations; and if from want of skill or care, from a wrong taste, or unlucky habits, he should fall into something less graceful, proper, or pleasing, still the marks of warmth and earnestness, that accompany all he utters, from the genuine workings of his soul, will, on hearers of any candour, make an impression which the most correct or elegant address, if unanimated and unfeeling, can never produce. By the way, how comes it about, that many preachers, who on a variety of topics in conversation, and upon other occasions, deliver themselves naturally, forcibly, and agreeably, no sooner enter the pulpit, than, as if some incantation had seized them in a moment, they assume looks, and tones, and a manner, the very reverse? Would this be possible, were they thoroughly penetrated, and roused, by the important objects that then employ them? I should think, not.—In short, Sir, when your heart flies out into your discourse, the hearts of your hearers will fly out to meet it.

They

They will love you as their friend, no lefs than refpect you as their paftor; and by fo zealous and fo faithful a manifeftation of the truth, you will commend yourfelf to every man's confcience, in the fight of God.—Mark this laft idea of the Apoftle on the prefent fubject—" In the fight of God." What a motive! What a principle! How encouraging and infpiring to a confcientious Minifter!

It was the third point I propofed for your confideration*. The influence which a powerful fenfe of the Omniprefent Deity, and an intimate correfpondence with him, will have on your general conduct, on your ftudies, on your miniftrations, on your addreffes to him in public, as the mouth of your people, and in your private intercourfe with them, as their counfellor, comforter, and friend, and in fine the happinefs which muft refult to yourfelf from the whole, I wifhed briefly to reprefent. Not that I fuppofe you to be ignorant of thefe things, or that I apprehend them neceffary

* Here, the time being elapfed, and the preacher exhaufted, he waved this part of his plan, and concluded with a few fentences. But perhaps the ferious reader will forgive his publifhing, at the defire of fome refpectable judges who heard the reft, what he had prepared on that head, though he was prevented from delivering it.

neceſſary to be preſſed upon you; but only that I might " ſtir up your pure mind by way of re-" membrance," from a ſolicitude to ſee you excel in whatever can contribute to your uſefulneſs and felicity.

The principles you early imbibed, and the reputation you have uniformly preſerved, make it, I am confident, wholly needleſs to caution you againſt open immorality, or ſecret vice. But you are not ignorant, that more than mere decency or ſobriety is required in the character of a Chriſtian Miniſter. You are not ignorant, that you muſt be " an example to the believers in word, in con-" verſation, in charity, in ſpirit, in faith, in purity." The Scripture commands it; and the laws of your profeſſion give the world a right to expect it. The world indeed is apt to expect, at leaſt to require, too much from perſons of our function; forgetting that " we are men of like paſſions" with others; or rather willing to find an apology for ſin in the frailties of thoſe who condemn it, as if we pretended to angelical perfection. But ſtill it is certain, that we are bound by every rule of conſiſtency and propriety, to ſtudy a peculiar elevation of mind and ſanctity of manners. And how are theſe to be acquired or maintained? By living, by thinking, by acting, as in the preſence of God.

God. "Walk before me," faid the Lord to Abraham, " and be thou perfect ;" that is, as righteous and pure as the condition of mortality admits.

A communion fo fublime, by often calling forth the principles of piety into act, and winding up the foul to it's moft pathetic keys, will prevent that languor and dullnefs, which are ready to fteal upon it, from a conftant familiarity with grave fubjects, will preferve you from the infrigidating power of furrounding indifference, and keep alive in your mind a particular fenfibility that will render the impreffions of religion more vivid, and its motives more efficacious. But I muft leave you, Sir, to conceive the influence, which thefe will have on your deportment and intercourfe with fociety ; and I muft leave your people to tell, how peculiarly engaging the truth will appear, where they fhall fee it manifefted in the life and converfation of their Minifter, no lefs than in his fermons. A conduct like this indeed will be more convincing, perfuafive, eloquent, than all thefe put together ; at the fame time that it will give every one of them an additional force and attraction. It will be a living fermon, animated with the very fpirit of piety and goodnefs.

I will

I will not now attempt to describe the difference perceived, by persons of discernment, between that preacher, whose mouth speaks out of the abundance of his heart, with warmth and pathos, and whose practice is a lively copy of his doctrine; between that preacher, I say, and him who only performs his exercises in the pulpit as a task, and who behaves out of it, as if he had never appeared there, or as if he thought himself no way concerned to enforce his precepts by his example. The difference in fact is so great, that it may be felt much more easily than expressed. And it will, in a higher or lower degree, be felt by every serious mind, as devotion is cultivated by the former preacher, or neglected by the latter.

Devotion, or fellowship with God, in the rational and genuine acceptation of these words, I consider as the life and soul of the Ministerial function, or if you will, as a kind of presiding and inspiring genius, that gives it direction, vigour and sublimity, where nature has imparted tolerable talents, and where education has improved them.

I mentioned the influence it will have on your Studies in the way of your profession, as well as on your general conduct and character in that respect. By placing yourself, if I may so speak,

under

under the more immediate illumination of the "Father of Lights," and with the earneftnefs of faith afking wifdom from him " who giveth to all liberally," you are affured that you fhall receive it. And this very affurance will cheer and quicken your honeft endeavours to improve in practical knowledge, and " all fpiritual underftanding." Then, by feeing " light in God's " light," to ufe the elevated language of the Pfalmift, you will be enabled to view divine objects through a divine medium; which will reprefent them, as they really are, fo fuperlatively fair and glorious, that you cannot but be inflamed with admiration, and eager to paint them with affection and force. Your mental eye, glancing from earth to Heaven, from Heaven to earth, will behold fuch profpects of all that is moft important to man, as fhall not only imprefs your own mind with the deepeft ferioufnefs, but alfo difpofe and qualify you to exhibit them in the moft ftriking manner to others. Having, as it is expreffed by St. John, " an unction from the holy one, and " knowing all things," connected with the nobleft exercifes and fweeteft pleafures of the foul, you will diffufe through your difcourfes a correfpondent unction, a certain happy mixture, or high favour of piety, peculiarly agreeable to the better

part

part of your hearers. Such indeed, can very readily perceive the wide diſtance between a teacher of religion, who recommends it by confiderations drawn from the fund of his own experience, and one who borrows his arguments only from a common-place theology: juſt as it is eaſy for a man of feeling and obſervation, to diſtinguiſh the ſentiments, of a real friend on the ſubject of that beautiful and exalted union, from the talk of a mere pretender, who never knew it's charm.

What ſhall I ſay farther of the animating influence, which your faculties will derive from that firſt and beſt principle of true devotion, a ſovereign deſire to pleaſe God, by doing good to his creatures? If, for the honour of preſerving a ſtate, or even defending an individual, or perhaps gaining but an inconſiderable advantage to a client, the orators of ancient days, after acquiring with infinite aſſiduity the richeſt ſtores of knowledge, and ſtudying with no leſs care the higheſt models of ſtyle and elocution, ranſacked their memories, and worked up their imaginations to a pitch of enthuſiaſm, that often tranſported their hearers;—ſurely the Chriſtian orator, who wiſhes to deſerve the name, will judge no application and no effort within his power, too much for the glory of being " a fellow worker with God," in the ſalvation of men,

You,

You, my reverend Brother, will not wonder, if these last words call up to my remembrance the ever venerable image of your and my Master, "Jesus "Christ, and him crucified," whom our Apostle preached with such distinguished zeal, as "the "wisdom of God, and the power of God to sal- "vation." When you contemplate the attributes of the Almighty, as displayed with transcendant lustre in the person of the Son, and in the work of redemption executed by him; when you survey the inestimable benefits flowing from it, through time and eternity, to a degenerate world, and reflect on the consolations and the hopes which you yourself immediately derived from the same source; —when you feel your mind warmed and raised by views like these, in hours of devout meditation, with what gratitude will you devote your studies, your labours, your life to the service of so meritorious a master! With what ardour will you come forth from your retirement, fraught "with " the blessings of the gospel of peace!"

You have this day, amongst other points of importance, been very properly interrogated concerning your faith in Christianity; "and you have professed a good profession before many witnesses." From your solemn declarations, so clear and evangelical, I am convinced you will never join that

unnatural

unnatural brood of preachers, if preachers they may be called, who affect to cry up the precepts of morality as all in all, but seem "ashamed of "the Gospel of Christ," though the only system that has ever secured to those precepts full respect, and uniform obedience, from such as cordially embrace it. The men I speak of either wholly sink the honours of it's Divine Author, whom "God hath exalted to be a Prince and a Saviour," the Mediator, Ruler, and Judge of mankind, or they mention his blessed name with reluctance, and treat the peculiar doctrines of his religion, if indeed they vouchsafe to introduce them, in a style that has "no relish of salvation in it." I suppose they are afraid of being laughed at by the sceptics of the age, were they to proclaim those "good tidings of great joy," that inspired the heavenly host with harmony and gratulation, that had been foreseen by rejoicing patriarchs, predicted by enraptured prophets, desired by expecting nations; that had employed the counsels of Heaven from the foundation of the world; to prepare for which, it's revolutions had long conspired, and to propagate which, through a wondering universe, was the business and the boast of Evangelists and Apostles!

X When

When I call to mind the disciples of Socrates, who gloried in publishing the doctrines, and recording the virtues of that truly great and extraordinary man, I cannot but love them for their affection and fidelity to their master, no less than I admire them for their writings; as on the other hand I am offended, not merely at the defect of faith or of devotion, but at the defect of taste, of sensibility, of consistency, in the characters I have been describing. To me, indeed, the disciples of Socrates appear to have excelled them in all respects. Among the rest, they were much more devout: they expressed themselves in a manner much more delightful; and in many things the philosophy of Plato coincides very happily with that of Christ. From Plato, from Xenophon, and the other respectable lights of heathen antiquity, you will never scruple to borrow a wife or a pious sentiment. But still you will look upon them, in comparison, as inferior stars, that " hide their diminished heads" before " the splendor of the sun of righteousness."

I mean not by these remarks, for which I make no apology, to deny that there may be very honest and virtuous men in the profession, who still retain a degree of reverence for the Founder of Christianity, as they are pleased to call him; though from some

some peculiar cast of mind, or unhappy turn of books and conversation (unhappy I must needs think it,) their reverence seems to be far from being exalted; and if we may conclude from the tone of their discourses, they are not much disposed to adopt the language of St. Paul, where he says to the Corinthians, " the love of Christ constraineth
" us, because we thus judge, that if one died for
" all, then were all dead; and that he died for all,
" that they who live should not henceforth live
" unto themselves, but unto him who died for
" them, and rose again;" or where the same Apostle tells the Ephesians, " for this cause I bow my
" knees unto the Father of our Lord Jesus
" Christ, of whom the whole family of heaven and
" earth is named, that he would grant you, ac-
" cording to the riches of his glory, to be strength-
" ened with might by his spirit in the inner man;
" that Christ may dwell in your hearts by faith,
" that ye being rooted and grounded in love
" may be able to comprehend with all saints,
" what is the breadth, and length, and depth, and
" height, and to know the love of Christ, which
" passeth knowledge, that ye might be filled
" with all the fullness of God."—Shall I confess, that when I read such passages as these, with numberless more from St Paul and the other Apostles of

our Lord, I cannot but regret, that even his moſt affectionate ſervants in our days are not more affectionate, and more awake to whatever concerns the advancement of his name, or the triumphs of his croſs; though, let me add, I would not have his name uſed like magic, or his croſs worſhipped with ſuperſtition.

The commanding influence, which a rational, and, withal, a fervent ſpirit of Chriſtian piety will have on your various Miniſtrations, I muſt not pretend to ſet forth at large. This in general may be obſerved, that he who ſeriouſly conſiders himſelf as called by Providence to " beſeech men " in Chriſt's ſtead, to be reconciled unto God," will not dare either to diſſemble or to trifle with his hearers. Am I employed to addreſs immortal ſouls, as a Miniſter of Jeſus, concerning the " one thing needful," from motives reſpecting both them and myſelf, the moſt pleaſing and the moſt awful? Are they, and am I, paſſing with rapidity, through a ſtate of probation, to an everlaſting ſcene? When I arrive there, muſt I give an account of this miniſtry to him " whom God hath " ordained to judge the world in righteouſneſs?" Bleſſed Saviour, " who is ſufficient for theſe things?" But though I rely on thy grace alone, without which I feel that I can do nothing effectually; yet

yet I feel alſo, that I muſt exert my utmoſt endeavours to ſave myſelf, and them who hear me:—What uprightneſs, zeal, diligence, fortitude, perſeverance, may not be expected from him who laying his hand upon his heart, often holds this language " in the ſight of God?"

The impreſſion which a ſuperior ſenſe of religion, cultivated by proper conſiderations and exerciſes in private, will produce on your Public Devotions, when you are addreſſing God as the mouth of the people, will be more particularly viſible. Then indeed you will appear in your element. Your pureſt affections, and higheſt principles, will then be kindled together. The praiſes, the thankſgivings, the confeſſions, the ſupplications you utter, will evidently be the effuſion of a full awakened ſoul to the Father of mercies and of mankind, under an immediate conviction of his preſence and perfections, of his ſuperintending providence, and infinite compaſſion in Chriſt Jeſus. From communion with him in your cloſet, the tranſition to a more open one in his temple will be eaſy and natural. You will ſpeak to him in the name, and on the behalf of your fellow worſhippers, with freedom and pleaſure, from a conſciouſneſs that you do not forget them when they are abſent, but " make mention of

" them

"them in your prayers," as St. Paul frequently tells us he did of the primitive Chriſtians in his.

Shall I venture to remark, that as far as my obſervation has gone, of thoſe who preach with very laudable ability, but few comparatively pray, as might be wiſhed, with copiouſneſs, ſolemnity, readineſs, and fervor. Why? Becauſe they have not beſtowed the ſame attention and ſtudy on this part as on the other. They have not taken pains early to lay in a ſtore of proper materials, to form a taſte for devout exerciſes in ſecret, to acquire a habit of pouring out the heart before God, unreſtrained by the fear of byſtanders, on the different occurrences of life, and the various ſituations of a pious and reflecting mind. Hence, if I miſtake not, the dryneſs and formality ſo frequently attending the performance of this duty in public; the want of affection, fluency, and compaſs; with ſo little accommodation to the occaſions and circumſtances that ariſe. And hence it often happens, that none but conſcientious worſhippers find any diſpoſition to join with ſeriouſneſs in a ſervice, rendered thus uninviting, though if differently conducted it might prove as attractive and delightful, as it is neceſſary and incumbent.

You may believe, I mean not to recommend that familiarity of air, briſkneſs of manner, or flippancy

flippancy of ſtyle, with which ſome have appeared as if they talked away to their Maker, inſtead of addreſſing him " with reverence and godly fear." If, in ſpeaking to his fellow mortals, a preacher betrays marks of forwardneſs, the more judicious amongſt his hearers will naturally be hurt by ſuch indecorum. But they will much more readily forgive him, than if he ſhould be guilty of the ſame behaviour in ſpeaking to the great Eternal. Humility, Sir, undiſſembled humility will always become us; but never ſo well as when we approach to him " in whoſe ſight the Heavens are not " clean," and it's ſublimeſt inhabitants " cover " their faces with their wings." In a preſence ſo tranſcendantly great and holy, let our ſouls bow with the profoundeſt awe: let our words, looks, and demeanour, expreſs no ſentiment, and no temper, but what is perfectly confiſtent with the moſt ſolemn veneration, and the moſt abſolute dependence.

He, who diſcharges this duty as he ought, will ſeldom be attended to with entire indifference; but the pious and the thoughtful will always join him with ſatisfaction, and often with rapture. Touched by the ſacred fire that glows in his heart, their's will burn within them. If ſuch a metaphor may be allowed, they will feel, in it's happieſt and moſt ſalutary effects, the electricity of devotion. Shall I add, that the power and beauty of the divine principle in the human breaſt, are never perhaps more conſpicuous, than when a Chriſtian Miniſter is ſeen, by his people around him, under it's actual operation, breathing forth the ſoul of benevolence and piety, in prayer for them, for himſelf, and for all mankind? When he afterwards turns his addreſs to thoſe very people, with the tenderneſs and ſolemnity which the preceding exerciſe has imprinted on his mind, I leave you to judge whether they will eaſily reſiſt the pleadings of that man, at the tribunal of conſcience, who could plead ſo eloquently and ſo zealouſly at the throne of grace.

That the intereſts of thoſe, who call themſelves Rational Diſſenters, have for a conſiderable time been declining, is acknowledged and lamented by their beſt friends. To what muſt we impute it? Chiefly, I apprehend, to the decay of that fervent and devotional ſpirit, which diſtinguiſhed a number of their predeceſſors, both amongſt the people and the miniſters. It was that ſpirit, which conſtituted the moſt eſſential difference between them and many of the eſtabliſhment. Without that ſpirit indeed, which alone can give life, ſtrength, and efficacy to every thing ſerious and good, where

is

is the mighty odds of ufing forms, or of not ufing them, of worfhipping in a church, or in a meeting? The modes and tenets may in fome refpects be different: but where " the power of godlinefs" is wanting on both fides, the predominant character of coldnefs and worldly mindednefs will be the fame. Yet, after all, what is there in the moft reafonable fyftem of religion you can fuppofe, that fhould deprive it of ardor, or leffen the affection of it's profeffors, or it's teachers? Ought not that ardor, and that affection, to keep pace with the intrinfic excellence of the fyftem itfelf? And might it not be hoped, that where the views are principally directed to what is moft vital and fubftantial, the mind would take the deepeft intereft, and the heart would beat with the ftrongeft zeal? Such, in truth, would be the cafe, if falfe refinement, and dry argumentation, dignified with the names of politenefs and philofophy, joined to a torrent of diffipation that carries away all orders of men, did not counterwork the moft important confiderations. By what means the people, or the minifters, of any denomination, are to be fortified againft fo fpreading an evil, it is not eafy to tell. In the mean while, it would furely be much for the honor of thofe who now hear me, were they to unite their endeavours in setting an example of holy fervor, and to " shine as lights in the world," amidst the clouds of sensuality and scepticism that thicken around them.

How your living and acting as " in the sight of " God," will affect your intercourse with men, and particularly with those committed to your pastoral care, it would be agreeable, if it were requisite, to explain. But you will readily conceive, from your own experience, that laying open your heart habitually to the common Parent of men, in the name of their common Saviour, must habitually dispose it to the practice of every thing liberal and benign. A devotional preacher, such as I have delineated, will be found the kindest counsellor, the tenderest comforter, the warmest and most sympathetic friend. The lively sense of spiritual and immortal objects, which he brings with him from retirement, will mix with his conversation, and to speak in the emphatic style of Scripture, will " season it with salt, so as to minister grace to the hearers." He will seldom indeed pass any time in company, without taking occasion to introduce or insinuate something serious, moral, sentimental, or instructive. But in doing this, he will be governed by a prudent regard to persons and circumstances. True religion

affects

affects nothing auftere, and nothing unfeafonable. The moft pious man will naturally be the moft affectionate and the moft complacent. It is not piety, but fuperftition, or bigotry, that produces a gloomy temper, or forbidding manners. St. Paul, as we have feen, was a pattern of benevolence and courtefy. And we know, that his Mafter and our's was the perfection of charity and meeknefs.

Whatever opportunities occur, for promoting the welfare or confolation of others, efpecially where their higheft interefts are in queftion, you will embrace with alacrity, from principles which no unworthinefs, or unkindnefs on the part of men, can conquer, namely, the love of God, and of his Son. There may indeed be numbers, with whom thofe principles will not oblige you to cultivate an intimacy. In this refpect, it will much import your peace, your reputation, your fafety, to practife great circumfpection. But the more you relifh the duties and the joys of religion, the lefs you will be inclined to aflociate with thofe that have not a tafte for them, and the more you will be attached to thofe that have. When alone, you will give yourfelf diligently to reading, meditation, and prayer, with the other neceflary preparations for your public labours. A

devout

devout and ftudious turn will fave you from the danger of being feen too often in gay affemblies, or by uncandid obfervers. In this way you may be thought lefs polite, or too referved; but I am perfuaded you will find yourfelf a gainer on higher accounts. When you ftep into fociety, your chief delight will be " in the excellent ones of the earth ;" and you will be particularly pleafed, when you difcover fuch amongft your flock. On them you will gladly beftow the largeft fhare of your efteem and attention; and from them you will learn many things conducive to your greater comfort and ufefulnefs; at the fame time that I have the fatisfaction to affure you, thofe I think of are as far from a pert affectation of fuperior knowledge or fanctity, as any fet of people I have ever feen. In truth, the beft minds are always the moft unaffuming.

And now permit me, before I conclude, to touch on fome of the happy effects, that will refult to yourfelf from an ardent and elevated fpirit of piety, in the difcharge of your minifterial office. The work in which you are engaged is arduous and laborious. But it's toils and difficulties will be greatly foftened,—may I not fay, frequently converted into fweetnefs, by profecuting it " in the fight of God," with zeal and unction; by the

joy

joy of finding, as I truſt you will find, that "your labour of love" is not unſucceſsful: and by the cheerful increaſing hope of divine aid, and final acceptance. Your reflections on a conduct thus honourable, thus animated, thus ſuſtained, cannot fail to inſpire a magnanimity, that will ever preſerve you from deſcending to the little, verſatile, and ignoble arts of popularity, which enſlave and diſgrace too many of the profeſſion. They will make you "bold as a lion," to encounter any danger or diſcouragement, that may ariſe from one quarter or another. The more you venerate the cauſe of truth, righteouſneſs, and religious liberty, as the cauſe of God, you will aſſert and plead it with the greater fortitude, "whether men will hear, or whether they will "forbear." If ſome ſhould miſtake, miſrepreſent, calumniate, you will appeal from their ignorance, from their falſehood, and from their malignity, to an approving conſcience, and to the unerring Judge. You will remember too, that "the diſciple is not greater than his Maſter, nor the ſervant above his Lord;" and you will have the conſolation to know, that he who is at the head of the univerſe, and for whom you are "rea-"dy to ſuffer the loſs of all things, will never leave "nor forſake you."

With

With respect, indeed, to your external situation, you must, under God, depend, in a great measure, on the steady attachment of those who hear you. But surely, the greater and better part of them will not be apt to relinquish a Pastor who acts in the manner and on the principles before suggested.

It may with truth be said, for the body of the people called Protestant Dissenters, in general, but particularly in London, and the commercial and manufacturing cities and towns throughout England, that they have long approved themselves very kind and liberal to their Ministers: and few I believe, of that number have as yet been left to struggle with hardships, comparable to those, which are suffered by thousands of worthy Clergymen in the established Church.—What pity were it, if the very affecting representation, lately published on this last subject, by one of her most learned, moderate, and deserving Prelates, should not meet with the attention and regard it merits!

To resume the point before us, as I am sure that no man, of a spirit truly religious, will ever sacrifice his integrity to his gain; so I verily believe, that whilst you continue, by manifestation of the truth, to commend yourself to every man's conscience in the sight of God, he will from time to to time raife up thofe who will honor and protect you, for his, and for your work's fake. As to the Members of this Society, I will pledge myfelf for them, that they will go on to give you all the encouragement in their power, as long as you are at pains to deferve it, that is to fay, as long as your connection with them fhall laft. They are candid, and they are generous. I owe them that teftimony.—What fay you, my friends? Do I over-rate your character? If this young man proves faithful to you, may I not engage for you, that you will not be wanting to him? If I ftill retain fome intereft in your hearts, allow me to ufe it in favor of my fucceffor. Let me hope, that you will ferioufly attend to his inftructions, earneftly pray for a bleffing on his labours, and unanimoufly concur to ftrengthen his hands. So fhall you live together in peace and piety on earth, and he will at laft have many enlightened and fanctified fpirits " to prefent before God as his " joy and crown in the day of the Lord."—How happy fhall I be to meet and rejoice with him and you, my much loved and ever refpected hearers, in the abodes of immortal friendfhip! Amen.

SERMON VII.

THE BREVITY, UNCERTAINTY, AND IMPORTANCE OF HUMAN LIFE*.

---

* Preached at the Proteſtant Diſſenting Meeting-Houſe in Hammerſmith, the Twenty-ſecond of June, 1783: on occaſion of the ſudden Death of the late Rev. GEORGE TURNBULL, Paſtor of the Church of CHRIST there.

THE BREVITY, UNCERTAINTY, AND IMPORTANCE OF HUMAN LIFE.

PSALM XXXIX. 4, 5.

LORD, MAKE ME TO KNOW MINE END, AND THE MEASURE OF MY DAYS, WHAT IT IS, THAT I MAY KNOW HOW FRAIL I AM. BEHOLD THOU HAST MADE MY DAYS AS AN HAND BREADTH: AND MINE AGE IS AS NOTHING BEFORE THEE: VERILY EVERY MAN AT HIS BEST STATE IS ALTOGETHER VANITY.

IF any thing, Men and Brethren, can add to the folemnity of the prefent occafion; if any circumftance can increafe the weight and importance of our fubject; if there be a confideration more powerful than another, to awaken ferious reflection, to imprefs the thoughts of death upon the heart, and to create in both preacher and hearers, a peculiar intereft in the affecting bufinefs of this day—it is the *manner* and the *ftate* in which

which the subject has been transmitted to us. When you are informed of these, you will readily discern, and, I trust, approve the reason which determined my choice of a text, in addressing you, at this awful hour.

Know then, my dear Friends, that the very last act of your late Pastor's life; the last exercise of his ministry, in the view of your edification, was to make choice of this very text, and to frame a discourse upon it; which, had he lived three days longer, he would have delivered from this place, as the improvement of the death of a valuable friend, well known to many of you, whom he had just attended to the grave.—Having made his last earthly meal, with his accustomed temperance and cheerfulness; having taken leave of the earthly friends who were about him, with his usual serenity, sweetness, and benevolence; at peace with God, at peace with himself, and at peace with all men, he retired to his closet, and impressed, as it appears, with the great object of his public ministrations; impressed with the solemn and mournful service of the preceding day; impressed with the sad duty he had to fulfil, on the approaching Sabbath; he had turned to this very passage of Scripture, as the subject of a funeral sermon for his departed friend; had
arranged

arranged his thoughts upon it, with all that order, accuracy, and diftinctnefs, which you muft have often remarked in him; had committed his ideas, in fhort hints, to writing; then commended himfelf to God, compofed himfelf to reft;—and expired.

I confider, therefore, the text, the fubject, and my departed friend's method of treating it, as a facred, and a valuable legacy, bequeathed by him to me, for your ufe, and my own. May God grant us wifdom to ufe it wifely and well.

" If one went unto them from the dead," reafoned the rich man in torment, furely " they will" believe and " repent." Well then, O men, one already in the arms of death, one now dead, comes to you, fpeaks to you, in the perfon of the dying creature whofe voice you now hear: the fpirit of your late excellent Minifter now accofts you by my tongue. That fpirit of his had often devifed many things for your inftruction; it was ever watchful for your good; it was ever attentive to, and ready to improve occafions of communicating ufeful knowledge,—but alas! you knew not, my much efteemed Father, my Friend! you knew not, that Providence was about to enforce your doctrine upon the people of your charge, the people of your love, by an argument fo powerful and

and tender; you knew not that your own deceafe, was to be the forcible and pathetic application of your fubject.

" Lord make me to know mine end, and the " meafure of my days what it is:" Thus, with holy David, meditated the pious Saint, whofe removal from us we fo juftly lament, and thus he prayed; and God has granted his requeft; God has infinitely exceeded his expectations. He defired to *know* his latter *end*; he was engaged in deep and earneft thought on his frailty and mortality; when lo, that very night, the God whom he worfhipped, put an end to all anxiety about that interefting event, " fhewed" him " the " path of life," conducted him through " the " valley of the fhadow of death," to his " pre- " fence," where there " is fulnefs of joy," and to his " right hand," where " there are pleafures " for evermore."

In the view of difcourfing to you, from the paffage which I have read, our worthy friend had propofed,

I. To treat of the great and interefting *object* of the Pfalmift's prayer to God, namely, that he might be made to *know* his *end*.

II. To

II. To confider how, or by what means, Providence effectually teaches men this all-important leffon.

III. To point out fome of the reafons and ends for which good men defire, and God beftows fuch ufeful and neceffary knowledge. And

Laftly, He intended to apply and improve the fubject, by delineating the character, and recommending the example of a good woman, lately one of yourfelves, as a perfon of fingular meeknefs, modefty, humility, prudence, and piety.

I fhall adhere fcrupuloufly to the hints which Mr. Turnbull has left behind him, for two reafons : firft, becaufe I confider myfelf as thereby fulfilling the defire and intention of the dead : and fecondly, becaufe, perhaps, better materials for the purpofe, could not eafily have been furnifhed.

I. We are to confider the *object* of the Pfalmift's requeft to God, that is, what he defires to be made acquainted with, when he prays, " Lord, make " me to know mine end, and the meafure of my " days, what it is." And,

1. It expreffes a defire to be made fenfible how *fhort* life is : a point, however obvious, of which men are ftrangely ignorant ; or what amounts to

the same thing, about which they are strangely indifferent; though one of the most important that can engage the human mind. It is incessantly presented to our view: yet we incessantly lose sight of it. Scripture, reason, feeling, all press the consideration of it upon us; but some vanity appears, and we forget that we are not to " live always."—" Our Fathers, where are " they? The Prophets, do they live for ever?" Consult the record; examine the bills of mortality; and what do you find written? " Adam " lived nine hundred and thirty years—and he " died." " All the days that Methuselah lived, " were nine hundred sixty and nine years,—and " he died:" and a thousand years when expired, are but " like yesterday when it is past; or as a " watch in the night." But even that antediluvian standard is greatly reduced; and human life is not now measured, as in the patriarchal ages, by centuries of years: No: it falls greatly short of one. " The days of our years are threescore years " and ten: and if by reason of strength they be " fourscore years, yet is their strength labour and " sorrow; for it is soon cut off, and we fly " away.*" " Man that is born of a woman is

of

* Psalm xc. 10.

"of few days, and full of trouble. He cometh forth like a flower, and is cut down: he fleeth also as a shadow, and continueth not†." "Behold, thou haſt made my days as an hand breadth: and mine age is as nothing before thee: verily every man at his beſt ſtate is altogether vanity. Selah‡." "Thou carrieſt them away as with a flood: they are as a ſleep: in the morning they are like graſs which groweth up: in the evening it is cut down and withereth." "We ſpend our years as a tale that is told." "My days are ſwifter than a weaver's ſhuttle," "My life is wind," "I am made to poſſeſs months of vanity." What is your life? "It is even a vapour, that appeareth for a little time, and then vaniſheth away."

As Scripture thus, in every page, inculcates the brevity of life, ſo Nature, in every object which we behold, and experience, in every event that paſſeth over our heads, bring it forcibly to the heart. If we go into the city, what do we meet? A multitude of buſtling ſhadows fluttering up and down, ourſelves ſhadows like them. If we ſtep into the field, every plant under our feet, while it ſhrinks from the preſſure, admoniſhes us of our

own

---

† Job. xiv. 1, 2.—‡ Pſal. xxxix. v.

own frailty; the firſt tree that preſents itſelf, in ſilent, but pathetic eloquence, ſeems thus to addreſs us: "The hand which planted me is ſhrunk "up and withered; the eye, which with delight "beheld my gradual increaſe, is cloſed for ever: "the head, which at noon repoſed under my "ſhade, lies low in the tomb. Frail ſon of the "duſt! Conſider me, and learn wiſdom. I af- "ford thee ſhelter and inſtruction to-day; but "thou paſſeſt quickly away; and to-morrow "I ſhall ſhelter and inſtruct another, and not "thee."

If we reſort to the houſe of God, there, the ſame awful voice reſounds in our ears. Who erected this edifice? Who occupied theſe places ten, twenty, thirty, forty years ago? Who filled this pulpit the laſt Lord's day ſave one?

If we retire to our own houſes, inſtead of the beloved friends whom we lately beheld there, and "with whom we took ſweet counſel," we only meet the vacant ſeats which uſed to receive them; the books which they were wont to read; the little works which they performed; the lifeleſs pictures that reſemble them; ſome affecting memorial or another that they *were* ours, but *are* ours no longer.

If

If we retreat within our own brittle clay tabernacle, we perceive the harbingers of mortality, we feel " the witnefs of death within ourfelves:" fome fpring in the machine relaxed, fome member out of order, fome prop decaying, fome faculty impaired: " the keepers of the houfe trem-
" bling, the ftrong men bowing themfelves,"
" the grinders ceafing becaufe they are few, and
" thofe that look out of the windows darkened.
" The filver cord" ready to be " loofed, and the
" golden bowl broken." And with fo many monitors, fo many proofs of the fhortnefs of life, is it poffible to lie down in fecurity, and to hold this extravagant language, " What fhall I do, becaufe
" I have no room where to beftow my fruits?
" This will I do: I will pull down my barns,
" and build greater, and there will I beftow all
" my fruits and my goods: And I will fay to my
" foul, Soul, thou haft much goods laid up for
" many years: take thine eafe, eat, drink, and
" be merry‖." Shall the worm that may be crufhed in a moment, and which muft perifh in a day, exalt itfelf as if it were immortal?

2. David when he prays, " Lord make me to
" know mine end and the meafure of my days,"
defires

‖ Luke xii. 18, 19.

desires to be impressed with a deep sense of the uncertainty as well as *shortness* of life. Could we securely reckon upon our little portion of existence, it were something: were our poor three-score years and ten, fenced on every side from danger, disease, and death, there were something like an excuse for the giddiness of youth, the confidence of manly strength and vigor, the self-complacency of beauty, the conscious superiority of talents; but alas! "In life we are in the midst "of death;" "we know not what a day may "bring forth;" exposed continually to "the "terror by night, and the arrow that flieth by "day; the pestilence that walketh in darkness; "the destruction that wasteth at noon day."

Every step that we tread is through the midst of certain perils, or hidden snares. Every element is pregnant with death. Every climate, every season, every situation teems with death. The roaring waves swallow up their thousands in a moment. The convulsed earth opens her jaws, and whole cities with their inhabitants perish. The fertile plains, and those who cultivated them, are deluged with a sea of liquid fire. The tainted air hurls destruction on a devoted world, in the blast of every wind. The fervent heat of the tropics, and the bleak air of the pole, contend in their efforts

efforts to waste and to destroy. The excessive labour, and the meagre subsistence of poverty, oppress life; the languor and intemperance of affluence, undermine and corrupt it. The genius of manufacture and art, like the subtle thief of the night, steals, without warning, upon his unsuspecting prey, and levels him with the ground; war, the bold robber of the day, stalks at noon through " garments rolled in blood;" pale famine, voracious as the lean kine of Pharaoh, devours the fat and the strong.

Do the aged and the weak alone die? Measure these graves; mark well these inscriptions; compare these dates. They are but " a span long." Here the blossom never blowed: there the rude hand of the tempest, shook the tree, and dashed its fruit prematurely on the ground. Do the aged alone die? Consult your own bitter recollections; enquire at that mourner; step into your neighbour's house; " woman, wherefore weepest thou?" It is the cry of the widow I hear, whom God has just bruised; " the desire of" whose " eyes," He " hath taken away with a stroke;" " it is Rachel " weeping for her children, and refusing to be " comforted, because they are not."—What is the conclusion of the whole matter? " Surely " every man walketh in a vain shew:" " when
" thou

"with rebukes doft correct man for iniquity, thou makeft his beauty to confume away like a moth; furely every man is vanity." Life extended to its utmoft length, is but a moment, and that moment, in its beft ftate, *uncertain.*

3. The pious foul in pouring out this requeft, " Lord make me to know mine end, and the " meafure of my days, what it is;" feems earneftly defirous to be inftructed how *important* life is. The true improvement of the *fhortnefs* and *uncertainty* of life, is not, to count it a trifle, to expofe it unneceffarily to danger, to be carelefs and indifferent about the prefervation of it; but, becaufe it is *fhort*, to acquire wifdom as foon, and to do good as diligently as we can. Becaufe it is *uncertain*, and we cannot " boaft ourfelves of to-" morrow," wifdom calls on us, " to do with " our might whatfoever our hand findeth to do: " for there is no work, nor device, nor know-" ledge, nor wifdom in the grave, whither we " are going:" and to " work out our own falvation with fear and trembling, while it is called to-day" before " the night cometh."

The *importance* of life is to be eftimated from the wifdom of Him, who is the Author of it. " God created man in his own image;" " God " breathed into man's noftrils the breath of life, " and

" and he became a living foul:" " his visitation
" preserveth our spirit." " The" very " hairs of
" our head are numbered of Him." Not a plant
grows in the field, not an insect crawls on the
ground, or flutters through the air, but has its
end and its use; for it is God " who feeds the
" ravens," who paints and " clothes the lilies of
" the field;" and he does nothing in vain:—
" and are not ye much better than they?" If the
vegetable and animal tribes possess an acknowledged *importance* in the scale of being; if the
lily and raven form consequential links in their
respective chain of existence; How much more,
man, the Lord of all, the glory of all; and every
man in his own particular sphere? While humility, under a sense of weakness, worthlessness, and
imperfection, says, " I am a worm, and no man,"
devotion, as on eagle's wings, exalts the foul to
the throne of God, saying, " my Father who art
" in Heaven:" while nature points to the tomb,
and the stern decree proclaims, " dust thou art,
" and to dust thou shall return," religion unveils
the glories of Paradise, and " mortality is swallow-
" ed up of life."

The *importance* of " the life that now is,"
must be estimated from the connection it has with
" that which is to come." The beauty of the
spring

spring is short and fading, but the glory of summer, and the abundance of autumn depend upon it. Youth, the morning of life, is quickly over; but, if it has been neglected or mispent, a noon of disorder, and an evening of remorse and despair succeed. Now, life is our birth into existence, rather than existence itself; it is the morning, not the day; it is the spring, not the year, of our duration. It may be of little importance, where I am, what I do, how I am disposed of, for ten or twenty years; but where, and what I am to be, to eternity, is a serious matter indeed: and the eventful hour is at hand, which shall thus decide the character and state of every one. " He " that is unjust, let him be unjust still: and " he which is filthy, let him be filthy still: " and he that is righteous, let him be right- " eous still: and he that is holy, let him be " holy still*."

The *importance* of every man's life must be estimated, from his relation to others; from his consequence and influence in society. That can never be insignificant, which affects the wisdom, the virtue, or the happiness of mankind. And who is so unconnected, who so insignificant, as
neither

* Rev. xxii. 11.

neither by his piety or profanity, as neither by wisdom or folly, as neither by his virtue or vices, as neither by his life or death, to have occasions ministered, of serving, or of hurting his family, his neighbourhood, his country?—Religion will never permit a man to consider himself as a solitary individual: for the language which it holds, is, " none of us liveth to himself, and no man dieth to himself," and the man whose doctrine this is, exhibited an illustrious example of that excellent spirit, when he represents himself as in doubt which to prefer, his own immediate glorification, or a longer continuance in the world, for the good of mankind; and he seems generously disposed to give up the former, to the latter; " What I shall choose, I wot not.
" For I am in a strait betwixt two, having a de-
" sire to depart, and to be with Christ; which
" is far better: nevertheless, to abide in the flesh
" is more needful for you. And having this
" confidence, I know that I shall abide and con-
" tinue with you all, for your furtherance and joy
" of faith; that your rejoicing may be more
" abundant in Jesus Christ for me, by coming
" to you again."*

Finally, the *importance* of life must be estimated from the everlasting consequences which flow from its

* Phil. i. 23.—26.

its improvement or abuse. Others may be affected by our good or ill behaviour while we live; but our character and conduct can affect ourselves alone when we die. "Behold *now* is the accept-
" ed time; behold *now* is the day of salvation,"
" and the revelation of the righteous judgment of
" God" is at hand, " who will render to every
" man according to his deeds: To them, who
" by patient continuance in well doing, seek for
" glory and honour and immortality, eternal life:
" But unto them that are contentious, and do
" not obey the truth, but obey unrighteousness,
" indignation and wrath; Tribulation and an-
" guish upon every soul of man that doeth evil,
" of the Jew first, and also of the Gentile."

Now, my friends, if the life of man be thus *short, uncertain* and *important*; and if, with all that present and temporal, all that future and e- ternal importance, men be disposed to waste and mispend it, surely a serious spirit has reason to " ask" this " wisdom of God," " from whom co-
" meth down every good gift and every perfect,"
" Lord *make* me to know mine end, and the mea-
" sure of my days, what it is."

II. The second Article, in my deceased friend's bequest, is, The consideration of the *means* by which, Providence is pleased to teach men this

this useful and necessary lesson. These he has marked down in so many plain short words, 1. Experience; 2. The Word: 3. The Spirit of God. And we will continue to walk in the path which he has marked out for us.

There is, evidently, in this subdivision, a gradation of thought and reflection, as it arose in the mind, which was undoubtedly the result of knowledge and feeling; and which, had he been permitted himself to explain it to you, would probably have been to this purpose:

1. God makes men to know their " end and " the measure of their days" by *experience*, when he drives them, by some stroke of his providence, from a dry, general, ineffective acknowledgement of the vanity of sublunary things, into a heartfelt, awakening, active persuasion of it. No one is so silly as to disbelieve, or to deny, the certainty and suddenness of death; but who is so wise as to live under the habitual impression and belief of it? What all readily admit as a general proposition, all are disposed, at times, to reject in its particular application. So deeply is the love of life implanted in man, that neither poverty, nor pain, nor neglect; nor old age, loaded with all these, is able to extirpate it: and we fondly cherish the delusion, that we shall live a little longer, and longer—till we are dead indeed. We

are convinced of the truth; but we act, as if the fact were otherwife, or as if we had no concern in it. Examples admonifh in vain, for " all men think all men mortal, but themfelves." God therefore makes us *experimentally* to know our end, by putting forth his hand, and touching fome of our vitals: He kills us in part, that we may know we are not immortal. He wounds the hand, that the heart may apprehend the blow which threatens it. He makes us to die again and again in others, to prepare us for dying ourfelves. But with no other means of knowing, and of improving our latter end, except the memorials of it, which are continually before our eyes, and the premonitions which we frequently feel in our own perfons, we fhould be apt to fall into many errors, with regard to its proper ufe and end. One man would peevifhly defert his ftation, another fink into torpid indolence and inaction, and a third would diffolve in diffipation and excefs, faying, " let us eat and drink, for to-morrow we die." To prevent, therefore, or to rectify, fuch dangerous miftakes, God is pleafed to employ,

2. *His word*, to lead men to the right knowledge and improvement of their approaching diffolution. In this view, Mofes prays, in another Pfalm, " So teach us to number our days that we

" may

"may apply our hearts unto wisdom." The Bible instructs us how to "use the world so as not to "abuse it." It guards us equally against oppressive melancholy, sullen discontent, and thoughtless riot. While it forbids us to think of *living* here *always*, it condescends to teach us to "pass the time of our *sojourning* here, in the fear of God." While it confers due weight and importance upon human life, it writes entire disapprobation on the romantic, visionary, and seductive views which men are apt to entertain. Here, as in every other case, Scripture points out the golden mean, where wisdom and happiness dwell. It points out the narrow way, that leads between anxiety, and levity; between fond attachment, and listless indifference. It inspires fortitude without rashness, and caution without timidity. It enables us to enjoy life with moderation, to employ it creditably to ourselves, and usefully to others; and to meet death with fortitude.

But are the ears of men always open to reason? Is Scripture truth always received with that reverence and submission which it ought to command? Does the word of God uniformly produce its intended effect? Then men would have but

* Psalm xc. 12.

but to read, in order to be wife, and good, and happy. But " they will not hear, they will not lay it to heart." God therefore, in pity of our dulnefs, perverfenefs, thoughtleffnefs, vouchfafes to give life and efficacy to the outward means, to the conclufions of *experience*, and the dictates of *the word*, by fending forth according to his promife,

3. His quickening *spirit.* Men need not to be told the mighty difference, in point of effect, which the fame truths, and the fame events produce upon their minds, at different feafons, and in different fituations; for men vary from themfelves as much as they do from one another. The heart, to day, is " harder than a piece of the nether mill-
" ftone;" to-morrow, it is melted like wax."
" The word, at one time, is as the founding brafs,
" and as a tinkling cymbal," at another " a ham-
" mer that breaketh the rock in pieces," quick and
" powerful, and fharper than any two-edged fword,
" piercing even to the dividing afunder of foul and
" fpirit, and of the joints and marrow: and is a
" difcerner of the thoughts and intents of the
" heart*." This vifitation of Providence makes no more impreffion upon me than upon the corpfe
in

---

* Heb. iv. 12.

in the church-yard; but I feel that ſtroke, in every particle of my frame. What makes the difference? What diſtinguiſhes the corpſe from the living man? The preſence or abſence of the vital, or the perceptive principle. The deaf and the dead hear not: the blind and the dead ſee not; and therefore muſic and colours preſent their allurements in vain.—What reduced chaos into form? What made man a living ſoul? Who raiſeth the dead? " The ſpirit of God moved " upon the face of the waters:" " God breathed " into man's noſtrils the breath of life, and he " became a living ſoul." " If the Spirit of him " that raiſed up Jeſus from the dead dwell in you, " he that raiſed up Chriſt from the dead ſhall " alſo quicken your mortal bodies by his Spirit " that dwelleth in you." It is he who " con- " vinceth of ſin, of righteouſneſs, and of judg- " ment." It is he who " guides men into all " truth:" it is he who " taketh the things" of Chriſt, and " ſheweth them" unto us. He is promiſed, and he is given, to " teach us all " things, and to bring all things to our remem- " brance." " Where the ſpirit of the Lord is, " there is liberty." O Lord " ſend the ſpirit of " thy Son into our hearts." We obſerve not, read not, hear not, as we ought; " we know not what we should pray for as we ought." May the Spirit himself " help our infirmities, making " intercession for us with groanings which cannot " be uttered."

III. We may enquire, For what *ends* good men desire, and God vouchsafes to bestow, this knowledge? The

1. And most obvious lesson taught us by the certainty of our latter end, is *humility*. Death, and every harbinger of death, aims a deadly blow at the pride and glory of man. Vigor wastes, and beauty fades, as these stern messengers approach. " Naked came we out of our mother's womb, " and naked shall we return thither." Greatness is soon to be neglected, merit to be forgotten, and power to be trampled in the dust. Be thy possessions, O Man, be thy accomplishments what they may, yet a little while, and they shall be thine no longer; for time is hastening to inscribe thy tomb with this mortifying reflection,

> How lov'd, how valu'd once avails thee not,
> To whom related, or by whom begot:
> A heap of dust alone remains of thee:
> 'Tis all thou art, and all the proud must be.

Is pride, then, made for man, who must " say to corruption, thou art my father, and
" to

"to the worm, thou art my sister and mo-
"ther?" Does it not become man to be *humble*, who is assured that the course of a few years, at most, will dissolve all connection between him and the world, will reduce his body to loathsomeness and deformity, will blot out the remembrance of him from among men, and summon his spirit to the judgment of God? But there is not merely a decency and propriety in *humility*; there is an amiableness and excellency in it, that entitle it to hold a first rank in the catalogue of moral virtues, or of Christian graces. Stript of it, all other qualities are naked, unseemly, and offensive. Learning is disfigured with pedantry, courage degenerates into ferociousness, and beauty is rendered shocking and disgustful through affectation. *Humility* is the shade in painting, which makes the figures to rise, and shine, and strike and please. Are we called of our divine Master, to "learn" of him? It is not, by healing the sick, walking on the water, or raising the dead; but by being "meek and lowly in "heart." Is the "mind that was in him" recommended to our notice and imitation? What mind is it? It is, when "he made him-
"self of no reputation, took upon him the form
"of a servant, and *humbled* himself." And when

men have attained the image of Chrift, they have arrived at the higheft glory of which their nature is capable. Happy are they whom a deep fenfe of their approaching end, is daily improving in the fpirit and practice of it. As the certainty of death is a loud and conftant call to *humility*, fo the uncertainty of the time of its arrival, is an argument equally powerful, to the practice of a

2. Leffon of much importance, namely *watchfulnefs*. He who knows man's duty and his intereft in all their extent, preffes this duty, in connection with the motive to it, with reiterated earneftnefs and zeal. " *Watch* therefore; for ye " know not what hour your Lord doth come." " *Watch* therefore; for ye know neither the " day nor the hour wherein the Son of man " cometh." " *Watch* and pray." " *Watch*, " for ye know not when the Mafter of the houfe " cometh; at even, or at midnight, or at the " cock-crowing, or in the morning, left coming " fuddenly, he find you fleeping. And what I " fay unto you, I fay unto all, *Watch*." " If " therefore thou fhall not *watch*, I will come on " thee as a thief, and thou fhalt not know what " hour I will come upon thee." Human life is a perpetual warfare; a ftate of conftant expofednefs to open affault, or fudden furprize. The good foldier of Jefus Chrift, therefore, knowing that the enemy

enemy will come, will only be folicitous that he be not taken at a difadvantage; will ftudy to prevent the fhame of being caught by his Commander off his poft, or flumbering upon it; and feek to efcape the danger of being overtaken by the foe, unarmed, unexpecting, unprepared. The life of a Chriftian, then, is,

3. An *habitual preparation* for death: not that he is continually doing the office of a fentinel, continually under arms, conftantly awake; but he has laid his account with unexpected hardfhip and danger; he holds himfelf ready to march, to fight, to die, upon the fhorteft notice. The preparation of a wife man and a Chriftian, for death and eternity, is not the reluctant, conftrained, perturbed devotion of a criminal condemned, who reads, meditates, and prays, with the halter about his neck. No; it is the calm, compofing piety, which conftitutes and promotes acquaintaince with God, which fweetens life, which difarms and deftroys death, and anticipates immortality. One, fuch as was our departed Friend, has no need to be alarmed at an unexpected fummons. For he is " *always* ready, " having his loins girded about, and his light " burning," as one who is always *waiting* for his Lord. " Let me die the death of the righte-" ous, and let my laft end be like his!"

The laſt branch of the taſk, which good Mr. Turnbull had preſcribed to himſelf, was to delineate the character of a valuable friend lately dead. But here, though he has ſketched the outline, I muſt not preſume to fill it up, nor pretend to finiſh the portrait. For this, many among yourſelves are much better qualified than I am, from your knowledge of the character in queſtion. Inſtead, therefore, of attempting to follow him, in deſcribing a perſon whom I did not know, I will detain you for a few moments, while I ſpeak a little of himſelf, whom I knew well, and loved much.

There is a natural curioſity excited, upon the death of men who have acted in public characters, to know the particulars of their parentage, birth, and education; to learn the circumſtances which determined the choice of their ſeveral profeſſions, or which attended the diſcharge of their reſpective employments. I ſhould have been happy in poſſeſſing the means of gratifying you, in theſe reſpects, upon the preſent occaſion: but I have neither had leiſure nor opportunities for making the enquiries neceſſary for this purpoſe; and the perſonal intercourſe which I have enjoyed with this good man, during an intimate friendſhip of twelve years, was generally employed on

ſubjects

subjects of a very different nature. Besides, I am disposed neither to set, nor to follow the example, of diving into the secret history of private families, in order to publish what is of no importance to be known, or which had, perhaps, better be forgotten than remembered.

I will, then, speak of Mr. TURNBULL, such as he was when I found him, and such as he has continued to be ever since; after his character was formed and fixed: such as he was in himself, independent of ancestry, alliance, country, or any of those circumstances, which, being entirely *without* a man, are neither to be extolled nor undervalued, and are the objects of neither praise nor censure

The Reverend GEORGE TURNBULL, for the last twenty-five years, Pastor of this Church, possessed a variety of excellent qualities, such as do not always meet and unite in the same character; and which are perhaps the more estimable, from being less common. Without pretending to make an exact enumeration, I will give a few instances, just as they present themselves to my mind. In him I found and admired, strong masculine sense, blended with child-like plainness and simplicity of manners; the solidity of age, with the purity of infancy; a profound understanding, with an ingenuous

genuous heart, a candid spirit, and an open countenance.—In him met genuine unaffected piety, and happy cheerfulness and sweetness of temper; habitual, serious veneration of GOD, habitual kindness and good will to men. Religion was, in him, the smiling mother which allures the offending child to hide his blushing face in her fond maternal bosom, not the angry father, whose frown drives the transgressor into distance and concealment. He possessed very extensive learning, and knowledge both of books and of the world, but so veiled under diffidence, modesty and humility, that length of time, and intimacy of conversation, were requisite to discover them; but then, they were of course valued the more, from the beauty of the covering which attempted to conceal them.—What is always the case, with every man of real learning and ability, he ever discovered a most obliging and winning deference for the opinion of others, with a decent and manly firmness in maintaining his own. He could bear contradiction without passion, yield with dignity, and conquer without enjoying the insolence of triumph. While his piety, experience, and understanding, rendered him a fit companion for the grave, the wife, and the aged, with a pleasantness of disposition, peculiar to himself, he accommodated

commodated his deportment to the vivacity, gaiety, and cheerfulness of youth. He was one of the few old men, whom young people are fond of. He gained upon their hearts by the moſt engaging and affable attention; by condeſcendingly and kindly entering into their views: He was the pleaſed obſerver, not the rigid cenſor, of the mirth whereof he did not always chuſe to partake. His preſence was a reſtraint on nothing but folly and impiety.—His own religious ſentiments, both with reſpect to doctrine and church government, were long ſettled and eſtabliſhed; and they were the reſult of deep and ſerious reflection, of extenſive enquiry and thorough conviction; but he had not learned the confidence and ſelf-ſufficiency of thoſe who ſay of their own ſect, " ſurely we " are the people, and wiſdom ſhall die with us." He treated the ſentiments of honeſt men of all deſcriptions, with candor and liberality. A well cultivated underſtanding, being ever to be found in company with decency of ſpeech and enlargement of heart. Hence he lived in friendſhip with all, was cheriſhed and reſpected of all, has died regretted of all.

Such was the Man. The Miniſter you well knew; his public labours, his private communication, his doctrine and manner of life, all the time that he went out and in among you, during

the

the period of his Miniftry. But you know not, for you heard not, faw not, the fecret breathings of his heart; his midnight interceffions, his morning cries at the throne of grace, in your behalf; his evening facrifice of praife and thankfgiving. The God, to whom they were prefented, and who alone was confcious of them, will, we truft, hold them in everlafting remembrance. They have already fallen back in a tide of bleffednefs, into the bofom of him by whom they were offered up, and as a diadem of glory they now encircle his head; and they will long continue to defcend, as the dew from Heaven, in the grace of the Almighty upon your fouls. Thus, by the prayers and interceffions which he poured out day and night, before the eternal throne, by the word which he preached, and which I hope you will long remember, and by the life of faith and holinefs upon the Son of God, which he lived in the flefh, " being dead he yet " fpeaketh," and will continue to inftruct and comfort you. And, from the dark cloud, which his fudden removal has fpread over your heads, may copious fhowers of " fpiritual and heavenly " bleffings in Chrift Jefus," fall down to refrefh and fructify this fpot, that it may produce abundantly " the fruits of the fpirit, love and peace " and joy in the Holy Ghoft." And thus, death fhall prove great gain, not only to himfelf, but alfo unto you. Amen.

ADDITION

TO

SERMON VII.

ON FUNERAL SERMONS, MONUMENTAL INSCRIPTIONS, AND THE BURIAL SERVICE.

THE love of fame is as natural to man as the love of life. To be careless or prodigal of either, is an argument of great intellectual or moral derangement. But this passion, like every other, may easily be, and frequently is, carried to excess, and becomes criminal, whenever it is gratified at the expence of duty and conscience. In the estimation of Solomon, " a good name" fairly acquired, and honourably supported, " is rather to be chosen than great riches:" but, like riches, it is a very uncertain portion: for as " riches certainly make themselves wings, and fly away as an eagle towards heaven," so " the bubble reputation," a possession still more flimsy, frequently bursts in a moment, vanishes " into air, thin air," and leaves the possessor " poor indeed," without even the miserable consolation of knowing the thief who robbed him of his treasure. The wise man, in another passage, gives " a good name" the preference to " precious ointment,"

ointment," and emphatically subjoins, "the day of death is better than the day of one's birth." Why is it so? Because death seals a man's character, and secures his reputation. While he yet lived, it was liable to forfeiture by misconduct, and was exposed to the breath of calumny; but now he is dead, his virtue is put beyond the reach of human frailty, the tongue of slander is put to silence, and his honest fame is established as on a rock; and thus he still lives in his better part.

We, accordingly, find men justly solicitous that their reputation should survive the body. Reconciled to the fatal hour which is to restore "the dust to the earth as it was," the eager eye contemplates posthumous honours, the greedy ear anticipates the eulogium which is to be pronounced, after it is no longer capable of hearing. When this serves as a stimulus to merit praise, the love of fame is not only innocent, but highly commendable. Of the multitudes, however, who are continually dropping into the grave, how few can be said to have lived? Of the generality, the whole history shrinks into one short sentence, *He was born—and died!*—And had it not been better for many of those whose memory has survived their ashes, and better for the world, if their names could have been "interred with their bones," and quietly consigned to everlasting oblivion? But history has erected a monument for them, similar to that which justice rears for more atrocious offenders, whose

gibbeted

gibbeted limbs and rattling chains commemorate only crimes and the punishment of them, objects from which the eye turns away in horror and disgust. When the insignificant, the worthless and the criminal are subtracted from the aggregate of mankind, how sadly are the numbers reduced! And when, from the remainder, we farther subtract the silently, calmly, unostentatiously meritorious, who lived and died in the shade, who shrunk from fame as seduloufly as others hunt after it, how few remain to be the subject of just panegyrick in life, and to furnish matter for the sculptor, the orator and the historian, when they are dead! how few, to realize the Poet's enchanting view of Elysium—

> * Hic manus, ob patriam pugnando vulnera passi:
> Quique sacerdotes casti, dum vita manebat:
> Quique pii vates, et Phœbo digna locuti:
> Inventas aut qui vitam excoluere per artes:
> Quique sui memores alios fecere merendo:
> Virgilii Æneid: vi. 660.

Even when proper subjects occur, to dispense praise with propriety is both a difficult and a delicate task. If in any case, here it is impossible to hit the exact

---

* Here patriot bands, who for their country bled:
And holy priests, who lived what they taught:
Inspired bards, fraught with celestial fire:
Sages, whose rare inventions bless mankind:
And who, by virtue, purchas'd honest praise
From grateful future ages.

exact medium between the too little and the too much. The partiality of blood, of friendship, or of gratitude, is ever expecting and exacting more; the spirit of envy and detraction, so prevalent in the world, thinks that much less might have served; and where is the wisdom and discretion that can draw the line?

Monumental inscriptions are, in many cases, a voluntary tribute to departed excellence; and, like every other species of voluntary offering, generally favour fully as much of the giver as of the receiver. Being frequently in verse, the Poet is under a temptation to exhibit himself too much, and his subject suffers in proportion. Hence the smallness of the number of classically pure and correct, of historically just and true, and of poetically elegant and sublime epitaphs. Mr. Pope, who so greatly excelled in various other kinds of poetical composition, failed egregiously in this. Not one of his epitaphs is there, that does not present one or more glaring defects; as every candid critic must be sensible, who will take the trouble to peruse Dr. Johnson's analysis of them, in the conclusion of his life of that great Poet. And if Pope failed, who shall boast of having succeeded; But he failed, perhaps, because he was a Poet. For poetry is too nearly allied to fiction to admit of its conveying simple, unadorned truth only: and an epitaph ought to be, at least, strictly true. But neither is the number of excellent monumental inscriptions in prose very considerable. They are generally deficient in respect of
simplicity,

simplicity. Aiming at something brilliant, powerful, uncommon, the Author degenerates into quaintness and conceit. Antithesis, and other cold, laboured figures of speech, affectedly decorate the tomb, just as the undertaker's formal company of mutes, and plumes of feathers, adorned the funeral procession, and made " the groundlings stare." The treatment of the dead is no easy undertaking. Unless the heart speak in the funereal train, speak from the pulpit, speak on the marble; may no unfeeling varlet be permitted to lay out my poor remains; and no stupid panegyrist put me a second time to death, by mangling my memory; " and not a stone tell where I lie."

Monumental inscriptions, I said, are, frequently, a *voluntary* offering; but funeral sermons are, for the most part, *a task imposed*, and, in a multitude of cases, a cruel task indeed. For it is expected, that, according as worldly rank, or family pride, or capricious vanity, or a paltry pecuniary consideration may prescribe, the preacher is to sacrifice truth and decency, by ascribing, in the tropes of a funeral oration, sense to a blockhead, generosity to a sordid miser, honesty to a notorious knave: and by dispensing the kingdom of heaven, the reward of the faithful, to a wretch whom he knew to have lived in the open violation of all God's commandments, and to have died without one penitential sigh, and without one ray of trembling hope. At the best, the indiscriminate honour of a funeral sermon soon ceases to be any distinction at all. If the same

mark

mark of public respect is put on the idle, the frivolous, the dissipated, as on the industrious, the useful and the sober-minded, the foundation of morals is undermined, the profligate is hardened in his wickedness, and goodness is defrauded of its just recompence of reward. Hence, accordingly, we have likewise but very few tolerable funeral sermons. They must, from the very nature of the thing, degenerate into mere frigid common place, violate sacred truth, or, in speaking truth, give offence, and provoke resentment.

France has produced many more, and far more excellent funeral sermons, than our own country. Previous to the late important Revolution there, encomiastic eloquence was the great exertion of literature and genius. Every military atchievement, every Academic admission, every royal birth, marriage or decease, gave birth to a thousand eloquent harangues. To excel in this species of composition was to be in the direct road to fame, favour and fortune. Flattery was there more glibly swallowed, and more liberally rewarded, than with us, and therefore more dexteroully administred. It was *fashionable* to attend exhibitions of this sort. When *Bourdaloue*, *Massillon*, or *Bossuet* mounted the pulpit, the Church was more crowded than the Theatre; blue ribbons graced every pew, and Princes of the blood flocked from *Versailles* to *St. Sulpice* to hear a Sermon. This made good preachers, and has enriched the republic of letters with innumerable exquisite funeral orations: and it presents a striking contrast to our 30th

of

of January exhibitions at Westminster Abbey, and St. Margaret's Church, where the Chancellor, attended by a single Lord or two, represents the whole British Peerage; and the Speaker, Clerk, and Serjeant at mace appear in the name of all the Commons of England. It is no wonder if such frigid attendance should produce but cold oratory. But in perusing the elaborate harangues pronounced in honour of a *Marie-Therese*, of a *Condé*, of a *Turenne*, of a *Conti*, &c. I quickly lose sight of the departed subject, and feel my mind engrossed with the living orator; and when I lay down the book, it is not the princess, the potentate, or the hero that I admire and praise, but *Father Bourdaloue, the bishop of Meaux, Flechier*, or *Massillon*. This is, to me, a proof that funeral eulogia are composed to celebrate not the dead, but the living. And the orator must possess little celebrity indeed, if he is not better known to the world, and of more importance in it, than most of the persons whose memory he is employed to embalm. It were to be wished, therefore, that the practice of funeral sermons were either wholly laid aside, or confined to subjects of real, well-known, and generally acknowledged worth; and this, for the sake of the deceased, as well as of survivors; for injudicious praise has frequently a tendency to rouse slumbering censure; and the world is disposed to ask, When, and Where, were the virtues exhibited, which the orator so pompously displays from the pulpit? Silence is the best, and most suitable eulogium of the generality of mankind.

mankind. The pious, modest, and humble, desire no other; the vain-glorious, insignificant and worthless should be permitted to pass as quickly as possible to the land of deep forgetfulness. Is it not passing strange, that death, and its mournful, humiliating concomitants, should be preposterously forced into occasions of ministring to the pride of life?

Were there however, no greater danger to morals, than what arises from the indiscriminate profusion of praise, in extravagant epitaphs, and injudicious funeral harangues, the practice might be left to be cured, by the pity and forbearance of the benevolent, and the freer of the sarcastic and malignant; but there is real and serious danger to both morals and religion from a solemn and important branch of the public service of our established Church. The burial-service, so powerfully impressive, is in one respect faulty, and the more, that it *is* so powerfully impressive. The body of every one, without distinction, is consigned to the grave " in sure and certain hope of the resurrection to eternal life." By whom, it may be asked, Is this glorious hope, in every case, entertained? By the worthy Clergyman who reads the service? Alas, he knew nothing of the party, in innumerable instances, till he came to the Church-yard, to *do his duty*, as it is called: perhaps he well knew the deceased to have lived and died a profligate; has a thousand times lamented his impenitence, and looked forward with fear and trembling to the hour of dissolution, which

was

was to hurry him into the presence of a righteous judge. Is this hope expressed by the mourners or spectators? They are often precisely in the same state with the minister, they know nothing that can serve as a ground of such hope; or they know too much to be consistent with it. Did the man himself live and die in this blessed hope, and is the voice of it now issuing from his tomb? We trust this is the case with myriads, and " blessed are the dead who die in the Lord." But are there not others, whom no stretch of charity can comprehend in the number of the redeemed of the Lord, and over whom we are constrained to " sorrow as those who have no hope:" who lived " without God in the world," and expired without hope, expired, it may be, setting at nought the faith and hope of the Gospel as " a cunningly devised fable?" Would we therefore place a man on the tribunal of the great Supreme, and permit him to pronounce his brother's doom? God forbid. No, let not man presume to judge at all; for God emphatically challenges the right of Judgment as his own. " To me belongeth vengeance, and recompence:" " Vengeance is mine; I will repay, saith the Lord."

I beg leave to subjoin, as a good reason why fallible man should not presume to judge; we have seen some meet death with confidence, whose lives, apparently, did not warrant composure and joy, in that awful hour; while persons of much purer character, more exalted piety, more unequivocal goodness, have trembled at the approach of the king of terrors, and expressed the most tormenting anxiety about their future state. Too great stress is often laid on the *frame* and *feelings* of the dying, which depend on a thousand contingent circumstances that do not, that can not, affect their real state. It is, undoubtedly, pleasant, it is edifying, it is animating, to behold a dying friend " filled with peace and joy in believing"—" rejoicing in the hope of the Glory of God;" but I will not afflict myself beyond measure, because the sun of my Christian friend set under a cloud.

In North-Britain the dead are consigned to the grave in solemn and profound silence. And, except in the case of eminent public character, or of distinguished excellence, no funeral eulogium is pronounced from the pulpit.

The republication of the preceding discourse, has furnished me with an opportunity of suggesting these hints. Had I not considered them as nearly affecting the interests of decency, morality and religion, on a point of universal importance, they should have been suppressed. My own career is drawn so much nearer to a conclusion. The lapse of twelve years makes a deep impression on the person, faculties, and condition of a man above forty. I must be preparing to follow my respectable friend. He had provided his own funeral sermon without knowing it.

I am

I am confcioufly and intentionally laying up materials for mine. When, and by whom they are to be employed, is for HIM to determine, " in whofe hand my breath is, and whofe are all my ways."

END OF VOL. I.

www.ingramcontent.com/pod-product-compliance
Lightning Source LLC
Chambersburg PA
CBHW020307240426
43673CB00039B/727